Between Two Worlds

Between Two Worlds

....

JEWISH WAR BRIDES
AFTER THE HOLOCAUST

ROBIN JUDD

THE UNIVERSITY OF NORTH CAROLINA PRESS

Chapel Hill

Designed by Jamison Cockerham
Set in Arno, Scala Sans, and Parkinson Electra
by codeMantra

Cover photograph from the United States Holocaust Memorial
Museum, courtesy of Flory Kabilio Jagoda.

Manufactured in the United States of America

LIBRARY OF CONGRESS CATALOGING-IN-PUBLICATION DATA
Names: Judd, Robin, author.
Title: Between two worlds : Jewish war brides after the Holocaust / Robin Judd.
Description: Chapel Hill : The University of North Carolina Press,
[2023] | Includes bibliographical references and index.
Identifiers: LCCN 2023023173 | ISBN 9781469675442
(cloth ; alk. paper) | ISBN 9781469675459 (ebook)
Subjects: LCSH: World War, 1939–1945—Women—Europe. | Holocaust
survivors—Marriage. | Jewish women in the Holocaust. | War brides—United
States—History—20th century. | War brides—Canada—History—20th
century. | War brides—Great Britain—History—20th century. | Intercountry
marriage—History—20th century. | Jews—Migrations. | BISAC: HISTORY /
Wars & Conflicts / World War II / General | SOCIAL SCIENCE / Gender Studies
Classification: LCC D804.47 .J83 2023 | DDC 940.53/18082—dc23/eng/20230522
LC record available at https://lccn.loc.gov/2023023173

For

KENNY

the song of my heart

CONTENTS

ILLUSTRATIONS

ABBREVIATIONS

Between Two Worlds

INTRODUCTION

Just as they did every Wednesday evening, thousands of American households gathered in their living rooms, kitchens, and parlors on May 27, 1953, to discover which audience member would be honored by the popular television show *This Is Your Life*. Each week, the show surprised one of its guests by taking them through a retrospective of their lives, reuniting them with long-lost family members, friends, roommates, and rescuers. *This Is Your Life* honored a wildly diverse group of people, including World War II veterans, actors, educators, physicians, housewives, and survivors of natural and humanly orchestrated disasters.[1]

On that May evening, viewers listened to the familiar crescendo of the opening credits and eagerly followed the show's creator and host Ralph Edwards as he moved slowly from the back of the theater to the front, ostensibly searching for that week's honoree. Ralph chatted with one guest after the next, eventually pausing beside a beautiful young woman. Dressed in a fashionable bolero jacket, blouse, and white gloves, she quietly introduced herself as Hanna Kohner; indeed, she was so soft-spoken that Ralph leaned in and asked her to repeat herself. A careful listener might have noticed her accented English, but most viewers likely were wondering whether the handsome actor sitting next to her was that week's surprise guest. Instead, an astonished Hanna learned that she was the honoree. As Ralph escorted her to the stage, he revealed to the audience that, despite her appearance, Hanna had lived "a lifetime of terror." She might look "like a young American girl," but she was a survivor of "Hitler's cruel purge of German Jews." With that shocking, albeit saccharine, introduction, the television host presented a survivor of the Holocaust to thousands of American viewers, many of whom knew little

1

about the Nazi atrocities. Over the course of that evening, audience members encountered survivors of the concentration camps, camp liberators, and American military veterans, including Hanna's husband.[2]

Hanna Bloch Kohner has received some attention as one of the first Holocaust survivors introduced to the American public, but little notice has been paid to her unique immigration story.[3] The television show's producers touted Hanna's transformation from a victim of the Nazi terrors to a glamourous young wife without acknowledging how she had journeyed to the United States in the first place. Hanna had come to the United States as a "war bride," a foreign civilian married to an American soldier serving abroad. She was one of over 200,000 women who immigrated to America as spouses of military personnel in the immediate aftermath of World War II.

Unlike many of her fellow war brides, Hanna had met her husband, Walter Kohner, a full decade before the fighting in Europe ceased. The two were childhood sweethearts in the Bohemian spa town of Teplitz-Schönau. The Nazi rise to power and Hitler's 1938 annexation of the Sudetenland, where Teplitz-Schönau was located, interrupted their youthful romance, and radically altered their lives. Walter escaped to the United States, where his brothers already had immigrated. Hanna hoped to follow, but she had no family members living in the United States who could serve as her sponsor. As Walter created a new life for himself in Los Angeles, Hanna encountered the growing Nazi persecution of the Jews. Almost overnight, the Nazis introduced a wide number of repressive laws. They stripped Jews of their citizenship, mandated that Jews disclose their property, and prohibited Jews from patronizing recreational spaces, like neighborhood parks. Hanna fled to Amsterdam, where, after having lost touch with Walter, she married Carl, a fellow refugee. She did not remain safe for long. The Germans occupied the Netherlands in May 1940 and issued their first anti-Jewish laws in October of that year. In January 1942, the Nazis began the forced movement of Jews in the Netherlands, first sending foreign and stateless Jews to the Westerbork transit camp in the northeastern part of the country. The Nazis deported Hanna and Carl from Amsterdam to Westerbork, later to Theresienstadt in northwestern Bohemia, and then to Auschwitz in southern Poland. In November 1944, they sent Hanna to Vöcklabruck, a subcamp of Mauthausen, located in upper Austria.

When the Allies reached Vöcklabruck on May 5, 1945, Hanna was malnourished and exhausted, but euphoric that she had survived. Eager to discover whether any of her loved ones had lived through the Nazi terrors, she left Austria and slowly made her way to Amsterdam. Soon after she arrived there, she discovered that the Nazis had murdered Carl in Auschwitz. Later she would learn that her parents also had been killed. She felt devastatingly alone and fell into a depression.

Unbeknownst to Hanna, Walter now was a soldier in the US Army, serving in Luxembourg. When he learned that Hanna was alive, he searched for her in their childhood town of Teplitz-Schönau. When he found no trace of her there, he continued on to Prague and then Amsterdam, where he finally located her and proposed marriage. Walter and Hanna married in October 1945. A few months later, the United States passed legislation that allowed military spouses like Hanna to immigrate more easily than other aspiring émigrés who fell under the immigration quotas established in the 1920s. Hanna immigrated to the United States as a war bride in July 1946.[4]

In the chaos and pandemonium that followed the attempted genocide of the Jews, several hundred European and North African Jewish women, such as Hanna, and a few dozen Jewish men married American, British, and Canadian military personnel. The smallest number of these Jewish noncombatants originated from North Africa, but most of the Jewish war brides were part of the surviving remnant of European Jewry. Born in countries spread across Europe and North Africa, they had spent the war years in camps, in hiding, and passing as non-Jews, and now, in the aftermath of their liberation, frequently found themselves far from their homes in places marked by unfamiliar cultures, practices, and languages. Other Jewish war brides had spent the Nazi years in Soviet-occupied territories and fled to Germany, Austria, or Italy when the war ended. Jewish war brides married Jewish and non-Jewish military personnel, most of them born in the United States, Britain, or Canada. Some, like Walter, had been immigrants or refugees themselves. They were originally from part of the ever-expanding Nazi Reich, had left their homes in the 1930s, came to the United States, Britain, or Canada as children, teenagers, or young adults, and then enlisted in the military during the late 1930s or early 1940s.[5]

Between Two Worlds: Jewish War Brides after the Holocaust tells their stories.

. . . .

The war bride phenomenon long preceded the October 1945 Luxembourg wedding of Hanna and Walter. Studies of world history include disparate examples of soldiers, officers, and rulers marrying noncombatants during times of fighting. Attitudes and policies concerning these relationships differed depending on time period, site of encounter, and the military force in question.[6]

Of the three countries studied here, the United States, Britain, and Canada,[7] Britain had the lengthiest history of regulating the marriages of soldiers. Imagining women as a threat to military discipline, British governments historically mandated that their military personnel receive permission to marry. If military commanders refused their soldiers that clearance and the soldiers married anyway, the British military denied support to the wives and their children, referring to them as "off the strength" of the regiment. In contrast, women "on the strength" of the regiment, whose husbands' petitions for marriage had been approved by their military superiors, received care and, if applicable, assistance in journeying to their husbands' homes.[8] For much of the nineteenth and twentieth centuries, the United States made no such distinction and did not mandate commander approval when its military personnel wished to marry. In part because of the paucity of relevant cases, until the late nineteenth century the United States did not even codify its policies concerning the ability of soldiers to marry when serving abroad. In 1870, the United States first formalized this right but clarified that it would not be responsible for the dependents' care or immigration.[9]

During World War I, as many more military personnel expressed interest in marrying noncombatants abroad, Britain, Canada, and the United States each crafted regulations that permitted active-duty soldiers to marry foreign women. While they were not alone in considering the marriages between noncombatants and military personnel serving abroad, these three countries paid particular attention to this growing phenomenon. The British military continued to require commander authorization when military personnel wished to marry, more severely penalized those soldiers who did not heed their commanders' sanction, and generally assumed the responsibility for wives and ensuing dependents, much as it had done for the women "on the strength of the regiment" in previous centuries. More than it had in the past, marriage abroad was considered appropriate recompense for military service, but British regulations concerning these marriages still were drafted with the hope that they would protect the reputation of country and military.[10] The Canadian Expeditionary Force (later the Canadian Corps), formed during the First World War, was highly receptive to foreign spouses because many of them originated from Britain, of which Canada was a dominion. To safeguard its military's standing and to guarantee that the women who would come to Canada would be "worthy" of admission, the Canadian government mandated that military superiors vet the fiancées before marriage. Imagining the new wives as future mothers of the nation, the Canadian government

4

permitted marriages abroad and developed family reunification policies that shouldered much of the responsibility for the women's care and transport.[11]

Concomitant US military policies diverged from those crafted in Britain and Canada in two ways: they did not consistently mandate commander approval, and they did not offer any new significant support to the spouses. During World War I, Gen. John Pershing, commander in chief of the American Expeditionary Forces, believed that military marriages could improve the reputation of US troops abroad and therefore placed few restrictions on the rights of military personnel to wed. Despite such an allowance, however, he resisted becoming involved in the care or transportation of foreign spouses. Men could marry foreign noncombatants, but they were responsible for their transport to the United States.[12] American military personnel quickly found that the high cost of travel and the dearth of ships available made it difficult to bring their wives home. In addition, some learned that their marriages would be declared void by their home state laws, which forbade marriages of persons of different races, and which penalized those citizens who had wed in violation of those laws. After World War I ended, the US military began to establish new restraints: all active American military personnel needed their regimental commander's approval before marrying. The US would make no significant change to its stand on transport, however, until after World War II.[13]

Hanna and Walter were part of a wave of military marriages that took place during and after the Second World War. During this period, marriage laws increasingly restricted how, why, when, and who could marry, and immigration policies vacillated between embracing this new type of family and worrying about the risk these foreign spouses posed to their new homes. The World War II Canadian infrastructure concerning war brides was the most extensive, due, perhaps, to its substantial involvement in the care and migration of spouses during and immediately after the First World War.[14] While the Canadian military slowly added restrictions to increasingly vet the foreign noncombatants marrying its military personnel, the government guaranteed spouses expedited entry, promised to pay for their ocean and rail transportation, and offered wives the citizenship or domicile status of their husbands.[15] The US military similarly enforced a greater number of checks on the ability of soldiers and officers to marry foreign noncombatants and, for much of this period, made military personnel responsible for their wives' transport, albeit with a reduced rate of travel. Beginning in December 1945, however, the US Congress passed the first emergency legislation for military spouses. Public Law 271 allowed for foreign spouses of American military personnel, both women and men, to circumvent existing quotas. This temporary law, which was set to expire after three years, was followed in 1946 by the Alien Fiancées and Fiancés Act (GI Fiancées Act), which also permitted intended brides and grooms to enter the country as nonimmigrants. The American government arranged and funded the immigration of war brides and fiancé(e)s to the United States. Both the US and Canadian governments, along with the Red Cross, organized assembly and immigration processing centers for these women and men and outfitted ships for their travel.[16]

British policies similarly implemented strong controls over potential spouses, but early on, spouses immigrating to Britain faced paradoxical treatment. The UK permitted expedited entry for spouses and fiancées, but it did not create a unique infrastructure to support their migration or acculturation. They were permitted to enter but lacked the support networks necessary to travel easily or integrate quickly. British officials likely did not imagine the need for such an infrastructure. The country had been devastated by the war and needed to focus on major recovery efforts. Moreover, it saw far fewer war brides than Canada and the United States. Less than 20,000 war brides made their way to Britain during this time.[17] In contrast, between 1944 and 1948, over several hundred thousand people, mostly women, but also some children and men—took advantage of the special visa exemptions offered by the war brides' legislation in the United States and Canada. In the United States, war brides numbered over 200,000 and constituted nearly 22 percent of all legal admissions. Canada witnessed the arrival of a total of 64,451 servicemen's dependents—43,454 wives and 20,997 children. Most of the war brides and dependents came from Britain.[18]

These policies were not ethnically or racially neutral. The United States, Britain, and Canada constructed systems of immigration and acculturation that favored white Protestant families. Within the United States, many states prohibited interracial marriages, and many commanders refused their personnel the permission to marry if the marriage would not be recognized by the soldier's home state. The legislation regulating the entry of US war brides included only spouses deemed racially admissible under the national origins quota system. While in 1945, American immigration law included no provision for Asian wives of US service members, by 1946, Congress extended the act to include Chinese immigrants, and in 1947 it allowed admission regardless of race if the marriage occurred within thirty days of enactment.[19] Canadian and British discussions did not revolve as explicitly around race, although their policies, like those of the United States, were certainly racially constructed.[20] Furthermore, while policies allowed for male and female civilian spouses, the legislators crafting and implementing these and the British and Canadian regulations imagined that most military personnel were male and that most civilian spouses were female.

. . . .

The marriages between Jewish survivors and military personnel fit into this history but have largely gone unnoticed. Many scholars include those individuals who later became Jewish war brides in their studies of the Holocaust and immediate postwar period but omit them when these fiancé(e)s and spouses left the displaced persons (DP) camps, refugee centers, or temporary residences, that is, when the men and women became war brides or war fiancé(e)s.[21] Studies of European and British war brides similarly pay little, if any, attention to religious and ethnic minorities among the war bride communities, often focusing their narratives on white Christian European and British women.[22]

Between Two Worlds: Jewish War Brides after the Holocaust argues that the Jewish war bride experience is worth exploring. Jewish war brides and their spouses engaged creatively with the problem of survival in the aftermath of trauma. Looking to Jewish spaces, languages, cultures, and bodies, they claimed some agency while simultaneously wrestling with the horrors of their pasts. *Between Two Worlds* focuses on their doing so during five key moments: liberation, encounter, courtship and marriage, immigration, and acculturation. The couples frequently met and dated one another in sites imbued with Jewish meaning: Zionist youth circles, synagogue services, clubs for Jewish soldiers, and DP camps. Their memoirs, diaries, and letters emphasized the centrality of Jewish ritual, history, and affiliation, beginning to imagine a European map with a Jewish presence while concomitantly insisting that their Jewish lives only could be continued outside of the former Nazi Reich. In their new homes, some created lives with spouses who shared common histories, languages, and cultures; others envisioned future Jewish lives with partners who had little personal knowledge of the Holocaust; a third sought out relationships and communities that would leave their Jewishness behind.

Former victims, soldiers, community leaders, nongovernmental organization (NGO) workers, family members, and military officials also looked to marriages between Jewish civilians and Allied military personnel to suggest ways that Jews and Jewish communities could pick themselves up and move forward after personal and communal trauma. They, too, discussed Jewish spaces, languages, cultures, and bodies during liberation, encounter, courtship, immigration, and acculturation. Some Jewish chaplains, NGO officials, and military family members believed that these Jewish war brides and fiancé(e)s helped to address the loss suffered by world Jewry during the Holocaust. In their view, these Jewish women—and they almost always imagined them as women even though a small number of them were men—would help reproduce and repopulate Jewish life, albeit in locales that were radically different from prewar Europe. Other contemporaries revealed different views of Jewish communal reconstruction. Some European and North African Jews criticized women who married soldiers rather than Holocaust survivors. Similarly, Jewish women's organizations often voiced displeasure with these "hasty marriages," lamenting their impact on unmarried Jewish women and worrying about a "spinster crisis."[23] In its analysis of postwar Jewish community building, *Between Two Worlds* emphasizes the uneven, prolonged, and sometimes unhappy experiences of reconstruction and recovery. It highlights that rebuilding was inherently and inevitably ambivalent and complex.

A second theme considered by this book emphasizes the multiple communities in which the Jewish war brides took part, and the sense of unbelonging that followed them as they moved among these different circles. Depending on time, place, and context, Jewish war brides made their way into and out of several disparate circles and spaces: including those of war and peace, military and civilian, Jewish and Christian, survivor and occupier, and home and abroad. The Jewish war brides moved from liberation sites to temporary mixed-gender and mixed-religion communities to Jewish DP centers to residences and camps formed explicitly for military spouses and finally to their new homes in the United States, Britain, and Canada. They frequently experienced inclusion and exclusion. Their heightened sense of not fully belonging in any one space often encouraged them to reflect on what it meant to be a Jew, wife, woman, and mother—or man, husband, and father—in the aftermath of the Holocaust. When talking about their Jewish identities, bodies, emotional health, and status as parents, children, and siblings, they painted complicated pictures of postwar Jewishness, victimhood, womanhood, and manhood.

Third, Jewish war brides and their spouses offered a touchstone for considering larger issues concerning marriage, immigration, and citizenship. Even before the United States, Britain, and Canada passed legislation permitting military spouses to circumvent existing immigration quotas, contemporaries assumed that the civilian brides and grooms would, one day, immigrate to the homes of the newly married military personnel. On the one hand, war brides were envisioned as fitting compensation for dangerous military service. On the other hand, these foreigners, who would eventually become parents and citizens in a new nation, were distrusted; an emphasis was placed on their being well vetted and acculturated. The degree to which marriage and family reunification would outweigh the protection of the nation-state—and vice versa—would come to depend on time and place, eventually becoming entangled with Cold War concerns. In the United States, such discussions would even reach the Supreme Court.

. . . .

Such a study faces several challenges, not least the confusing, tricky, and contested nature of the very terms employed. During the immediate postwar period, the individuals studied here would not have referred to themselves as "survivors"; some would never define themselves that way.[24] Before 1961, people generally used a wide array of words in English, Hebrew, Yiddish, and German to refer to the group that would eventually be considered the "collective of survivors." These included "refugees," "liberated Jews," "Sordey HaShoah [survivors from the Shoah]," "Verfolgte des Naziregimes [persecutees of the National Socialists]," "Geschädigte [wronged parties]," "She'erit Hapletah," "Iberlebene / Sheyres Hapleyte [surviving remnant]," and "displaced persons." Some of these terms were self-reflective, used by the survivors to categorize themselves as individuals who had lived through Hitler's regime.[25] Jews in occupied Germany, for example, first used the term "She'erit Hapletah / Sheyres Hapleyte" to refer to those Jews liberated from camps in Germany; over the course of the 1940s, the category was expanded to encompass Jews living in occupied Germany, Austria, and Italy, regardless of their experiences during the war, although some continued to insist that the term alluded only to those liberated from the camps. In contrast, the term "displaced person" was applied externally. Introduced in November 1944 by the Supreme Headquarters Allied Expeditionary Forces (SHAEF), it referred to Jews and non-Jews—many of whom temporarily lived in the displaced persons camps established by the Allied forces—displaced by World War II. The International Relief Organization enlarged the definition to include anyone who "has been deported from or has been obliged to leave his country of nationality or of former habitual residence, such as persons who were compelled to undertake forced labour or who were deported for racial, religious or political reasons."[26]

After the trial of Adolf Eichmann in 1961, more and more people began to use the term "survivor" to refer to those who had been directly persecuted by the Nazis and who had lived under Nazi rule. American psychoanalyst William Guglielmo Neiderland, himself a refugee from Nazi Germany, first used the term "survivor syndrome" in 1961 to refer to a mental condition suffered by those who survived Nazi persecution.[27] In her *Eichmann in Jerusalem* (1963), Hannah Arendt employed the word "survivor" when speaking of those who had "survived the war in one form or another of Nazi captivity."[28] Increasingly, "survivor" became invoked and expanded to include multiple wartime experiences; the television series *Holocaust* (1978–79), Claude Lanzmann's documentary film *Shoah* (1985), Steven Spielberg's film *Schindler's List* (1993), and the opening of the US Holocaust Memorial Museum (1993), each circulated the term in the public arena.[29]

Between Two Worlds employs a broad definition of the term "survivor," even though some of the women and men examined here never used the term for themselves. Encompassing those who lived under Nazi domination, direct and indirect, and survived displacement, persecution, and/or discrimination by the Nazis and their collaborators, it includes Jewish refugees, prisoners, camp inmates, displaced persons, the "infiltrees," and new immigrants, all diverse individuals who experienced a wide range of suffering and struggles across Europe and parts of North Africa. As one interviewee made clear, her story was "not a Holocaust story of concentration camp, Poland, Auschwitz," but she was a "survivor" nonetheless.[30]

A second category used throughout the book is "military personnel." This refers to the men and women who operated in a wide range of capacities for the Allied and occupation forces. Most of the individuals studied here served in the British Royal Air Force, British armed forces, Canadian Royal Air Force, First Canadian Army, US Air Force, and/or US Army. Because of the geographic and religious focus of this work, there were few examples of military personnel who served in a naval force and then met and married Jewish civilians living in North Africa or Europe, but I integrate their stories when I can.[31] I also include narratives of those who were in military formations attached to the Allied forces. The greatest number of those were men who served in the Jewish Brigade, a military formation of the British Army established in September 1944. The Jewish Brigade included more than 5,000 Jewish volunteers, mostly from Palestine. They fought in Italy from March 1945 until the end of the war in May 1945 and were stationed along the Italian border with Austria and Yugoslavia, and later in Belgium and the Netherlands. In those capacities, members of the Jewish Brigade had several opportunities to engage with local Jewish civilians. *Between Two Worlds* does not assume that all military experiences were alike. When relevant, it mentions the service and role of the soldier or officer and tries to highlight the similarities and differences among experiences and national military policy.

This book employs the terms "Jewish war bride" and "Jewish war fiancé(e)" to refer to those women *and* men who married—or became engaged to—military personnel serving abroad.[32] In North America, the term "war bride" first was invoked in 1914, when the United States took part in a Mexican border conflict.[33] While the phrase tended to be used most frequently in the United States and Canada, this book utilizes it to refer to the spouses—usually women—whether or not they married military personnel from those countries alone.[34] Transnational narratives can be messy, and *Between Two Worlds* tries to highlight moments of sameness and difference across place and time while also offering a clear, readable narrative.

This book considers Jewish hurt, recovery, and reconstruction in the aftermath of the Holocaust. As such, it limits its examination to those Jewish war brides and fiancé(e)s who were generally considered by the rabbinic authorities at that time to be Jewish: individuals born to two Jewish parents, to a Jewish mother and a non-Jewish father, or who had converted to Judaism.[35] This book does not assume that Jewish noncombatants only married Jews or that Jewish military personnel only married Jewish noncombatants. Indeed, chapters 3 and 5 discuss non-Jewish military personnel who sought to marry Jews, Jewish survivors who wished to marry non-Jewish soldiers and officers, and Jewish soldiers who requested permission to marry non-Jews.

When conducting research, religious affiliation was not always initially apparent and additional work was required to identify the spouses' religious identities. Depending on time and location, some official paperwork omitted any mention of religion. Moreover, newspaper articles concerning the war brides—one means of identifying couples to research—infrequently revealed religion unless the paper in question was a Jewish one. Ruth Applebaum is a case in point. In January 1946, the *Chicago Tribune* featured her as a newly arrived bride in that city; the article made no mention of her Jewishness nor of her experiences during World War II. When she was featured in a second article by the same newspaper in 1955, the reporter briefly referenced her life in the Nazi Reich but omitted any allusion to religion.[36] Stories such as hers would become folded into this study as additional materials were procured about the spouses themselves.

Like the military marriages of World War II more generally, the number of Jewish civilians who married Allied military personnel serving in Europe or North Africa is difficult to quantify. Particularly after June 1945, many couples married outside of military settings. As chapter 3 sets out, several of these men and women no longer needed to rely on their chaplains to marry them. Some received their commanders' approval and then married in local synagogues, churches, registry offices, or city halls. Others risked censure when they did not seek military permission but married locally anyway. Another group did not marry in Europe or North Africa at all. They received military permission to marry but waited to do so until they could reunite with their fiancées in Britain, Canada, or the United States. Some war brides and fiancé(e)s circumvented the formal war transportation channels; they came to the United States, Britain, or Canada privately, without requesting travel on a war bride ship, whose logs allow scholars to find and track the military personnel's dependents.

Finally, this project relies on memory as a historical source. Several of the women and men studied here began to speak publicly in the late twentieth century about their experiences during the war. Several published Holocaust memoirs. Some created works of theater, musical performance, and art concerning the Shoah.[37] These individuals—and dozens of other war brides—also participated in interview projects, often consenting to being interviewed multiple times. I rely on these texts, along with contemporaneous archival sources. The interviews, memoirs, and works of art offer comprehensive understandings of the complex encounters among liberators and liberated and distinct narratives of trauma and rebirth, but they also are characterized by the flaws inherent to any text shaped by memory.[38] Throughout the project, I try to tease out the ways testimonial narratives convey historicity, bearing witness to the subjective meanings and experiential discontinuities for the individual narrator. I aim to account for the messiness inherent in remembering a decades-long relationship that began in a moment of trauma. Scholars have been critical when survivors are held up as "secular saints."[39] I strive not to romanticize these relationships or the actors involved, but I make note of the language the survivors and their spouses used when discussing their own encounters and relationships.

. . . .

Between Two Worlds underscores the importance of studying the Jewish war brides and their spouses. Even though they were few in number, the Jewish war brides touched thousands of lives. They impacted the chaplains who approved of and then officiated at their marriages, the Allied authorities whose policy decisions structured the couples' fates, the nongovernmental officials who were involved in immigration and acculturation efforts, the high court justices who considered their rights and privileges, the non-Jews who lived and traveled with Jewish spouses, and the family members and friends who often unknowingly heightened the Jewish spouses' sense of failing to belong.

At the core of this book are questions concerning the meanings, limitations, and possibilities of postwar reconstruction, marriage, immigration, and acculturation. War paradoxically "fractured and created families,"[40] something that was so true of the Jewish war brides and fiancé(e)s who lost parents, spouses, children, siblings, and friends to the Nazi terror and then created entirely new transnational households. Throughout liberation, encounter, courtship and marriage, immigration, and settlement, these Jewish war brides entered, remained in, and exited several different communities and circles. Finding themselves both similar to and different from other Jews, migrants, war brides, citizens, survivors, and stateless people, the Jewish war brides charted their own path, one that has been mostly ignored by the historical record. Their understudied stories are at the heart of this book.

1

I Thought Liberation
Would Be a Happy Story

THE WAR ENDS

When the Nazis and their allies invaded Yugoslavia in April 1941, fifteen-year-old Flory Kabilio, her mother Rosa, and her stepfather Michael lived in Zagreb. Flory's *nona* (grandmother), uncles, aunts, and cousins lived in Sarajevo, about 230 miles away, and after Germany rapidly partitioned the country, Flory and her family lost touch with them. Refugees fleeing the "Jerusalem of Europe" reported that the Nazis and their allies had destroyed Sarajevo's Great Sephardic Synagogue and made the city's streets unsafe for its Jews. Flory and her parents worried about their relatives and agonized over their own safety as they experienced increasing harassment and anti-Jewish violence. Daily life for Jews in Zagreb had become extremely difficult. Jews had to register with special government authorities, wear badges identifying themselves as Jews, live in specific areas, hand over their property and businesses, and refrain from working in a wide range of professions.[1]

As the anti-Jewish harassment intensified in Zagreb during the spring of 1941, Flory's parents devised a plan for them to flee the city. Flory—and then Rosa and Michael—would travel seven hours by train to the Croatian port city of Split, where they would be met by a close family friend. The Italians had formally annexed Split, and the Kabilios had heard that, unlike the German military, the Italian army refrained from implementing anti-Jewish laws. Hoping that they would be safe in Split, they and thousands of other Jews made the trek from cities and villages across Yugoslavia to the port city. But Split did not remain a sanctuary for long. Locals destroyed the synagogue and Jewish-owned businesses and homes, and, beginning in the summer of 1941, Italian forces interned Jewish refugees. Within a few months of the Kabilios' arrival in the Croatian city, they were sent to an Italian-controlled refugee camp on the island of Korčula. Flory and her parents lived there for over a year. She spent her days offering music lessons to other refugee children and wandering among the island's olive groves, sandy beaches, vineyards, and pine forests, likely scavenging for food.[2]

Flory, Michael, and Rosa had hoped to stay in Korčula for the remainder of the war. However, in October 1943, as Italian forces withdrew from Yugoslavia and the Germans approached, British and partisan forces suddenly evacuated a group of Jews from Korčula to southern Italy. Recognizing that Jews on the island would be at risk when the Germans arrived, these soldiers insisted that all women and children leave immediately.[3] Flory and her mother were swept up in the first round of evacuations. Her stepfather Michael, who had been granted permission to temporarily leave the island, was not. When Flory and Rosa were pushed onto a tugboat and forced to leave their few remaining possessions behind, they had no idea whether they would be reunited with Michael or even survive the harrowing journey at sea. Upon reaching Bari, then under British control, they experienced "liberation" with some ambivalence. They were alone, with no financial resources, in a city where they knew no one and, because they did not comfortably speak Italian, could not easily communicate with the residents.[4]

Sala Solarcz lived hundreds of miles—and worlds—away from Flory. Her liberation took place two and a half years later. In fact, in October 1943, as Flory and her mother landed "safely" in Bari, Sala began her tenth month as a prisoner in Auschwitz and her thirty-sixth month in confinement. Sala's wartime experiences had begun earlier than Flory's. In September 1939, she was outside with her siblings when she spotted German airplanes flying overhead. Close to several military bases, Sala's lakeside town of Seroc, Poland, experienced heavy bombing during the early days of the war. Fearing for their own safety, Sala's large Hasidic family gathered a few of their most treasured items and traveled the twenty-five miles to Warsaw. The Warsaw Jewish community was the largest in both Poland and Europe, and the Solarcz family hoped to find refuge there.[5]

The family's flight to Warsaw failed to protect them. Once they reached the capital, they had to separate. Demands for housing outpaced availability, and it was impossible for them to all dwell under a single roof. Shelter, food, and fuel were difficult to acquire in a city that had been crowded even before the war had begun. Warsaw was besieged by both a continuous stream of refugees and heavy air attacks and artillery bombardment. After German troops occupied the city on September 29, 1939, conditions swiftly deteriorated for Sala and the other Jews there. Violence on the streets became commonplace, and the German civilian occupation authorities increasingly implemented anti-Jewish measures. In November, they required Warsaw's Jews to identify themselves by wearing white armbands with a blue Star of David. They soon confiscated Jewish-owned property, dissolved prewar Jewish organizations, closed Jewish schools, and compelled Jewish men to participate in forced labor. One year later, in October 1940, the Nazis required all Jewish residents of Warsaw to move into a designated area, which the authorities later sealed off from the rest of the city with a ten-foot-high wall.[6]

Sala lived in the Warsaw ghetto for over a year. In December 1941, the German authorities deported her to a second ghetto outside of Lublin. In 1942, they sent her to the nearby Nazi extermination and concentration camp system of Majdanek. Between 1942 and 1945, Sala was forcibly moved from one camp to the next: from Majdanek to Auschwitz, from Auschwitz to Ravensbrück, and then from Ravensbrück to Tachau. In mid-April 1945, the Nazis compelled her and hundreds of other prisoners to undertake a 100-mile march from Tachau toward Dresden. Dozens died on the journey. Those who survived were severely malnourished, exhausted, and ill. Many suffered from typhus, typhoid, and frostbite. When they learned from German civilians on April 25, 1945, that they were "free," Sala was in the Saxon town of Oschatz, about 35 miles from Dresden and approximately 450 miles away from the village of her childhood.[7]

Sala experienced the news of her freedom with confusion. She only comprehended a few words of German, so it was difficult for her to follow the conversations around her. Moreover, after years of imprisonment, she could not fully fathom that she could move freely. She continued to fear German repercussions if she moved on her own without permission. Sala also suffered from deep loneliness. As she surveyed the physically ravaged landscape

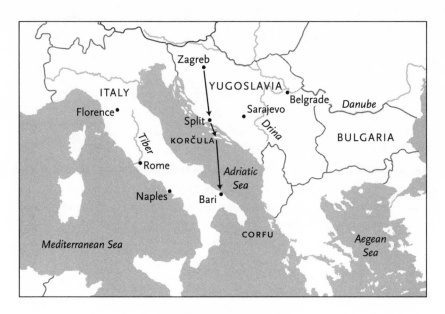

Flory's Wartime Movements

around her, she thought of her many siblings and half-siblings with whom she had escaped to Warsaw six years earlier. Standing on the streets of the ruined Saxon city, she had no idea whether any of them had survived.[8] Since 1939, Sala had witnessed the deaths of countless Jews; she recognized that it was unlikely that there were many survivors within her family. Her own survival, however, gave her some hope that perhaps one of her many siblings or cousins also had endured the terrors of the war. "All I wanted to know," she remembered, was "if someone from our family survived."[9]

· ·

The early months of liberation left their mark on millions of individuals: victims of the Nazis, perpetrators, collaborators, civilians, Allied military personnel, and NGO volunteers. How and when they experienced liberation varied. When the Allied Forces emancipated Nazi prisoners from the camps of the Reich, not everyone experienced the moment in the same way. Some felt a release from captivity in spaces that were not camps: the emancipation of people in hiding, those participating in partisan efforts, victims whose death marches were interrupted by lines of combat, and individuals who "passed" as non-Jews. Former victims were spread across Europe and North

Sala's Wartime Movements

Africa in Poland, Ukraine, France, Belgium, the Netherlands, Egypt, Greece, Italy, Algeria, Tunisia, and Germany.[10] Liberation narratives preceded Victory in Europe (VE) Day on May 8, 1945. Allied successes at the battle of El Alamein, a town on Egypt's Mediterranean coast, allowed for liberation to begin for some North African Jews as early as November 1942, although it was during the spring and summer of 1943 when Allied military moves forced the Germans to retreat from North Africa. This led to the liberation of the majority of Jews there, opened a second front against the Axis powers, and resulted in the invasion of Sicily and the Italian mainland.[11] Just months after the Allies invaded Italy, British and American soldiers extended safety to Jews and other victims of the Nazis living in southern Italy. It was during this period that partisan and British soldiers moved Flory and her mother and, later, her stepfather, to Bari.

After May and June 1944, many more individuals would emerge from experiences of immobility and incarceration. During the late spring, Allied forces progressed into France on the western front and liberated Majdanek on the eastern front. As the Allies moved toward Germany—with the Americans, British, and Canadians arriving from the west and the Soviets approaching from the east—they liberated people in captivity and in hiding.[12] Twenty-three-year-old Clara Heller, a Romanian-born Jew, experienced liberation in

September 1944, when British forces freed her, her mother, and two of her siblings from their eighteenth hiding place: a small home on Stadion Street in Hoboken (now southern Antwerp), just blocks from the stadium where German soldiers held their sporting events.[13]

Of course, the largest number of civilians experienced liberation during the spring of 1945. Like Sala, Gena Goldfinger learned of her freedom in April 1945, just weeks before VE Day. Just sixteen when the Nazis arrived in Kraków, Poland, Gena had been incarcerated for six years: first in the Kraków ghetto and then in a series of different camps, ending at the Bergen-Belsen camp complex in lower Saxony. On April 15, 1945, following a local truce reached three days earlier, British forces announced to the camp inmates that they were liberated. Gena was one of 14,000 Jewish women of Polish, Hungarian, Czechoslovak, and "Greek" origin "freed" at the camp.[14]

Especially before May 1945, shifting military borders and tenuous military victories made many experiences of freedom fragile.[15] Flory remembered that the ongoing fighting in Italy made her worry that liberation was in doubt. She and her mother reached Bari days after British Commonwealth forces captured the airfields around Foggia and one month after the September 1943 armistice signed between Italian and Allied forces. But both Britain's hold on Bari and the armistice itself were vulnerable. The German military began to strike against Italian forces almost immediately after the announcement of the armistice, launching surprise bombings on Bari well into the early winter of 1944. The surprise attacks on Bari and its surrounding airfields and villages only reinforced survivors' perception that liberation had not yet fully materialized, and they readied themselves to flee if the war turned against the British in southern Italy.[16]

Ever-changing lines of combat similarly shaped Clara's liberation experience in Belgium. After being freed in September 1944, Clara and her surviving family members had been too frightened to venture far from their hiding place. At first, their lack of financial resources, concern about missing family members, and fear of repercussion hindered their movement.[17] But, six weeks later, when the Germans began a concentrated attack on the port city, Clara and her family stayed at home because of the bombings. In the fall of 1944, the Nazis launched varying attacks to regain Antwerp, one of the only deep-sea ports between the Mediterranean Sea and the English Channel that had not been destroyed. Over the course of six months, the Nazis dropped 750 V-1 and V-2 missiles on the city. Ninety thousand properties were damaged or destroyed, and 3,400 civilians and 700 Allied service personnel were killed. Until the Allies secured all of Belgium in late February 1945, Clara and her family remained in the Stadion Street house, worrying that their freedom might be temporary.[18]

Even after the fighting ended in Europe, victims of Nazism could not simply return home, locate family, or move about freely.[19] In many places across the continent, Allied military personnel restricted Jewish survivors' movements, attempting to keep refugees and DPs in place. This policy, which affected all noncombatants, not just Jews, had been established in June 1944. That month, the Supreme Headquarters Allied Expeditionary Forces (SHAEF) directed military units in occupied areas to collect refugees and DPs in assembly centers and supply them with material needs until their repatriation.[20] Because SHAEF's original expectation was that refugees would wish to return home and because the Soviets demanded that their citizens be returned to the Soviet Union, early DP camps were organized in such a way to allow for DPs to be sent to their prewar residences; staff separated Western and Eastern Europeans, with each pointed toward their geographic destination in anticipation of their repatriation.[21] Many Jewish survivors resided, at least temporarily, in an Allied displaced persons camp located in the occupied zones of Germany, Austria, or Italy; like all DP center residents, they often were not permitted to leave without the authorities' permission.[22]

Military personnel offered several justifications for restricting migration. First, retaining people in place allegedly safeguarded the movement of Allied personnel and commodities, which was especially important because many Jewish survivors, DPs, refugees, and returnees failed to migrate in ways anticipated by the SHAEF and UN Relief and Rehabilitation Administration (UNRRA) authorities. Several Jews rejected repatriation as an option, instead expressing an interest to journey to the DP camps with large Jewish populations, to locations that had been rumored to house their loved ones, to cities to which their traveling companions wished to relocate, and/or to Palestine or the United States. If such mass migrations were to occur, they would have disrupted the Allied supervised flow of people and goods, defied Soviet demands for the "return" of their citizens, and overwhelmed newly reinstated border controls.[23]

Military leaders also worried that mass migration would exacerbate the existing housing crisis. Allied bombings had destroyed large residential areas; in Germany, for example, about 25 percent of housing units were demolished.[24] Allied personnel, liberated slave laborers, death march survivors, and those who survived years of hiding all required housing, as did the refugees fleeing advancing Soviet troops and those who had been bombed out of their homes. In the immediate postwar period, Allied forces asserted their control over housing priorities in occupied territories and, to do so, frequently tried to keep people in place. In areas already under the control of local or national authorities, those powers, too, insisted on regulating movement to contend with housing shortages.[25]

Military, civilian, and voluntary-agency powers also worried that mass migration could trigger or contribute to a public health crisis. Refugees and displaced people carried with them the illnesses caused by malnutrition, forced labor, displacement, and overcrowding. During the war, sanitary conditions and city infrastructures had collapsed; hospitals lacked medicine and medical personnel; and people were scared and hungry. The Allies had learned from earlier experiences that they needed to better limit the spread of disease, which they believed they could accomplish by feeding, fumigating, and sheltering civilians. They took advantage of new inventions such as DDT and vitamins but insisted that they needed people to remain in place to implement these novel tools.[26]

SHAEF and NGO personnel were particularly concerned about people leaving the former Nazi camps, sites thought to pose acute risks. The now-freed inmates could spread diseases and might be unable to recover from illness if they were no longer in locations with some, even if limited, medical care. There were, of course, grounds for such concern. The Bergen-Belsen camp complex had a prison population of 60,000 that was so devastated by disease and malnutrition that one-sixth of its liberated population died within a few weeks of being freed. These newly liberated people remained desperate for medical help, food, and clean water. To manage their care and to prevent the further spread of disease, staff would evacuate only a small percentage of the former prisoners for immediate medical attention. They divided the survivors into three categories: those for whom immediate assistance might make the difference between life and death, those likely to die, and those likely to survive. They also adopted the slow methodological regime of DDT dusting, washing, and cleaning those deemed likely to survive. For this process to be effective, everyone needed to stay in place.[27]

Gena was one of the thousands of people who remained at Belsen after the war. She recovered quickly from the effects of malnutrition and forced labor, and she responded well to DDT dusting, washing, and cleaning. Her mother, Estera, however, contracted typhus, the louse-borne disease that claimed the lives of many of the Bergen-Belsen survivors. Estera eventually mended, but the two remained at Belsen for several months after liberation, only leaving the camp first when Gena married and then again when they immigrated, separately, to Britain.[28]

Disease and fear of disease similarly immobilized survivors in areas under Soviet occupation. After liberation, Sala remained in Oschatz for several weeks because one of the women with whom she wished to leave Saxony had contracted typhus. Indeed, nineteen of the few hundred women who had been forced to march with Sala had died in Oschatz, many from disease and malnutrition. Unlike Gena, Sala had been at liberty to go, but she waited until her friend was released so that they could travel to Berlin together. The difference in Gena's and Sala's experiences lay in the policies of the occupying powers. The Soviets were less likely to keep people in place and did not enforce a quarantine in the former prisoner-of-war camp where Sala and her friend resided.[29]

Even if liberated survivors were sufficiently healthy to travel and had permission to do so, destroyed roads and infrastructure, a lack of financial resources, fear of sexual assault, and local hostility posed significant obstacles to their movement. Survivors had to rely on limited means of transport: foot, truck, wagon, and, if fortunate, parts of the civilian transport system that remained intact, either because they had not been destroyed during the war or because they already had been rebuilt. Ironically, Allied strategic bombings, one of the multiple tactics that had helped to liberate victims, had destroyed the very means survivors required to return "home" or reconnect with lost family members. Years of bombing raids had destroyed railroad facilities, roads, bridges, and filling stations. "There was no way to travel," remembered Sala. To get to Berlin and then to journey from Berlin to Hannover, she and her traveling companions traversed long distances by foot and by hitch-hiking with NGO or military personnel.[30]

Journeys from one city to another, or even within one city, required tremendous time and energy, but despite the difficulty of travel, Sala and her friends insisted that they leave Oschatz as soon as they could. Reports of rape by Red Army soldiers circulated among the survivors, and they feared for their physical safety.[31] In fact, liberation often coincided with sexual violence—and the fear of that violence—at the hands of Allied soldiers who sought out sex and, on occasion, companionship.[32] "We were terribly afraid of any soldier, of any man," Sala later remembered. "We tried to make ourselves miserable looking. So they would come in and leave." While Sala had hoped that Soviet military personnel might spare Jews, many Red Army soldiers did not differentiate among non-Jewish and Jewish women; one soldier sexually assaulted one of Sala's traveling companions even as she continued to protest that she had been a Jewish victim of the Nazis.[33] Narratives about, and experiences of, sexual assault pushed many survivors to try to leave Soviet jurisdictions quickly, shaping how they experienced and remembered liberation.

It would be misleading to suggest that concerns about sexual pressures existed only in the East. Certainly, the ubiquity of sexual violence in the Soviet zones was unique,[34] but American, British, and Canadian soldiers also participated in acts of banditry, sexual assault, and sexual humiliation. Servicemen often pursued women as "a prize for conquest" and engaged in sexual activity in exchange for food, protection, or shelter.[35] In Bari, Flory witnessed British and American military personnel bartering food and shelter for sexual favors, and she herself was a target of unwanted sexual advances from soldiers at the British depot where she worked.[36] Soon after her liberation, Clara similarly expressed concern that soldiers might take sexual advantage of her and her sister. The night her future spouse, Daniel Isaacman, met Clara, he wrote to his parents about this fear, indicating that it had "kept her at home." Daniel supposedly only persuaded Clara to spend time with him when he presented himself as a fellow Zionist and not as an American soldier. "I convinced her . . . not to let my uniform fool her. . . . I was a *shaliach* [Zionist emissary] sent from the states to organize Gordonia [land of Israel]."[37]

Several Jewish chaplains serving overseas also noted the risk of sexual assault for female survivors. In April 1945, American Jewish chaplain Robert Marcus expressed his concern about 1,000 Jewish female forced laborers the Allied forces had recently liberated. He requested that these women be evacuated immediately, in part because of their vulnerability to abuse from the Soviets and other DPs.[38] A few months later, the Jewish Welfare Board received reports from four additional Jewish chaplains that Jewish women faced the threat of assault in some of the DP camps.[39]

Many Jewish civilians remembered liberation as the moment when they began to acknowledge the enormity of their losses.[40] Even though news of her freedom was imminent, Clara's liberation experience intertwined grief with relief. The day before British forces arrived in Antwerp, members of the resistance felt sufficiently emboldened to come to the Hellers' hiding place and share with them both that they would be freed and that Clara's brother, Herschel, had been killed in an Austrian labor camp. For Clara, liberation could no longer mean what she had hoped for during her time in hiding, namely a return to their previous life. "There really is no going back," she recalled thinking; "nothing will ever be the same."[41] Hungarian-born Judith Magyar Isaacson similarly described liberation with ambivalence. Judith, her mother, and aunt had survived forced labor in Auschwitz and at a munitions labor camp in the town of Hessisch Lichtenau. But, in the immediate aftermath of being freed, they came to realize that their survival was unique among their community and family. Judith's uncle and father had died; her aunt had gone back to Hungary "expecting all these people, and they were gone." News of these murders shaped Judith's decision to remain in Germany with the American GI she recently had met. There would be no much-anticipated family reunion; she would not return to Hungary.[42]

Because of the fragile medical and emotional states of many survivors, liberation frequently coincided with the severe illnesses and deaths of family and friends. Many of those liberated from the camps, hiding spaces, and forced marches were on the verge of passing away, and thousands of people perished during the days following liberation. In Bergen-Belsen, where the gravely ill and starving prisoners had been packed together without food, water, or basic sanitation, many died from starvation, typhus, and dysentery even as British, Canadian, and voluntary medical forces arrived. "People were dying like flies," Gena remembered.[43] For Gerda Weissmann, liberation had been marked by the death of her closest companion, Liesl. Gerda had been interned in several different concentration and labor camps and later was one of 350 female Jewish prisoners who survived a 480-mile death march that had begun in Upper Silesia and ended in Czechoslovakia. Gerda and Liesl were liberated by the US Army less than twenty-four hours before the announcement of the war's end on the European continent, and Liesl died one day after their rescue, likely from an injury caused by a bullet from an American fighter plane. Gerda, who later married one of her liberators, recalled that while she had long imagined that "liberation would be such a happy story," Liesl's death forced her to experience it differently.[44] "I am alone," she soon would write to her uncle in Turkey; "none of my closest friends survived. . . . There is no one close to me. . . . I am so homesick, so lonely."[45]

Survivors' experiences of postwar loneliness, liberation, mobility, and immobility also were shaped by the hostility they encountered—or expected to encounter—from their current or former non-Jewish neighbors. When Jews returned "home" in search of family, friends, and lost possessions, they often faced resentment. Non-Jewish neighbors had gained financially by looting Jewish property during the war, an act Judith described as "treasure hunting."[46] If forced to return Jewish possessions, non-Jews could face serious economic repercussions. In Antwerp, Clara and her surviving family conceded that their former neighbors would never return the possessions they had stolen from the Hellers' home and business. She and her family determined that it would be safer for them to locate a new place to live and find different means of supporting themselves rather than return to their prewar home and business.[47] The Kabilio family also lost all of their possessions and their residence, and Michael's Zagreb tie factory now was in the hands of a Croatian neighbor. Not only did he and Rosa recognize that the journey to Zagreb from Bari would be arduous and costly, but they also knew that there was little to return to—and that they might not be kindly received.[48] Fears of the hostility they might encounter from former compatriots kept them in Bari long after the war had ended.

Violent expressions of xenophobia and antisemitism similarly prevented Sala from returning to her hometown of Seroc. Almost as soon as she learned of her freedom, Sala heard that it would be dangerous for her to go back to Poland, where Jews had become caught up in the struggles between right-wing groups, clustered around the underground organization affiliated with the Polish government-in-exile in London, and left-wing ones, concentrated around the temporary government created by the Soviet occupation authorities. Anti-Jewish riots had broken out in several Polish cities, and Jews who journeyed to their hometowns were sometimes attacked and murdered on their way or upon arrival. In Poland, non-Jews killed more than 500 Jews between November 1944 and October 1945.[49] News of the lawlessness, sexual violence, and antisemitism in Poland prompted Sala and her friends to abandon their original plans of returning "home" and to travel instead to Berlin, where they hoped to reconnect with family and friends without risking their lives. Sala later discovered that one of her brothers had been a victim of the postwar antisemitic violence in Poland. Having survived the camps, he returned to Seroc and Warsaw and was murdered by a non-Jewish Pole.[50]

Hard economic conditions, communist takeovers, and growing xenophobia led to a new phenomenon: the rapid arrival of Jewish and non-Jewish refugees fleeing their "home" countries into Germany, Austria, and Italy. The American and British zones in Germany and Austria offered these refugees physical distance from the former residences that had again rejected them, illegal escape routes to Palestine, shelter and food, and opportunities to search for missing relatives and loved ones. In September 1946, American Jewish chaplain Herbert Friedman described the influx of refugees, bemoaning the fact that antisemitic violence was pushing thousands of Jews into the American zone. He had witnessed roads "clogged with refugees . . . tired sick hungry Jews," all "shoving across the border."[51] Several months earlier, Rabbi Philip Bernstein, the adviser on Jewish affairs to the US Army, alleged that there were far more people coming into Germany than could be housed. Claiming that these "infiltrees" entered the American zone at a rate of 10,000 per week, he worried that the "population in the American zone is now two and one half million more than it was before the war, whereas half the housing of the area has been destroyed by bombs."[52] The lack of sufficient accommodation was only one of many deprivations. Many of these DPs did not receive sufficient aid to meet an "acceptable standard of living." They lacked fuel, warm clothing, and food, scarcities worsened by the harsh winter and hot summer.[53]

Like many Jewish soldiers and officers, Bernstein insisted that these fleeing refugees deserved aid, but American and British authorities differed in their treatment of these individuals. US officials granted them the same assistance they extended to displaced people of Allied nations, meaning that those arriving in the American zones could seek help from DP camps and from organizations that aided victims of the Nazi terror now living in Germany and Austria.[54] In contrast, the British Control Commissions in Austria and Germany argued that the Jews who had "infiltrated" the British zones since August 1945 should not be regarded as displaced persons and refused to provide them with food and shelter. This encouraged many to attempt entry into the American zone instead, and, by the spring of 1947, there were approximately 153,000 Jews living there, while only about 14,000 Jews lived in the British zone in Germany.[55]

Outside of Germany and Austria, southern Italy also served as a site where significant numbers of refugees—not only Jewish ones—continued to arrive. The Allies expected about 30,000 non-Italians to migrate through northern Italy to their homes in Central and Northern Europe, but these migrants were joined by European Jews who were looking for ways to enter the United States or Palestine, legally or illegally.[56] The Jewish migrants often lived in UNRRA-established DP camps or in assembly centers created by the Jewish Brigade.[57] At these centers, the Jewish Brigade, often assisted by Allied Jewish military personnel, helped care for the refugees, taught Hebrew, and prepared the aspiring immigrants for their lives in Palestine. It was difficult for the authorities to distinguish legal DPs from Jewish refugees who entered with forged papers, and, by the winter of 1945–46, the immigration of Jewish refugees to Palestine through Italy had become a major problem for the Allied authorities.[58]

· ·

Wherever they were located, victims of the Nazi terror and those engaged with their liberation experienced these moments of freedom with mixed emotions. "That was liberation," explained one memoirist; "it wasn't simple."[59] Being rescued from the Nazis was exhilarating, but it also was uneven, prolonged, and, at times, miserable. Gena invoked that ambivalence into her nineties, when she insisted that April 15 was "the most important date" on her calendar, while also portraying liberation as a moment characterized by grotesque horrors.[60] Her husband Norman Turgel, a British intelligence officer whom she met at liberation, likewise remembered that period with ambivalence. On the one hand, he was proud of his role in freeing Bergen-Belsen's Jews and capturing its torturers and murderers. On the other hand, he could not let go of the chaos, death, and despair he had seen during the camp's liberation. In later testimony, he interlaced descriptions of his military triumphs and meeting his future wife with observations of the camp's depravities and desolation.[61] Norman's experience was representative of that faced by other Jewish military personnel who actively participated in liberation and recovery. As Allied military personnel journeyed through occupied Europe, they encountered victims who had been in camps, forced on death marches, spent time in hiding, and passed as non-Jews. They also determined whether they wished to become involved in relief efforts and considered whether they would obey policies regulating contact between military personnel and noncombatants.

Until they encountered the survivors, many Allied soldiers and officers who had heard reports of the Nazi treatment of Jews were naturally preoccupied with fighting—and surviving—the war. "I knew *something* about what was going on," remembered one Jewish veteran. "We had heard reports about some terrible things happening, but we just didn't know *what*. . . . We really didn't know anything at all about the horrible extent of it—the actual unimaginable—until we came on-site in a couple of places."[62] In the letters Daniel wrote to his parents from France, where he was stationed in July and August 1944, he paid little attention to the Nazi treatment of the Jews. Instead, he wrote about his daily life, his homesickness, and the fighting. But his letters grew more intense as he encountered—and then interacted with—Jewish survivors. As he moved through Germany and into Belgium, he sent panicked notes to his parents about European Jewry's "dire straights [*sic*]." Long having imagined that antisemitism would make a Jewish state a necessity, Daniel lamented "that which we prophesized [the destruction of European Jewry] has, alas, come true."[63] Nazi antisemitism had devastated European Jewry, and Daniel announced his intention to be a part of relief and recovery efforts. In his first letters, Canadian Royal Air Force (RAF) private Charles "Charlie" A. similarly focused on the food rations, his health, and his efforts to plan Jewish cultural and religious events for the "Yiddisha boys" at the base. When he was stationed outside Bergen-Belsen, however, his communications took on alarmist tones, describing the Nazi atrocities and outlining the extensive physical and emotional needs of the Jews he encountered.[64]

Refugee military personnel offered similar stories of shock and alarm upon encountering Jewish survivors. Perhaps slightly more informed about the Nazi terrors than their American-, British-, and Canadian-born compatriots had been, several Jewish soldiers who came from Central Europe but now were serving in the Allied forces described a roller coaster of emotions. They shifted from a concern about the families they left behind to a focus on the war effort, and then, later, to despair about the surviving remnant of European Jewry and the implications for their families and friends. Before and immediately after he was inducted into military service, American intelligence officer Kurt Klein, who later married Gerda, learned about some of the atrocities taking place in Europe. Kurt had come to the United States from Walldorf, Germany, in 1937. Until his parents' deportation, he and his siblings had received regular communications from them, describing the growing Nazi hostility toward—and harassment of—Jews. Kurt had hoped that his military service would take him to Europe, so that he might locate and assist his family. Yet he "did not fully perceive the gathering storm."[65] Returning to Germany as an officer, he slowly began to piece together a fuller picture of the Nazi horrors, but "the war was still going on" and he focused on his military duties.[66] Even when he and his fellow soldiers learned that 100 female Jewish prisoners had been abandoned nearby, they could not drop everything and go to them. "We were not in any position to do anything right then and there," he explained. It would not be until the following day, when they would travel to Volary, that he began to see for himself the "living skeletons . . . in various stages of disease or close to death" who required his help.[67]

Liberators simultaneously articulated confusion, revulsion, and distress over what they witnessed. "It was just simply something that one couldn't believe," Kurt remembered.[68] "Words would not give you half the idea of what it all looks like," one Jewish Canadian RAF transport driver similarly explained to his chaplain. The driver had difficulty processing what he was seeing and begged his "padre" to visit Belsen "and see with your own eyes, as I did, what was done to the Jews."[69] Such atrocities, penned an American soldier in a letter to his wife back home, "make some of the things that you have read about in the past seem like pleasant bedtime stories."[70] Invoking

Close-up portrait of Jewish serviceman Lt. Kurt Klein.
United States Holocaust Memorial Museum,
courtesy of Gerda Weissmann Klein.

the literary norms and imagery that would be repeatedly employed in future portrayals of the Holocaust,[71] members of the Allied forces described being overwhelmed by horrific smells, encountering individuals so malnourished that they "were nothing but skin and bones," seeing mass graves overloaded with bodies, and discovering enormous barracks crammed with suitcases, glasses, and shoes.[72] "I was . . . prepared to see the nude, emaciated dead bodies piled three, four, and five high on the street," one soldier wrote to his family. "It was only the living dead that I wasn't prepared for."[73] "We had become pretty accustomed to seeing dead and mangled bodies, but even the GIs were appalled and nauseated by the sights and odors at Dachau," another GI explained. "The picture of the dead lying in formless heaps of naked and starved, the moans of those not yet dead and the stench of those already dead was more than nightmarish. For even in a nightmare this couldn't be envisioned."[74]

The Jewish survivors required relief and support, and Jewish military personnel were uniquely positioned to help them. They were already on the ground, had access to supplies and means of travel, and sometimes had language skills that allowed them to communicate with Jewish survivors. Many were motivated by a sense of responsibility to their coreligionists.[75] Several Jewish soldiers and chaplains exchanged letters and reports describing the situation's urgency. "The situation here is terrible," wrote Daniel to his parents as early as December 1944. "Almost nothing is being done to alleviate their plight. . . . The sooner we act, the more lives we save, the more hearts we mend. . . . Our people are starving, and the liberation, so far, brought them nothing."[76] Rabbi Louis Milgrom, an American Jewish chaplain stationed with the Twelfth Tactical Air Command, sent similarly disquieting memos back to the United States recounting the destitute, diseased, and depressed Jewish survivors and refugees he encountered. He lamented that it was left to Jewish military personnel to help them and that "none of the Jewish organizations have thus far come to their aid." Without the military, he insisted, these Jews "would still be ill, and most would be unfed and unclad."[77] His contemporary, British chaplain B. M. Casper, also insisted that Jewish chaplains and soldiers needed to focus on European Jews who "have been forgotten and neglected," no matter what their other obligations might be.[78]

Casper and others became highly involved with aid and assistance.[79] They shared their rations, organized the collection of necessary goods, settled Jewish refugees in various DP camps, advocated on behalf of the Jewish victims, and set up makeshift hospitals. They also led religious services, traced missing relatives and loved ones, provided counseling and pastoral care, ran Zionist youth activities, smuggled Jews out of Europe and into Palestine, and wrote letters home requesting that family and friends send care packages to needy survivors.[80] One Jewish chaplain reported that he and his Jewish soldiers were "moving people to freedom as fast as we can, are solving family problems, doing social work, generally raising hell—and also serving 5 divisions and special troops."[81] Daniel similarly visited with Jewish survivors, worked with the Jewish Brigade to care for Jewish children, and distributed food items, blankets, and other goods that he likely took from the base. Indeed, his letters became so focused on his frenzied relief efforts that his father warned him against "overdoing it."[82] Nearly 250 miles away in Hannover, Germany, Abraham "Abe" Bonder, a Canadian Royal Air Force mechanic who, like

Daniel, had been involved in the Zionist movement, likewise expressed the urgency of helping the "remnants."[83]

While need prompted many Jewish military personnel to intervene, so, too, did the recognition that geography alone had saved them. Jewish soldiers and officers understood that had they themselves been living in Europe during the 1940s they, too, could have been targeted for extermination. Refugee soldiers were particularly sensitive to the ways immigration had spared them from witnessing the full "terrifying drama" of the attempted genocide of European Jewry. In his letters to Gerda, Kurt recognized that he was "fortunate" to have survived the Nazi ordeal. As he wondered whether he would have been designated for extermination along with his mother had he not left for the United States in 1937, he expressed his gratitude for having immigrated and for being able to return to Europe and visit some of the last sites where his family members would have been before their deportation.[84] American-, British-, and Canadian-born soldiers likewise drew comparisons between themselves and the European Jews selected for annihilation. In his letters home, Daniel frequently likened his family members to the Jews he met. He wrote to his parents that he often would try to "visualize what we would have done under the like conditions" and, in April 1945, after meeting his future wife, Clara, he described her siblings and mother as "a family just like ours." For Daniel, whose parents came to the United States from the Russian Empire, only luck and fortune spared him and his family from the Nazi genocide.[85]

Daniel identified an additional variable that pushed him to assist the Jews he encountered: a chivalrous notion that their generation of Jewish men were uniquely placed to help "save" the surviving remnant and, in turn, the Jewish people as a whole. During Passover, a holiday already focused on themes of redemption and survival, Daniel figuratively placed himself—and his fellow Jewish soldiers—at his parents' seder table. "How much I would have liked being there," he wrote. "But I was—for when you filled the wine cup for Eliyahu—it was for me—I and my generation are the Eliyahus who are to find the salvation for our people. Drink a toast to us, your youth."[86] A student of Jewish religion and history, Daniel's invocation of Elijah's cup was hardly accidental. The fifth cup of wine poured during the Passover seder goes untouched in honor of the prophet Elijah, who is believed to one day herald the advent of the Messiah. Passover not only commemorates the historical redemption of the Israelites from bondage, but it also invokes the future redemption of the Jewish people. That April 1945 holiday must have been heady for Daniel and his fellow Jewish GIs. In letters home and in missives to their chaplains, other Jewish soldiers similarly emphasized their responsibility for caring for the surviving remnant and helping the Jewish people recover. "It is my job now," one Jewish Canadian RAF transport driver insisted.[87]

. . . .

No matter what prompted their involvement, when Jewish (and non-Jewish) personnel participated in relief efforts, they often violated the military policies that delimited whether and how soldiers and officers could interact with noncombatants. These regulations, frequently referred to as nonfraternization policies, shifted considerably between 1944 and 1947, and sometimes shaped the nature of the encounter between military personnel and survivors. The policies tended to follow cultural affinities and experiences of war and liberation. Military officials permitted (but did not always promote) contact between soldiers and noncombatants in countries categorized as trusted allies. In places whose populations had allegedly been victimized by the Nazis, they also allowed fraternization, as long as those interactions preserved the reputation of the military forces and, in the American case, followed racially segregated lines.[88] As aid worker Miri Kugelman remembered, in these territories, soldiers could "fraternize but not loot."[89] Between the summer of 1943 and May 1945, that meant that military personnel and survivors in countries such as Italy, France, and Belgium could interact with one another with relative ease. In Bari, Jewish Fifteenth Air Force Battalion master sergeant Harry Jagoda visited the DP camps, distributed goods to Jewish refugees, and socialized with Flory and her family. In Antwerp, Daniel regularly attended local Zionist meetings, spent time with Clara and her sister, and organized activities for Jewish children. During that time, neither man faced any restriction on interactions with local and refugee Jewish communities.

After May 1945, however, Allied military officials began to limit contact between soldiers and noncombatants in several previously occupied countries. As the war in Europe waned, officials worried that German-born noncombatants in Belgium and Holland, whether or not they had been affiliated with the Nazi Party, posed a security risk. New policies crafted for these regions forbade anyone born in Germany or Austria, but now located in Belgium or Holland, from socializing with soldiers, gaining employment at army bases, or entering Red Cross clubs. This would impact the relationships between some Jewish civilians and military personnel. Tens of thousands of Jews had come to Belgium and Holland from central Europe before the war; many of those who survived the Holocaust and had returned to (or stayed in) Belgium and Holland now found themselves treated as former enemies.[90] The case of Elfriede "Friedl" H. offers one such example. Friedl had fled to Belgium from Vienna during the late 1930s and had survived the war in hiding. When she and Canadian RAF transport driver Sydney D. first met in September 1944, they socialized without any limitations. However, eight months later, new regulations restricted their relationship, limiting Friedl's ability to travel to her now-fiancé and/or socialize with his friends at local Red Cross clubs.[91]

The most stringent nonfraternization policies regulated contact in Germany and Austria. Here, too, Jewish noncombatants and military personnel found themselves affected. First announced in September 1944 when Allied troops entered West German territory, the early regulations prohibited all interactions, even everyday conversation, between members of the military and German and Austrian civilians. Military authorities agreed that a strict nonfraternization policy was necessary to "win both the war and the peace."[92] While they soon disagreed over the principles' implementation and called for each army of occupation to establish its own policy, the various miliary forces generally permitted soldiers to play with children, purchase goods from German and Austrian stores, and employ German and Austrian workers. However, the regulations diverged on matters concerning intimate social interactions, and multiple policies that regulated sexual relationships, travel, housing distribution, and marriage existed.[93] Some of these nonfraternization policies, particularly those concerning travel and marriage, continued to impact Jews living in certain locations.

Violations of the nonfraternization policies were rampant. Sexual encounters featured prominently in letters home, military newspapers, and pinups.[94] But there existed a second kind of violation, namely those everyday nonsexual interactions between military personnel and Jewish noncombatants. In crafting their policies, Allied officials had intentionally included Jews and other victim groups. Weighing the expediency of creating a uniform regulation against the importance of addressing humanitarian needs, military leaders determined that to keep matters clear and to be certain that the victims were not really perpetrators in disguise, the policies needed to include any person on German or Austrian soil.[95] The shifting nonfraternization regulations affected some European Jews and Allied soldiers. Jewish military personnel criticized the policies' inclusion of Jews and recognized that they themselves often violated the regulations. Military officials, one chaplain complained, could not differentiate between "Jews who are not American and who live in Germany today and other 'indigenous enemy personnel.'"[96]

Philip Bernstein called the policies "unjust" and worried that they would jeopardize the standing of those chaplains and soldiers who worked with European Jews.[97] Jewish chaplains' reports for the spring and summer of 1945 similarly lamented that they frequently breached military policy and articulated a need to do "welfare work on the QT."[98]

Until authorities relaxed the regulations in the fall of 1945, Jewish chaplains and soldiers continued their illegal work while simultaneously requesting permission to interact socially with European Jews, bring them food, and/or allow local Jews to worship with military personnel. But permission sometimes could be difficult to receive. In April and May 1945, Britain's Jewish Hospitality Committee for British and Allied Forces repeatedly was denied the authorization to host Jewish worship services and meals that would welcome Jewish civilians alongside British military personnel, and, one month later, American soldiers physically prevented German Jewish civilians from attending a synagogue service led by an American Jewish chaplain.[99] When military officials redefined the categories of "displaced person" and "Germany" in early autumn 1945, they excluded many Jewish civilians from the nonfraternization policies, a change rooted less in the lobbying efforts of military personnel than in the ongoing, coterminous talks concerning different victim groups' eligibility for assistance.[100]

. . . .

While Sala was ignorant of these official discussions, she was aware that definitions of DPs, Jews, and Germans shaped policies and, in turn, impacted her. Now living in the Ohestrasse DP camp in Hannover, the young survivor was frustrated that liberation did not mean that she could move about freely. She had spent much of her adolescence and early emerging adulthood incarcerated; while thankful for the roof over her head, the clothes on her body, and the food in her stomach, she had been angry that as a resident of a DP camp in the British zone, she had been encouraged to be "repatriated" to Poland, a country she no longer considered "home." Instead, Sala wanted desperately to settle in Palestine. She even had attempted to immigrate there illegally in August. Her escape had been thwarted and she had been unceremoniously returned to Ohestrasse. There, surrounded by Jewish survivors about her age, she participated in Zionist activities and plotted her escape from Germany.

Since Sala had learned of her freedom in Oschatz that previous April, the Polish-born survivor had been almost exclusively with people her age. In Oschatz, Berlin, and Hannover, Sala traveled, socialized, and resided with people in their late teens and early twenties. Most of the survivors Sala met were between the ages of eighteen and forty. It was rare for anyone over forty years old to have survived the harsh conditions of the concentration camps or hiding or for anyone under sixteen to have avoided selection to the gas chambers.[101] Moreover, the young NGO and military personnel she met were also approximately her age. Sala had countless encounters with young people, and those experiences rarely left a mark. One fateful meeting, however, would shape the rest of her life, an interaction that eventually resulted in courtship and marriage.[102]

2

I Found a *Chavera*!

....

JEWISH ENCOUNTERS
IN JEWISH SPACES

Sala Solarcz first crossed paths with Abraham "Abe" Bonder in September 1945 at the Rosh Hashanah celebrations at the Ohestrasse DP camp. The young survivor had dreaded the Jewish holidays without her family. She had no interest in socializing with the Jewish soldiers and aid workers, whom she knew would be visiting Ohestrasse. It was not the Canadian or British military nonfraternization regulations that kept her away. Instead, she felt that the Jewish soldiers treated Jewish DPs as if they were a spectacle, something to be watched and pitied, as if they were "monkeys to be observed in a cage." She wanted no *rachmanos* (sympathy), she just wanted to be left alone. But she was unable to sidestep Abe. The Montreal-born mechanic had long been interested in Jewish politics and community. An avid Zionist, he had met with surviving Jews in the Low Countries and Germany. Now, in Hannover, he noticed that Sala had removed herself from the celebrations. He approached her and, in Yiddish, asked after her welfare. According to their recollections, she was taken by Abe's earnestness and his ability to speak comfortably in her language. The two spent the Jewish holidays together and within weeks were considering marriage.[1]

The encounter narratives of Jewish civilians and military personnel such as Sala and Abe tell stories of loss, recovery, power, and unbelonging in the aftermath of trauma. Bookended on one side by the end of the Holocaust and, on the other, by marriage and emigration, accounts of chance meetings between survivors and the servicemen they eventually married offer paradoxical portraits of Jewish powerlessness and vibrancy. On the one hand, couples met one another during moments of horrific loss and trauma. On the other hand, in telling stories about how they met, survivors and the servicemen they later married inverted visions of a world in which Jewish historical actors lacked agency and control. Instead of a portrait of a continent *without* Jews, their encounter narratives offered an image of a world that *included* Jewish beauty, actors, languages, and cultures.

· ·

In the aftermath of the Holocaust, loss stamped itself onto the daily existence of European and North African Jews. When she encountered Abe, Sala recently had learned of the deaths of multiple family members and had failed to illegally immigrate to Palestine. Abe had arrived from the Low Countries to Germany just days after it had sued for peace. Over the course of his time in Europe, he had witnessed the horrors that had befallen the continent's Jews, as well as the physical devastation of European infrastructure and landscapes. He also had received dreadful news from home. His father had died suddenly, and his mother was ill. Shattered that he could not quickly receive compassionate leave and return to Montreal, he threw himself into recovery efforts. Soon afterward, he met Sala.[2] Likewise, Bella Lewkowicz, a French Jew who had survived the war in flight and in hiding, recalled that she crossed paths with Raymond "Ray" Ostroff, the American GI she later married, just as she came to the realization that she had "nothing to go to and nowhere to go." The Nazis and their French collaborators had murdered her brother, her father had died from malnutrition and disease immediately after being freed, and her childhood apartment had been destroyed and ransacked. The Philadelphia-born soldier to whom she would quickly become engaged was also processing the desolation he had witnessed as a combat soldier during the war and, later, as a member of the occupation force. Ray had landed in Normandy on D-Day, fought in both France and Germany, and helped liberate Jews who had been in hiding. Trauma was a core component of both Ray's and Bella's everyday lives.[3]

Of course, chance meetings could not wipe out trauma, resurrect lost loved ones, return stolen possessions, or replace ruined lives. But they could insert Jews, Jewish spaces, and Jewish beauty into the ravaged landscape, a Europe that had intended to be "without Jews."[4] In stories about their unexpected meetings, military personnel and Jewish civilians both expressed incredulity that they had crossed paths in the first place and emphasized their future partners' unique charisma and appeal.

It made sense that these couples later underscored both their surprise and their partners' attractiveness. In the early days of liberation, many servicemen and officers had come to imagine a Europe whose Jewish population had been decimated, and they often lamented to their families, congregants, and neighbors that they encountered more Jewish corpses than "live" Jews. Even when they met "live" Jews, many of the survivors would die within days, or even hours, of their encounter, since most of the Jews who remained alive were malnourished, diseased, and filthy.[5] Survivors, too, found it remarkable that they encountered military personnel who were Jewish. Former victims had spent years absorbing antisemitic discourses about themselves, and now they found Jewish servicemen in the role of victor and occupier. To be liberated "not only by an American, but by a fellow Jew" was wildly unexpected.[6]

Stories of chance encounters acknowledged the grotesque scenes in which the couples met while simultaneously depicting them as uniquely charming. It was practical for couples to tell stories in which they distanced their future romantic partners from the other "living dead," a strategy of disassociation commonly used when reactivating or recalling traumatic memories.[7] Gena and Norman distinguished Gena from the general prison population at Bergen-Belsen, where the two first crossed paths. The former prisoners were skeletal, unwashed, and "insect-ridden." Gena, however, was clean, blonde, and striking. Norman later insisted that she "looked bloated rather than thin," with attractive "features." "In my eyes," he recalled, "she looked beautiful."[8] Central to that origin story—and to Gena's desirability—was their shared surprise that the other was Jewish. Norman allegedly had assumed that the "blonde young woman" was a member of the Nazi SS hiding in the makeshift infirmary. When Gena revealed that she was Jewish, Norman later admitted he felt relief that the pretty woman in her prison uniform to whom he was attracted was a fellow Jew and not a perpetrator. Gena similarly expressed surprise that her handsome liberator was a Jewish officer "trying to track down the Nazis and to see justice done."[9] The couple shaped their encounter story in a way that recognized, but also disassociated themselves from, the horrors linked with their initial meeting. In their telling, their first interactions at Belsen allowed each to avow their Jewishness in a place where, just days earlier, one's Jewish identity could mark an individual for extermination. Ironically, their narratives also promoted images of Jewish beauty in characteristics previously associated with Germanness: blonde hair, striking features, and positions of power.

A year earlier, and nearly 1,200 miles away, Flory and Harry likewise expressed their astonishment at discovering their shared Jewishness and allure. When Harry invited Flory to an officer's dance, he assumed that the blonde-haired beauty was Catholic, "a Pollack."[10] Flory, who for years had not revealed to anyone that she was Jewish, had not even considered the possibility that the American soldier could be a Jew. The two only discovered their common religious identities when Harry suggested that they go to her parents' apartment to receive their permission to go to the dance. There, he noticed a *machzor* (Jewish prayer book for the High Holidays) lying on the table. Surprised, in a mix of English, Hebrew, and Italian, he disclosed that he was Jewish and asked whether they also were Jews. Their chance meeting allowed them to publicly affirm their Jewishness. In Flory's case, it also ended her family's attempt to conceal their Jewish identity and allowed her to imagine a Jew who was magnetic, powerful, and attractive. Harry drove a jeep, supposedly was so handsome that when he arrived in southern Italy, "the girls were all crazy" about him, and joked with those he met. His attractiveness, levity, and lightness were traits unlike those of the thousands of refugees with whom Flory and her family had been linked.[11]

Flory and Gena seemingly gained the notice of their future husbands because they were fair-haired women. In fact, hair appeared in several different encounter narratives. When Lala Weintraub, who had survived the war by passing as a Pole, first met Morris Fishman in the Hasenhecke DP camp, where Morris served as the director, Lala's blonde braids caught the director's eye. According to Lala, her hair resembled that of a non-Jew, and, as such, prompted Morris to inquire why the Jewish survivor sought help from an agency that assisted Jews. In this way, she contrasted herself with other Jewish DPs. They were "refugees and they had nothing," she remembered; "not that I had a lot, but I was young, I was fresh. . . . I looked like a shiksa [non-Jewish

Flory Kabilio playing her accordion.
United States Holocaust Memorial Museum,
courtesy of Flory Kabilio Jagoda.

woman]."[12] Jewishness, she implied, was not imagined to be beautiful (or youthful), but her hair and age were. Judith Summer (née Lederer), a survivor of the camps and a death march, similarly emphasized that her hair played a role in attracting her future husband's attention. The fact that she had hair differentiated her from other survivors at the hospital where she and her future husband, Sam Swerdlow, both worked. The Nazis had not shaved her head, which, she maintained, allowed her to remain attractive and which led Sam to assume that she was not Jewish. "What a difference it makes to a woman whether you're bald or whether you have your hair," she explained.[13] This emphasis on hair is consistent with survivor testimony more generally. In memoirs, interviews, and letters, many victims lamented the experience of being shaved, describing how the lack of hair made them feel subhuman, animalistic, and vulgar. After the war, survivors also frequently focused on a woman's hair to talk about sexual violence, sometimes looking to hair as what drew unwanted notice or fixing on it as a means to introduce the difficult topic.[14] It is possible that the encounter narratives emphasized the women's hair and non-Jewish features as one way to avoid thinking about wartime humiliations and depravations.

In addition to expressing astonishment that couples might share both Jewishness and attractiveness, encounter stories included a third category of disbelief, namely "surprise" reunions. These frequently involved the reuniting of foreign-born military personnel with the survivors they had been romantically involved with before the war.[15] Intimating that relationships such as these would have continued if the Nazis had not come to power, interviews, chaplaincy reports, and newspaper articles described couples who reunited even though their reunions were long assumed to have been impossible. In these "love will find a way" stories, narrators underscored the horrors of the war and the twists and turns following liberation, any of which would have been sufficient to have prevented the couple from finding one another again. They also hinted at the strength and forbearance of the soldiers and officers who "tracked down" their future spouses despite the many obstacles thrown in their way.[16]

The postwar encounter narrative of Walter and Hanna offers one such story of a "miraculous" reunion. Childhood sweethearts in Czechoslovakia, the two had been separated by the war. After her liberation in 1945, Hanna attempted to send word to Walter that she had survived the Nazi atrocities. When he discovered that Hanna still was alive, Walter, now a soldier in the US Army, "shook his head in disbelief." During his time on European soil as a refugee soldier, he witnessed unimaginable death and devastation. He had learned of the murder of so many family members and friends that it had seemed hopeless to have envisioned that his former girlfriend had survived, though news of her survival did not indicate where she had been liberated or had settled. The GI searched for her across Europe, eventually finding her in Amsterdam and proposing marriage.[17] Similar origin stories concerned the reunion in Nice of a couple who had dated as adolescents in Germany; the unexpected meeting in Hannover of a British ex-enemy alien serviceman and his former German-Jewish girlfriend; and the London reunion of an American GI with the girlfriend he had "left behind" a decade earlier.[18] These encounter narratives shared commonalties: the young couples all had spent time together in a Europe that had not yet witnessed the aftermath of Kristallnacht; the future grooms each emigrated from Germany, Czechoslovakia, or Austria during the 1930s and then eventually joined the US, British, or Canadian militaries; the female survivors all faced growing discrimination, harassment, and persecution and, in most cases, arrest, deportation, and internment; both the future husband and wife discovered at the war's end that the Nazis had murdered family members and friends; and each future groom overcame great difficulties and obstacles to locate the former romantic partner. In no case did the historical record reflect the challenges the couples faced when they "reunited." We do not know if they felt pressure to marry or if one harbored resentment of the other; instead, contemporary and subsequent sources underscored the miraculous discovery of a Jewish former lover presumed murdered or missing.[19]

While this theme was particularly relevant for encounter narratives concerning refugee soldiers and their prewar romantic partners, it was not limited to them. Other stories highlighted how extant social, familial, and geographic connections engendered new relationships in this landscape of loss. These narratives, like the ones concerning the reunions of former romantic partners, insisted on a Jewish continuity, real or imagined, that could withstand the horrors of the Nazi years. Anna Nathan and Karl Bergman's origin story focused on their shared childhood home of Trebechovice, Czechoslovakia. Like Walter, Karl had escaped Czechoslovakia in the 1930s, albeit for England, where he eventually joined the Royal Air Force. After the war's end, the RAF serviceman journeyed to his hometown to find out whether his mother or siblings had survived the Nazi atrocities. It was there that he met Anna, who, along with her first husband, had been deported to Theresienstadt, where she had given birth to a girl. Only the mother and daughter survived the war, and, in the spring of 1945, they made their way back to Trebechovice. Anna and Karl met because Anna's former brother-in-law had been a friend of Karl's and had requested that he bring food and clothing to Anna and her young child.[20] Other couples encountered one another through prewar social or familial networks, such as the American Jewish chaplain's assistant who met his future wife, the chaplain's niece, when the survivor came to the military base, or the Canadian soldier who encountered the woman he would marry when he returned to his family's hometown to search for his father's relatives.[21] Still others connected through recently created military-civilian couples who now introduced their friends and siblings to one another. Daniel and Clara, for example, plotted to bring Daniel's friend Reuben "Ruby" Gorewitz and Clara's sister Freide together; when the latter two became a couple, the four young adults became part of a "really wonderful foursome."[22] Downplaying their own traumas, these couples crafted origin stories that emphasized continuity after loss and hinted at possibilities of agency during a period in which many felt a lack of control.

· ·

Frequently highlighting an element of intentionality, couples reversed tropes of Jewish powerlessness when they told how they had met, inserting Jews and Jewish places, languages, and cultures into a landscape that had witnessed the physical destruction of Jewish neighborhoods and landmarks. Some of the couples' origin stories highlighted how Jewish physical spaces brought them together. Others looked to religion, language, culture, and belief. When they described having met in a Jewish neighborhood or at a synagogue service, Zionist meeting, or Jewish cultural event, these future spouses reified their sameness despite their intrinsic differences. By focusing on places, ideology, language, or practice, they linked their prewar cultural heritage with their postwar realities, suggesting that the Nazis and their collaborators had failed to wipe out Jewish life and culture. They crafted encounter narratives that told stories of active—and defiant—attempts to create postwar Jewish lives against the backdrop of death and destruction. Perhaps, too, they looked to Jewish spaces and culture to explain their immediate attraction to one another in the aftermath of genocide.[23]

Ray and Bella's origin story centered on Jewish neighborhoods and ritual objects in a France that had sought the destruction of those very things. Soon after arriving in Reims, a medieval city northeast of Paris, in 1945, Ray stumbled upon a neighborhood whose doorways still were affixed with *mezuzot*, ritual objects hung on the doorposts of Jewish homes. The son of a Jewish butcher, Ray had grown up in an observant Jewish household in Philadelphia. When he spotted the *mezuzot*, he immediately recognized their significance and began searching for Jews in the area. Standing in the doorway of one of those homes was Bella. She recently had returned to Reims and now was living with her mother and surviving siblings in a different apartment than the one she had been forced to evacuate years earlier. Ray approached her and, in Yiddish, asked whether she was Jewish. When he first arrived in France and learned details of the Nazi atrocities against the Jews, Ray had imagined a country erased of its Jewish population. Now, after meeting Bella in what had been a prewar Jewish neighborhood, he radically shifted his perception. There remained a small, but active, Jewish community in Reims. For Bella, too, the fact that an American GI approached her in Yiddish restored the prewar lingua franca of that neighborhood to her postwar apartment complex and sharply contrasted with the image of Jewish victimhood that she had unwittingly absorbed during the war years.[24]

Just as Bella and Ray focused on Jewish ritual objects and neighborhoods in their encounter narratives, other couples looked to the synagogue as the backdrop when describing how they first met. These stories frequently took place in Jewish places of worship that the Nazis and their collaborators had demolished, set afire, ravaged, and/or defamed, and that some Jewish military personnel then rebuilt and restored. The restoration of European and North African synagogues had been an important issue for many Jewish chaplains and soldiers during and immediately after the war. Volunteers removed trash and rubble, scoured the floors and walls, repaired broken windows, installed temporary lighting, and collected the torn vestiges of synagogue prayer and holy books. Whenever possible, they then utilized those reconsecrated spaces for Jewish worship.[25] In dozens of cities, Jewish chaplains and other military personnel organized religious services in reclaimed synagogues for soldiers, officers, and civilians who, in the words of one such chaplain, "had just passed through the valley of the shadow of death."[26] In the fall of 1944, American Jewish chaplain Aaron Decter helped to coordinate Rosh Hashanah services in a Paris synagogue whose building he and his men had cleaned and restored. He announced services in his military bulletin and on posters and relied on word of mouth to spread the news; he was overwhelmed by the response. "So many flocked to attend," he reported to the Jewish Welfare Board (NJWB), an organization that served Jewish chaplains in the military and veterans administration, that "many worshippers and attendees had to stand outside in support."[27] American, British, and Canadian Jewish chaplains similarly reopened synagogues for military personnel and civilians in Belgium, Italy, the Netherlands, and Germany.[28] Participants joyfully described the reclaimed synagogues as being "packed to capacity" and "charged with indescribable emotion."[29] They also specifically noted the presence of women. Visiting Europe in May 1945, Rabbi Aryeh Lev, the assistant to the chief of chaplains for the US Army and a member of the NJWB's Committee on Army and Navy Religious Activities (CANRA), found a newly renovated "gorgeous" synagogue that was half filled with female worshippers. Portraits of Jewish women at prayer reinforced a traditional coupling of femininity and spirituality; they also explained how some couples met.[30]

Describing their encounters at synagogues, couples returned the prewar places of worship to the postwar map. Sala Garncarz met her future spouse, Sidney Kirschner, at the historic eighteenth-century synagogue in Ansbach, Germany, at the first Jewish holiday services held in the Bavarian city after liberation. The Nazis had desecrated the synagogue during the war, but members of the US Army's "Famous Fourth Infantry" and other volunteers removed its rubble, scoured the synagogue floors, and made small repairs. When the Rosenbadstrasse synagogue reopened in time for Rosh Hashanah, Sidney, an American Jewish soldier, noticed Sala, a Polish Jewish survivor of several work camps. Sala later recognized the irony of having met her future husband at a synagogue in the very country that had sought the extermination of the Jewish people. She envisioned their encounter as a narrative of Jewish renewal. "It was the first time that we got together with so many Jews," she remembered. "And to see a shul in Germany. That was like, unheard of."[31] Such synagogue encounters, however, had been "heard of" and talked about. Meetings such as those between Sala and Sidney took place elsewhere in Germany, at rebuilt synagogues in Belgium, France, and the Netherlands, and in places of worship in Italy, Tunisia, Algeria, and Morocco that had remained intact during the war.[32] Encounters at prayer services suggested a shared commitment to living Jewish lives in places that once had been imagined to be stripped of Jewish life and culture.

Couples also shared stories of meeting at worship services in spaces that were not prewar synagogues, namely at military personnel hospitality centers and DP camps.[33] Created by diverse Jewish organizations during and after the war for Jewish officers and soldiers, hospitality centers existed in cities as diverse as Amsterdam, Reims, Frankfurt, Heidelberg, Bremen, Munich, and Paris, and were supervised by different authorities, depending on where they were located.[34] Britain's chief rabbi oversaw the British and Canadian Jewish hospitality clubs, with funding from disparate Commonwealth institutions, the NJWB established and ran their American counterparts, and the Va'ad Lemaan Hachayal (Association for the Well-Being of Soldiers) created clubs in Italy and other locations for members of the Jewish Brigade. No matter their sponsor, they tended to be patronized by American, British, and Canadian (and Palestinian, Free-French, and Free-Czech) military personnel, with a fair bit of overlap among them, and grew in number as the Allied forces gained footholds in areas previously under Axis control.[35] When the war ended, Jewish chaplains built new hospitality centers, which housed worship services and developed programs that included the participation of noncombatants. They organized dances, evenings of Jewish music, discussion groups, weekly motion picture viewings, and holiday meals.[36]

Strategically marketing the centers as spaces where men could meet "their fellows and new girl friends in the warmth of a home atmosphere," center directors—mostly Jewish chaplains—encouraged social mixing between

Jewish soldiers and Jewish women. Recognizing that Jewish military personnel were more likely to attend chaplaincy-sponsored events if women also did, they invited local Jewish women to worship services, dances, and lectures. Some also hired local Jewish women as secretaries to staff their centers or to serve as "hostesses" at their events; others collected cosmetics and stockings to distribute in order to attract a Jewish female clientele.[37] Many European and North African Jewish women patronized these centers even though they often expressed suspicion and fear of soldiers. Letters from soldiers and Jewish hostesses, as well as chaplaincy reports, indicate that mixed-gender events were popular, attracting several hundred participants.[38] In September 1944, American Jewish chaplain Harold Saperstein disclosed that he had organized Yom Kippur services and a break-fast "somewhere in France," in which he had encouraged soldiers to invite local Jewish girls. The chaplain had expected approximately fifty guests but welcomed over a hundred.[39] When the synagogue center in Heidelberg opened during Chanukah over one year later, its first worship service was attended by more than 200 GIs, as well as a "a liberal complement of girls." The Heidelberg director had not restricted his programming to religious services. Instead, he organized a dance to follow.[40] Soldiers and hostesses likewise recorded their appreciation of the opportunity to mix with Jews of the opposite gender. After attending his Jewish center's course on Amsterdam Jewish life, one Canadian Jewish soldier remarked that his only criticism of the weeklong program was that the class had concluded, rather than begun, with a dance. If the social event had been earlier, he explained, "we would have met more Jewish girls and in that way see [sic] more of Dutch Judaism."[41] A Jewish hostess similarly emphasized how important it was for her to interact with young Jewish soldiers and officers. In an article in the Heidelberg Synagogue Center's newsletter, she asserted that "a party with Jewish GIs and Jewish girls means much more than any other party." It was "a pleasure of the highest caliber."[42]

Several couples reported meeting at these Jewish sites. Gregor Shelkan, a survivor of the Riga ghetto and four different Nazi internment camps, met Bertha Kerson, the press aide to Gen. Lucius Clay, at the temporary site of Berlin's hospitality center, the American Jewish chaplain's residence. Gregor, a talented cantor and musician, had been chosen to lead Kol Nidre, the prayer service that commences Yom Kippur. Bertha was one of the people responsible for the event's coverage, though she also attended as a Jew who wished to observe the holiday. When the service ended, she relied on her interpreter to congratulate Gregor on his performance. The two found each other attractive and, through the interpreter, arranged to meet again.[43] Ria

Rabbi Dr. Isaac B. Rose next to his vehicle, Netherlands,
June 1945. Yad Vashem Artifacts Collection.
Donated by Isaac and Leesha Rose, Jerusalem.

Strumpf, a twenty-one-year-old German Jewish nurse who spent many years as a prisoner in Theresienstadt, similarly encountered Sgt. Harold Kessler at the center in Heidelberg, when its chaplain organized worship services and a dance to follow. The two crossed paths at the quick service and then again at the social event, making plans to see one another again.[44]

Just as several couples met in the hospitality centers originally designed for military personnel, many others met in spaces specifically intended for Jewish civilians, namely the Jewish displaced persons camps. Organized by fellow DPs, aid workers, chaplains, and UNRRA officials, the DP camps offered vocational training, immigration assistance, and clothing distribution alongside religious services, the distribution of ritual objects, musical performances, newspaper publications, theatrical programs, cabarets, and sing-alongs.[45] Military personnel frequently patronized—and sometimes even administered—these sites; one American Jewish GI recounted to his sister how his commanding officer, who was also Jewish, would take him and a few other GIs to the nearby camp to participate in the wide range of Zionist activities at the nearest DP camp even though it was some distance away. After one visit, he commented that he "had a hell of a good time. For hours I talked to the different people. . . . Then we sang for a good couple of hours. . . . I expect to be out there quite often, though it's quite a distance."[46]

While that soldier never created a long-lasting romantic relationship with any of the DPs he met, a few soldiers and officers established rapports that led to marriage. These couples encountered one another when the military personnel brought food and much needed supplies to the DP centers, helped settle arriving Jewish refugees fleeing from the east, and participated in DP cultural and social events.[47] Just as Abe met Sala B. at Rosh Hashanah services at the Hannover DP center, Morris encountered Lala in the Hasenhecke DP camp when she sought his assistance with her immigration application; American GI Mort Horvitz met Polish survivor Halina (Helena) Jakubowicz at the makeshift bar in the Regensburg DP center; Canadian RAF pilot Charles A. encountered his future wife at the Bergen-Belsen DP center; and Mayer (Michael) Abramowitz crossed paths with Rachel Kosowski at a DP camp in Berlin.[48] These origin stories frequently underscored the presence of Jewish culture and ideologies in a space that once sought their annihilation.

Some encounter narratives focused on the role Zionism played in bringing couples together. Eugenia Cohen, a Milanese Jew who had survived the war in hiding, met Reuven Donath, a member of the Jewish Brigade, at the Zionist-leaning Italian DP camp run by the Jewish Joint Distribution Committee (JDC) in Selvino. Eugenia, who had not grown up in a Zionist household, had begun to embrace the movement after the war's end. When liberated, the young survivor could not return home to Milan; her parents had been deported and her home destroyed. She decided to make her way from the Lombardy plains, where she had been in hiding, to the DP camp in Selvino. With no prospects, she volunteered to work at its children's home, which housed approximately 800 children orphaned by the Holocaust and was staffed by JDC volunteers and Jewish Brigade soldiers (the Palestinian unit of the British Army). While participating in Selvino's daily activities, Eugenia came to envision Palestine as a powerful symbol for her own renewal. When she met Reuven, one of the Jewish Brigade soldiers there, she saw no future for herself or other Jews in Europe and hoped to one day immigrate to Palestine, along with many of her young charges.[49] Reuven worked in Selvino at the behest of the Jewish Brigade. He had learned Italian in his Tel Aviv high school, and the Jewish Brigade had sent him to Selvino after VE Day to help prepare the children for their future lives in Palestine. He coached gymnastics, organized games, coordinated outdoor excursions, and helped bolster the learning of the Hebrew language.[50]

A little over 700 miles away, Clara and Daniel met at a meeting of Zionist youth in Antwerp. The child of Zionist activists and himself involved in the socialist Zionist movement in Philadelphia, Daniel participated in local Zionist activities whenever he could during his military service.[51] When he and Clara first crossed paths, she, like Eugenia, had imagined Palestine as her future home. Indeed, Clara remembered that when Daniel first attended her *hachshara* meeting, she had been leading a debate concerning whether the attendees ought to go to Palestine illegally or wait until they could migrate legally.[52] When he wrote to his parents immediately after encountering Clara, Daniel described the "bachura" (young woman) as a committed Zionist who "would fit in beautifully into our group at home." Walking "under a full moon," the young adults spoke of their "days in the movement." In that first letter, Daniel envisioned a budding Zionist-based friendship. "For if I found a *chavera* [Zionist female friend]," he wrote, "she too found a *chaver* [Zionist male friend]."[53]

Daniel, Clara, Reuven, and Eugenia emphasized the centrality of Zionist ideology and experience to their initial encounters. They were not alone. In the aftermath of the Holocaust, many young Jews flocked to Zionism. The surviving leadership of prewar Zionist youth movements joined with thousands of *shlichim* (emissaries) from Palestine and soldiers from the Jewish Brigade to encourage survivors to make Palestine their new home. They offered Hebrew Jewish educational programs, singalongs, and games; they debated the strengths and weaknesses of different forms of Zionism, studied Jewish history, and celebrated historical Jewish milestones; they created orphanages for children orphaned by the war and established camps and kibbutzim (farms) to prepare prospective immigrants for life in Palestine.[54] By mid-1946, thousands of young kibbutz members representing all strands of the Zionist movement lived at forty such training centers.[55] Like Clara and Eugenia, other Jewish survivors also met their future spouses at Zionist activities.[56]

Yet while Zionism animated political and cultural life in the DP camps, orphanages, and kibbutzim, it would be incorrect to suggest that supporters of the postwar Zionist project had been prewar adherents, or that postwar Zionism replicated the ideological strands and activities of prewar life.[57] Eugenia only came to embrace Zionism after liberation; in contrast, Clara had been involved in the socialist-Zionist Hashomer Hatzair movement before the Nazi invasion, but she found that Antwerp's postwar Zionist movements were unlike those that had existed in the 1930s. When she resumed her Zionist activities, she noted that the prewar groups, which once had been in opposition to one other, now had tentatively united to move their shared agendas forward. "We organized ourselves," she remembered. The Cultural-, Socialist-, Marxist-, and Political-Zionists now "called ourselves the Jewish Zionists. There was no division anymore."[58] Clara and her fellow Zionists felt strongly that unity was crucial to Jewish recovery and reconstruction. They organized *sichot* (discussion sessions), assisted other survivors, particularly hidden children, prepared local Jews for a life in Palestine, and encouraged Jews to publicly demonstrate their pride in being Jewish. She remembered wanting to "tell the world, to show Belgium that we are not afraid."[59]

These origin stories not only emphasized the importance of Zionist ideology and experience but also underscored the place of Jewish languages in those first meetings. When he described Clara in that initial March letter, Daniel sprinkled his correspondence with key Zionist terms: *ulam* (hall; large room), *kvutzot* (groups), *chaver, chavera, Gordonia*. He also boasted that the two communicated in Yiddish, a language that the young survivor spoke fluently because she had been raised in a Yiddish-speaking household and that Daniel knew imperfectly because he had been born to two Yiddish speakers. The American soldier recognized that language would play a significant role in their relationship. They were "two youths unable to live as they wished, unburdening themselves and living the life of *their ideal in words*"; speaking in Yiddish would allow them to share their pasts and create new futures.[60] Clara, too, paid attention to the place of language in their encounter. While she remembered Daniel's ability to speak Yiddish as unimpressive, she was taken by his earnest attempts to communicate with her and the other teens in their native tongue. She also noted that his Hebrew was "beautiful." Neither she nor her Zionist colleagues could speak or write in Hebrew, and they hoped that the American GI might tutor them in the language that they would need when they immigrated to Palestine.[61] While Clara may have known a few Hebrew words and spoke Yiddish flawlessly, Eugenia arrived in Selvino with no familiarity of Hebrew or Yiddish. Indeed, at the DP center, she communicated only in Italian, while the children under her charge spoke Yiddish, Hungarian, Romanian, and Polish. As she and the youngsters learned Hebrew together, she began having a shared language with the members of the Jewish Brigade, other volunteers her age, and the children in her classrooms. Hebrew could offer her a form of Jewish continuity and community in an Italy that she no longer considered home.[62]

Language played an important role in encounter narratives. On a continent where a vast array of cultural and religious institutions had been destroyed, the ability of civilians to communicate with Allied personnel in a shared language offered possibilities for different forms of cultural reconstruction. Certainly, some of the civilians were "too near death to enter into conversations."[63] But if the surviving Jews had the energy to speak with the military personnel they encountered, the language they employed during those meetings could be significant. Jewish civilians spoke dozens of different languages and dialects. While many Jewish adults from Eastern Europe knew

Yiddish regardless of which country they came from, children from the same region might not have had that same competency. Many of them only spoke the languages of the areas where they had lived or been confined during the war. Regardless of what language they spoke, few were fluent in English. Most Allied military personnel serving in the European theater spoke only English, but some American, Canadian, and British military personnel communicated proficiently with the civilians with whom they crossed paths. Chaplain Abraham Klausner remembered that when he arrived in Europe, there always seemed to be one soldier in his unit who could speak Yiddish comfortably. He boasted that he, too, could communicate with survivors from across Europe, even though his "American plain Yiddish" sometimes diverged from the specific dialects spoken by the Jewish DPs he met.[64]

Yiddish played a central role in Abe and Sala B.'s encounter, as well as that of Bella and Ray. When Abe noticed that Sala was avoiding the other military personnel, he approached the survivor, gently speaking to her in Yiddish, just as he did whenever he met Jewish survivors. The son of Russian immigrants who had arrived in Canada in 1919, he spoke Yiddish at home and in his parents' butcher shop where he worked after school. Over the course of their conversation, Sala became intrigued by the young mechanic who could carry a conversation in her native tongue, seemed genuinely solicitous of her wellbeing, and refrained from exhibiting any public display of compassion.[65] Likewise, when Ray and Bella first met outside of her building in Reims, Ray instinctively spoke to her in Yiddish. "He stopped me," Bella remembered, "and asked, 'Are you Yiddish?' I said, 'sure,' and that was the beginning." The couple would not have had any other shared language at their disposal. Ray grew up speaking Yiddish with his immigrant parents and spoke English outside of his home. Bella communicated with her parents in Yiddish and with her siblings and childhood classmates in French.[66]

In contrast, many refugee soldiers and their partners communicated in the secular languages of their youth. Kurt and Gerda each stressed the role German played when they first met. When the two first encountered one another at Volary, a town near the Austrian-German border, Kurt spoke to Gerda in German and was captivated by her grasp of the language when she invoked a poem by the German poet Johann Wolfgang von Goethe. "I could hardly believe that. . . . There was nothing that she could have said that would have underscored the grim irony of the situation better than, than [pause] what she did, and it was a totally shattering experience for me."[67] Likewise, when Karl first sought out Anna and her daughter in Trebechovice, he also instinctively spoke to her in Czech and German. The two would only begin to speak in English long after Anna immigrated to England and their daughter began to converse in that language.[68] Perhaps these shared languages helped refugee soldiers cope with their return to the countries they could no longer recognize and to homes, families, and communities that had been destroyed. Or maybe it was the familiarity of the native language that drew these couples together and later helped to solidify their relationships.

Even if they shared the languages and idioms of the civilians they encountered, some soldiers experienced some discomfort when speaking Yiddish or German in the presence of other military personnel. They had worked hard to prove their assimilability to their fellow soldiers or officers. Now, as military personnel heard them speaking German or Yiddish to Jewish civilians, they felt as if their alienness was highlighted.[69] This was Mort's experience. Having grown up in Wisconsin to observant Jewish parents, Mort was comfortable speaking German and knew some Yiddish, but he increasingly noticed—or at least imagined—that he was looked at askance by some military buddies when he flawlessly communicated with Jewish survivors in Germany. He envisioned this to be especially true as antifraternization politics were implemented at the end of the war. He found himself most comfortable speaking in Yiddish or German when he visited DP centers or Jewish hospitality sites. It was in one such space that he met his future wife.[70]

As some couples conversed at least somewhat comfortably in languages remembered from home and childhood, others clumsily took part in stilted conversations, desperately relying on a combination of sign language, the shared words they understood, and, if they were fortunate, a translator.[71] Lacking a shared language was especially common among civilians and military personnel who encountered one another in North Africa and southern Europe, where the Jewish civilians infrequently spoke Yiddish and the Jewish military personnel infrequently spoke French or Arabic. When they met in Algeria, Lydia Bendrien spoke no English and Harold Servetnick was unfamiliar with French. Lydia's father, who had invited a group of Jewish soldiers to his home that Friday night, had not given much thought to whether the military personnel could converse with him or his family. Lydia and Harold tried to capture one another's attention using hand gestures, eye rolls, and a few shared Hebrew words. They also relied on one of the cousins at the large dinner, who had studied English at school and tried to manage the conversation at the table.[72]

When military personnel had the luxury of a translator during initial encounters, they frequently made note of it as well as the impact of the translator's absence in later meetings. Connecticut-born Bertha was accompanied by a translator when she first met Gregor; after that initial Yom Kippur service, they had to depend on a limited number of shared German, English, Yiddish, and Hebrew words, a wide range of hand gestures, and dictionaries.[73] When they met at Bergen-Belsen, Gena and Norman spoke somewhat haltingly in German, which both had studied at school, but they relied heavily on Norman's translator. After Norman left Belsen, they had difficulty writing to one another because Norman could not use the translator's services for personal communications. Likewise, when Hungarian-born Judith I. met Vermonter Irving "Ike" Isaacson at an army base near the DP camp where Judith, her mother, and aunt lived, they also relied on the captain's friend to translate Judith's Hungarian and Ike's English. In contrast, the friend continued to accompany the couple until Judith acquired enough English to speak with her romantic partner.[74]

. . . .

Encounters in unfamiliar languages were likely just one more indignity in an already strange and tumultuous landscape. Many of the survivors and several of the military personnel had become accustomed to bizarre turns of event, hearing multiple foreign dialects, and relying on unspoken forms of communication. However, even when surrounded by languages they could not understand, Jewish military-civilian couples remembered their encounters as moments when they found ways to insert their agency and control while also acknowledging the horrors around them. Today, we have the self-satisfaction of tracing the moments of encounter forward. When reading Judith I.'s memoir, viewing Gena's wedding dress at the Imperial War Museum in London, or watching documentaries about Gerda, we know what takes place next. But Judith, Ike, Gena, Norman, Gerda, and Kurt did not. Surrounded by devastation and horror, these young adults were not necessarily thinking about a future with one another, even if they reshaped their encounter narratives to suggest that they were thinking exactly that. How, then, did these couples move from meeting one another to courtship and marriage? What possibilities were there for couples in war-torn North Africa and Europe to spend sufficient time with one another to begin envisioning marriage and then to act on those impulses?

3

Forgetting the "Stupid Crazy World"

COURTSHIPS AND MARRIAGE

Soon after Clara and Daniel met in March 1945, the American GI began to attend the *hachshara* activities frequented by the fiery young Zionist and her surviving siblings. While Clara's mother, Rosa, worried that the soldier's presence could damage her daughters' reputations, she was sympathetic to Daniel's longing for Jewish familial life and his dedication to Jewish causes. Perhaps, too, she realized that Allied soldiers could obtain foods unavailable to civilians and that Daniel might be willing—if not eager—to share those goods with them. Whatever the reason, within days of that first meeting, Rosa invited Daniel to join her and her children for Sabbath dinner, and Daniel walked the six miles from his base to the Heller household. Over the course of the evening, Rosa supposedly was struck by Daniel's earnestness and his serious attempts to communicate with her and her family in Yiddish. Clara became charmed by the soldier who spoke Hebrew fluently and

Yiddish imperfectly, played the violin, and articulated a solid understanding of diverse Zionist ideologies. Daniel was happy to be in the company of a Jewish family, celebrate the Sabbath, and flirt with an attractive Zionist. The GI hinted that he would be interested in returning to the Heller household, and Clara and her mother invited Daniel to come back. He did return, bringing with him food and other goods from the base.[1]

Daniel's letters depict a quickly developing courtship shaped by home-cooked meals, a shared dedication to Zionism, sexual attraction, love for music, and a commitment to taking part in Jewish recovery efforts. Writing to his parents daily, sometimes even multiple times a day, he described his and Clara's Zionist activities, deep conversations, and long walks. He quickly announced to his parents that, despite their different social, cultural, and economic backgrounds, he had fallen in love with the female survivor. "The more I get to know," he wrote, "the more I want to know. . . . She is an explication of my ageless dream, lovely intelligent, courageous and good." He and Clara were "narishe junge [silly youth]" who, together, could "forget this stupid crazy world for a while."[2]

There were many obstacles to their relationship. As Daniel noted, he and Clara came from radically disparate backgrounds, barely shared one language between them, and had homes on two separate continents. The war still was going on, and it was likely that Daniel, who had little control over his movement, would soon leave Antwerp. Moreover, while Clara's mother had come to support the young couple's relationship, Daniel's parents expressed ambivalence. Unsure that their son was sufficiently mature to commit to a relationship and worried that his wartime experiences had pushed him to act rashly, they urged Daniel to be cautious. Yet, despite these many obstacles, Clara and Daniel continued to spend time together. In late April, just over one month after they first met and about two weeks before the war formally ended in Europe, they announced their betrothal.[3]

Gena and Norman also declared their engagement that April. The two had met during the liberation of Bergen-Belsen, and their whirlwind courtship commenced less than a day after Norman, in his university-clipped German, surprised Gena by inviting her to dinner at the officer's tent. At first, Gena was reluctant, in part because the two had barely spoken when they worked in proximity to one another in the camp's hospital. However, after some deliberation with her mother and friends, she agreed to dine with him. The idea of a proper meal was enticing and an evening at the officers' tent would offer her an opportunity to leave the area where the British had quarantined the former prisoners. It would be the first night in several years that she would be free to exit the space that confined her.

After being sprayed with a disinfectant, a necessary measure for anyone leaving the quarantined area, Gena and a friend made their way to the cordoned-off space reserved for the British military officers and their guests. Norman stood by the entrance. He greeted Gena and her friend warmly, walked them to their table, and welcomed her to their engagement party. Gena thought he was teasing or wondered whether she had misunderstood him. But she had not. While she balked at the notion of marriage, Norman was undeterred, insisting that he had known of their fate from the moment he had learned she was Jewish. He also revealed a practical consideration for becoming engaged. The war in Europe was ending but had not yet concluded, and Norman and his troops would soon be transferring to another site. He wanted to guarantee Gena military protection. If she were his fiancée, he explained, the British forces would help keep her safe. Norman announced their engagement to the men present and gave Gena a formal written statement that established her as his fiancée. A few days later, he left Belsen. The two sporadically exchanged letters until Norman returned five months later to finalize their wedding plans.[4]

Many Jewish couples, like Gena, Norman, Clara, and Daniel, documented their progression from encounter to time spent together, to engagement, to the formal exchange of wedding vows. They told of courtships that developed in sites where many civilians lacked habitable spaces, electricity, clean water, means of transport, or opportunities for leisure. They described relationships that centered on love, food, a desire for companionship and sex, shared cultural values, and similar pastimes. And they discussed a series of military policies and regulations concerning marriage that were baffling and difficult to decipher. Like their recollections of their encounters, their memories of courtships and wedding ceremonies reveal glimpses into their different strategies for recovery. As these men and women spent time together in a landscape that had been devastated by war, they experimented with opportunities to insist on their own agency, while simultaneously facing a wide range of obstacles that reminded them of their limitations and powerlessness.

· ·

In identifying the tangible and intangible variables that moved couples from their initial encounter to their betrothal, Jewish survivors and military personnel described courtships that rested on learning how to communicate needs, feelings, and desires, even when they shared no common language. Despite having been raised by Yiddish-speaking parents, Daniel now was articulating emotions in a language he did not think of as his own; he requested a Yiddish dictionary from his parents so he could get his feelings across.[5] When he declared his love for Clara, he had to do so in a foreign language. "It was the first time in my life that I was romantic in Yiddish," he wrote in April 1945. "Its [sic] quite an expressive language."[6] Clara appreciated Daniel's attempts to communicate in Yiddish, but she later reflected that he "couldn't speak too well," which led to its own miscommunications and lost opportunities.[7] Sala K. similarly remembered feeling confident about her developing feelings for Sidney but disappointed that he was not fluent in Yiddish. When thinking back to their days of courtship, she insisted that "it wasn't real communication. It wasn't really like having a conversation easily." This made building a relationship difficult.[8]

Others found that a shared language drew them together. This was particularly true for refugee soldiers and the civilians they later married. When they met in Volary at liberation, for example, Gerda and Kurt may have recognized the gulf of differences between them, but they also acknowledged their shared comfort with the German language. Now they spent hours conversing in German in the hospital courtyard, walking in the fields surrounding the hospital, writing letters in German to one another, and sharing favorite German authors and works of literature.[9] Karl and Anna's shared German and Czech languages also motivated them to continue seeking out one another's company. In Anna's recollections, their common prewar culture, experiences, and networks encouraged Karl to inquire about his family's and friends' experiences during the war and motivated her to see him as a future husband.[10] Years later, she remembered that she "had an inkling that this was the kind of man" she wanted "as a father for my child."[11]

As they navigated how to communicate, couples spent significant time together participating in activities that centered on home, family, and community. They were drawn to these sites, in part, because they lacked other choices. Jewish survivors and military personnel courted in a Europe and a North Africa that were in a throes of a public health crisis, and where many communities lacked the infrastructure, habitable spaces, venues, and means of transport that engendered opportunities for entertainment. Yet they also participated in activities that revolved around community and home because those very spaces offered them measures of comfort in the aftermath of their wartime traumas. In their interviews, Bella and Ray tenderly remembered the centrality of Bella's family's one-bedroom apartment in Reims. Even though this was not Bella's childhood home—that had been seized and ransacked—they reenacted prewar rituals of family life. Bella, her sister, mother, and Ray ate "Jewish meals" in her mother's kitchen. "We didn't spend much time in the street, like the kids do today," she remembered, overlooking the fact that she and Ray went outside to escape the cramped apartment.[12] By welcoming Ray, Bella's family attempted to create a new sense of normalcy in their apartment, and Ray embraced the opportunity to spend time in a domicile outside of the base. Meals with Bella's family reminded him of his Philadelphia home and offered a sharp juxtaposition to what he had witnessed during the war and what his daily life looked like then.[13] Daniel and Clara also spent significant time in the residence where the Hellers had settled, observing some of the very rites that each of them remembered from their prewar adolescence and childhood. They celebrated the Sabbath by eating Friday night dinner with Clara's family. Their meals featured the foods of Clara's childhood—Romanian dishes—and culinary items that both Clara and Daniel remembered from their youth: "Ashkenazic stalwarts: roast chicken, kishke, and kugel."[14] At a time and in a place where home and family had been destroyed, spending time in a home, even a temporary one, allowed for a sense of rebuilding and recovery.[15]

Just as the home featured prominently in courtship narratives, so too did specific mutual pursuits and values. Several couples remembered the place of Zionist activities in furthering their relationship but noted that—like their new residences—this Zionism, too, diverged from their prewar movements. They now spent time together leading Hebrew singalongs, organizing Hebrew games with DP children, teaching the Hebrew language, supervising the care of orphans and "half-orphans," and participating in Brichah, a program to smuggle Jews into British-controlled Palestine.[16] During the few weeks they remained in Hannover together, Abe and Sala B. realized that they shared the dream of one day settling in Palestine. The couple attended local *hachshara* meetings and befriended some Zionist-leaning DPs and NGO volunteers, the latter of whom would be crucial to Sala's illegal emigration after Abe's demobilization.[17] Likewise, with other young adults in Antwerp and Brussels, Clara and Daniel sang songs "of hope, of rebuilding our land and ourselves," studied Jewish history, and celebrated Jewish historical events. They taught classes on Zionist ideology and promoted the superiority of the Zionist groups with which they had affiliated during their adolescence: the Shomrim/Ha-Shomer and Gordonia.[18] For Daniel, Zionism cemented their relationship even though they disagreed over whether the Shomrim or

Gordonia was the preferred form. "We two live in the very same world," he wrote to his parents. "Our hopes and aspirations are the same.... Our dreams are of the same pattern."[19]

Many couples likewise found that Jewish hospitality centers and DP camps provided them with the comfortable spaces in which they could spend time and develop their relationships. In a European landscape where military-civilian couples often aroused suspicion, the Jewish survivors and military personnel sought out places where they could participate in activities with others like them.[20] They attended bonfires, theatrical performances, workshops, and sports events hosted by the different DP camps, as well as dances, synagogue services, classes, and films offered by Jewish chaplains for their soldiers.[21] Mort and Halina courted at the Regensburg Jewish center where they had met, patronizing its meals, dances, and volunteer efforts; likewise, Isaac Rose and Leesha (Elisabeth) Bos, who had met during the waning days of the war in the Netherlands, spent most of their time at Amsterdam's Jewish Center, enjoying its worship services, theatrical revues, Zionist activities, and concerts.[22]

Courtships also rested on another form of common interest: sexual activity. Despite the unpleasant settings and lack of privacy, young couples cuddled, kissed, and engaged in sexual activities in parks, quiet corners, and clubs. Those survivors who discussed—or alluded to—sexual activity in their letters or interviews did so with ambivalence. Sexual contact offered embodied pleasure, as well as pain and deprivation. It could serve as an affirmation of life and a way to feel connected, but it also acted as a traumatic reminder of the impact the Nazi past had on their bodies and of sexual assault. With the return of their physical health, survivors were discovering or rediscovering their bodies. Nazi policies had deprived Jewish bodies of their secondary sex characteristics—emaciated women lost the fat in their breasts and ceased menstruating; Jewish men were shaved of their beards and often experienced impotence. Now, as survivors slowly began to recover, some articulated a lack of understanding of the physical changes they underwent during and after the war; they now alluded to how that unfamiliarity shaped their sexual lives. Ignorant about pregnancy and procreation, for example, Gena remembered panicking when Norman first kissed her, worried that she would become pregnant simply because their mouths touched.[23] Clara, too, quietly confessed that, in comparison to Daniel's past experiences, she had no knowledge of sexual matters.[24]

Perhaps because of these concerns, or maybe because of the ever-present workshops and warnings against premarital sex,[25] some couples took the warnings against premarital sex quite seriously and presented their limited sexual activities with both solemnity and innocence. One soldier described a "feeling of deep reverence" when he and his romantic partner embraced,[26] while Daniel portrayed his and Clara's first embrace as "sweet and refreshing."[27] Indeed, during the early days of his courtship, Daniel shared with his parents that he controlled his sexual desires when he was with Clara because he worried that certain sexual activities could "hurt" her.[28] Later, he revealed that he had implored Ruby to keep him in check. One evening, when the two soldiers were staying at the Heller home and Daniel had leaned in to kiss Clara, Ruby reminded him to restrain himself.[29] While it is unclear exactly what Daniel meant when he worried about "hurting" Clara, women who had faced risks of, or experienced, sexual assault during or after the war, also likely were apprehensive about sexual intimacy. While Clara never discussed sexual violence, she and her sister had articulated their fears of sexual assault at the hands of Allied military personnel.[30] None of the other women studied here linked sexual violence with their own relationships to sexual intimacy, but some detailed the sexual assaults of friends and family members or similarly discussed their reticence to become involved with soldiers or officers because of the fear of sexual assault.[31]

It is possible, too, that the couples positioned themselves as practicing sexual restraint or having no sexual knowledge as a way of demarcating themselves from the non-Jewish women who were involved with military personnel or with Jewish DPs. As discussed in chapter 1, in postwar Europe and North Africa, suspicion of women's sexual nature was widespread, as was the assumption that they used their sexuality to take advantage of Allied military personnel. This distrust expanded to include relationships between non-Jews and Jewish DPs. Here, too, lay a belief that non-Jewish women desired the rations received by Jewish DPs and sexually manipulated these men to obtain food, shelter, and clothing.[32] Perhaps by highlighting their supposed ignorance of sexual matters, Jewish women presented themselves as above suspicion.

Of course, becoming involved with a soldier or officer could bring real material advantages. Across Europe and parts of North Africa, people experienced a relentless absence of habitable places to sleep, fresh vegetables, fruits, fats, proteins, and fuel.[33] Deprived of necessities, many obtained goods through their interactions with military personnel who, themselves, had come to realize that cigarettes, chocolate, and canned meat were precious supplies. Courtship narratives described soldiers and officers wooing Jewish civilians with white bread, oranges, salmon, cheese, canned goods, and coffee, all food gifts that could be transformative, even lifesaving.[34] Food and fuel played a central role in the courtship of Leesha and Isaac in the Netherlands, the only Western European country subjected to hunger as a collective punishment. The two met soon after the winter of 1944–45, when 18,000 people died of diseases related to malnutrition or starvation.[35] Within hours of their encounter, Isaac provided Leesha and her fellow partisans with "cookies, crackers, matzot, cans of salmon, sardines, butter, kosher corned beef, bars of chocolates, and cigarettes." Whenever he visited, he would "shower" her and her friends with food, gifts that kept Leesha and friends nourished and allowed them to barter for other needed goods. These foodstuffs, ironically, came with a disadvantage. The other members of her circle lacked the contacts that would give them access to food and needed goods, and, at times, Leesha wondered if she was being judged or envied by her peers.[36]

Similar stories emerged from the DP camps where rations and NGO-authorized supplements rarely included fresh meat, eggs, vegetables, or fruit.[37] Lala told of a courtship that involved gifts of fresh vegetables and other difficult-to-obtain food items from Morris, as well as puritanical anger and resentment from her fellow DPs. Her relationship offered her the much-needed foodstuffs others lacked.[38] Rachel and Mayer likewise described a relationship that began when she requested a chocolate bar from Mayer, a US chaplain at the Wittenau DP camp. During their time together in Berlin, Mayer supplemented the family's rations with additional groceries and fuel.[39]

Military personnel obtained these gifts through legal and illegal means. Soldiers and officers shared their rations and collected extra provisions from fellow soldiers and officers. Just as they once had asked family and friends to send packages to the Jews they encountered across Europe and North Africa, they now beseeched them to mail their girlfriends canned goods, stockings, cosmetics, and clothing.[40] Even over sixty years later, Flory fondly remembered the "beautiful packages" from Harry's family and the foods he obtained from the PX, from seizing goods without permission, from selling cigarettes, and from the black market.[41] Daniel likewise requested that his parents send Clara canned goods, candy, and clothing and obtained foods on the black market; in her interviews, Clara recalled how crucial those foods were to the Hellers' postwar recovery.[42]

The underground economy, which peaked during the first three years after VE Day, featured significantly in courtship narratives. While every European country witnessed some form of a black market, there were certain locations where one could not be fed and clothed without relying on it, including parts of Belgium, Germany, Austria, and France.[43] While some enterprising Allied military personnel and civilians participated in large-scale endeavors in the black market—stealing gasoline, requisitioning army trucks, and amassing fortunes—most peddled basic commodities.[44] Of the illegally obtained and traded goods, none was more significant in European market culture and in stories about dating than the American cigarette.[45] There was a robust market for these cigarettes, which could be sold for several times their purchase value. Until 1946, American soldiers in occupied Germany could purchase ten packs of cigarettes for fifty cents at the PX and sell them for $100.[46] Morris used them to barter for food and extra gasoline. The local demand for cigarettes funded several of his and Lala's excursions, including their travels across Germany and Europe. "At that time," explained Lala, "people were crazy to get cigarettes."[47] Similarly, with a backpack of "booze and cigarettes," Daniel bartered for goods and services that the Hellers required: attorney's fees, fresh meat, and eggs. Whether or not they or their new partners smoked, military personnel such as Daniel and Morris could "woo" civilians with cigarettes and use them to support their courtship.[48]

The housing and work that military personnel commandeered for their romantic partners also played prominent roles in their stories about courtship. Like food, lodging was hard to procure in postwar Europe, and the Jewish survivors involved with Allied soldiers and officers competed for housing with local civilians, people fleeing the East, Allied military personnel, freed former prisoners, and displaced populations.[49] When Morris and Lala first met in the fall of 1945, she, her uncle, and her cousin lived in barrack-like accommodations where "there still was barbed wire everywhere." Morris quickly secured Lala a new room and a position filing papers; when he transferred to Passau, he obtained a tiny cottage and another job for her. Ike similarly helped Judith I., her mother, and aunt locate improved housing, first in a different DP center and then in the "picturesque resort town" near his new base.[50] As with Lala's additional food rations, Lala and Judith remembered their fellow DPs being jealous of their spacious accommodations and, in Lala's case, her work. They likely were. Even if the DPs had been involved with military personnel, the soldiers or officers would need to be highly enough ranked or sufficiently connected—like Morris or Ike—to successfully requisition improved lodgings.[51] Moreover, the DP camps frequently were in deplorable condition. Established on sites that once had been barracks, camps, hospitals, schools, apartment buildings, private residences, and hotels, they were overcrowded, accommodating anywhere between fifty and several thousand people. And, while the number of camps grew exponentially as more Jews fled from Eastern Europe, so did their populations.[52] Even after the release of the Harrison Report, which called for some improvements in the DP camps, living conditions remained substandard.[53] In September 1945, Judah Nadich, General Dwight D. Eisenhower's adviser on Jewish affairs, complained about one camp where 180 Jews resided with only 140 beds and 80 blankets.[54] The DP camps were "beyond imagination," one Jewish chaplain complained in 1946.[55]

Given the deplorable state of the DP camps, it is not surprising that some of the military personnel procured housing outside of the DPs camps for their romantic partners. When Flory and Harry began dating, Harry seized a large apartment that had been requisitioned by the military but was no longer being occupied by military staff. He quartered Flory and her parents there, moving them from the small apartment in which they had settled. Flory and her parents had avoided the overcrowded DP camps, moving from room to room in Bari. Now, staying in a spacious apartment with high ceilings and clean floors, Flory recognized how sharply her new residence contrasted with their previous lodgings and from the makeshift housing in Bari's DP camp.[56] Like Flory, Gerda also wished to reside outside of the DP camps, which she thought too closely resembled the Nazi camps where she had been incarcerated. When she settled in Munich after being released from the hospital, Kurt requisitioned a private room for her in a house outside of the city, a home he likely could procure because it had belonged to a member of the Nazi Party.[57] Gerda's housing, food, and work reinforced a growing sense of in-betweenness. She was aware that her relationship with Kurt gave her access to benefits other Jewish civilians and DPs lacked; she imagined that her fellow DPs were jealous of her; and while she had access to the base because of her work, she also felt most comfortable with the men and women with whom she shared languages, culture, and wartime experiences, namely other Jewish DPs. Even if they resented her, they understood her.[58]

. . . .

No matter what brought them together, many of the Jewish civilians and military personnel studied here decided to marry within a few months, if not weeks, of their initial encounters. News of transfer or demobilization—or concern about impending orders—frequently encouraged them to swiftly become betrothed. Several proposed on the eve of their demobilization. When Kurt discovered that he soon would be returning to the United States, he asked Gerda whether she might marry him and join him in New York. Likewise, after learning that he soon would be demobilized, Abe proposed marriage to Sala B., even though they only had met a few weeks earlier. In a letter to his chaplain inquiring how to speedily arrange for a marriage ceremony, Abe acknowledged that he might have been "rushing this a little too quickly," but he did not want to leave Sala behind without arranging for their future reunion, and marriage seemed to be the only path that could guarantee that outcome.[59] Other military personnel proposed as they were moving to new locations. Norman and Harold proposed while each had a year of service remaining. When Norman discovered that he and his men were leaving Bergen-Belsen, just seven days after meeting Gena, he proposed marriage; Harold asked Lydia to marry him when he learned that he would be leaving Oran for somewhere in France.[60]

When announcing their betrothals to families, friends, chaplains, and commanding officers, military personnel and their Jewish fiancé(e)s insisted on their exceptional bonds, just as they had done in their encounter narratives. They asserted that they now knew "what true love meant" and described their attachments as "genuine," "deep," "serious," and "delirious."[61] "I love you with a joyful intensity," Gerda wrote in an early letter to Kurt, "a feeling that I never knew existed and that blots out so much pain."[62] Perhaps those feelings were sincere; perhaps, too, military personnel and Jewish civilians were refuting contemporary assumptions that military-civilian relationships were superficial; or maybe those couples had begun to absorb and reiterate the themes they utilized when petitioning to marry. As Gerda, Kurt, and others would discover, receiving permission to marry was an arduous and legislated process and required them to prove their worthiness. Jewish civilians and military personnel lacked control over the standards for such merit and for whether, how, or when they could marry. This, too, threw into relief the instability that many of these couples felt in the aftermath of war and trauma.

Permission to marry was hard to procure in part because marriage and immigration were linked. As the United States, Britain, and Canada exited a traumatic war and faced a looming Cold War, an overwhelming refugee crisis, and stark economic challenges, military and governmental officials paired considerations of who should be permitted to immigrate with who should be allowed to marry. Officials all considered the impact future spouses could have at home and abroad and they framed their deliberations in gendered ways. Assuming that the intended spouses were women, they feared that disreputable wives could "embarrass the military service," negatively affect a husband's effectiveness on the battlefield, base, or at work, and place a burden on society.[63] Because they could enter their partners' countries as legal residents or new citizens, these potential spouses needed to be properly vetted; they had to be able to be a good influence, assimilate well, remain married, and not become a public charge.[64] Bureaucrats and officials frequently looked to moral order, racial and religious homogeneity, and political affinity to determine what constituted an appropriate spouse. Allegations of sexual impropriety, moral deviance, suspicious origins, and/or communist leanings could be sufficient grounds to question one's fitness for marriage.[65] So too could a potential violation of existing immigration laws and policies. No country would permit the admission of spouses who were ineligible for citizenship.[66]

These regulations, promulgated alongside other policies concerning marriage and citizenship, promoted a specific image of the morally respectable family.[67] American, British, and Canadian officials mandated commander approval, something that had been a long-standing policy in the Canadian and British militaries but was first formally implemented by the American forces in 1942.[68] They devised various forms of character checks, sometimes even launching investigations into the petitioners' standings in their home communities, and often required that both members of the couple demonstrate that they were healthy, of appropriate age, and unmarried.[69] No matter the specific restriction or paperwork demanded, all Allied officials insisted on some kind of delay—somewhere between four and six months—between the date of giving permission to marry and the date of the marriage ceremony itself. This, they argued, would guarantee the vetting of the spouse and the appropriateness of the match.[70]

Worried that military personnel might marry enemy or ex-enemy aliens, officials also developed policies concerning the fiancé(e)s' birthplace and current location. At the beginning of 1944, the United States, Britain, and Canada forbade all marriages between military personnel and civilians in Germany, Austria, and some formerly occupied regions, and, for much of 1945 and 1946, they continued to outlaw marriages to native-born German or Austrian citizens on lands that had been part of Germany in 1938.[71] "It is quite possible," the American acting adjutant general wrote, "that other undesirable marriages might be contracted if no general prohibition existed."[72] Over the course of the late spring and summer of 1945, the United States and Britain separately modified this blanket prohibition, permitting their military personnel to marry non-German- or non-Austrian-born civilians on German or Austrian soil.[73] Canadian officials, however, continued to forbid marriages when the potential spouse lived on German or Austrian soil, even if that individual had been born elsewhere. This was the policy that prevented Abe and Sala B. from marrying in October 1945, before Abe's demobilization. His chaplain acknowledged that soldiers might characterize the Canadian restrictions as "cruel," but he insisted that such a blanket prohibition was necessary because they had been warned that Germans pretended to be Jews to emigrate and escape punishment. He told Abe, "When you learn that 20,000 Nazis paraded around Paris as Jews and a goodly number got into Palestine on the same pretext, you realize that the authorities just won't take chances."[74]

Military officials depended on their chaplains to enforce these regulations.[75] In the United States, Britain, and Canada, chaplains, who had long been deputized to perform marriages, also offered workshops on married life, assisted with planning marriage ceremonies, and counseled couples. As one Jewish chaplain joked, they did everything but "pick the bride."[76] Now, commanders turned to them to investigate the potential couples more fully, and marriage interviews began to consume a significant amount of the chaplains' time.[77] Between July 1944 and May 1945, American Jewish chaplain Bert Klausner, who was stationed in both France and Germany, conducted forty-one marriage interviews and investigations.[78] He was not alone. In 1945, American Jewish chaplains serving on the European continent reported conducting approximately 7.5 marriage interviews each per month and Canadian Jewish chaplains about 4 per month, while British Jewish chaplains reported just a handful per year. Protestant and Catholic chaplains reported similarly.[79]

As Jewish chaplains became increasingly involved in vetting, supporting, or discouraging marriages abroad, they began to consider an additional set of religious queries concerning marriage and the ideal family unit.[80] While no formal military regulation looked to religion as a prerequisite for a "good" spousal match, many Jewish and Christian chaplains assumed that endogamy was essential to marriage, and they therefore rejected petitions crafted by interfaith couples.[81] In July 1945, Chaplain Isaac Rose, who himself was romantically involved with Leesha, denied the marriage request of a Canadian artillery branch bombardier born to two Jewish parents because his fiancée had a non-Jewish mother and Jewish father; Isaac thus asserted that "the girl" was not Jewish.[82] American Jewish chaplain Oscar Lifshutz likewise persuaded a Jewish GI to rescind his application to marry a non-Jewish woman because the chaplain could not condone intermarriage. Two years later, in 1948, Oscar was among a group of American Jewish chaplains who pushed rabbis serving on the European continent to confirm their commitment to approving only endogamous marriages.[83]

While Jewish chaplains often expressed skepticism over any non-Jewish civilian who wished to marry a Jewish soldier or officer, many exhibited particular animus toward non-Jewish women of German origin. Mimicking the discourse about fraternization more generally and the discussions about war brides in particular, Jewish chaplains described German women as deviants who wished to receive the higher food ration of Jewish victims, ensnarl soldiers as potential husbands, and emigrate. When a Canadian Jewish soldier serving in Holland requested permission to marry his pregnant German-born non-Jewish girlfriend, Canadian Jewish chaplains Samuel Cass and Isaac Rose expressed horror that there was "a German girl on the loose in Holland" and questioned the value of the couple marrying, even if there was a child involved.[84] Mayer Abramowitz likewise asserted that German non-Jewish women sought out "low grade Jewish GIs" to marry so they could leave Germany for the United States as war brides.[85] One British Jewish chaplain invoked xenophobic anxieties about both German women and British Jewish refugee servicemen, arguing that the latter were more likely than their British-born counterparts to become involved with non-Jewish German or Austrian women. In his view, these "ex-enemy alien soldiers" lacked "deep roots in English soil." Downplaying the fact that the British military treated its "ex-enemy" servicemen differently than British-born military personnel, the chaplain portrayed Jewish refugee soldiers as unpatriotic and German women as manipulative. While he offered an extreme view, he was not alone in asserting that Jewish military personnel might be attracted to Christian German women and should be forbidden from marrying them.[86]

While most Jewish chaplains agreed that they should dissuade their soldiers and officers from participating in interfaith marriages, they were divided over cases in which the fiancé(e)s sought permission to convert. On paper, Canadian Jewish chaplains were more stringent than their American or British counterparts, agreeing in 1944 that they would only participate in marriages in which both parties were "*borne* of the Jewish faith." This technically not only made intermarriage impossible but also prevented marriages between Jews when at least one of them had been born Christian.[87] Despite such a declaration, several Canadian Jewish chaplains behaved otherwise, approving of marriages between converts to Judaism and Canadian Jewish soldiers. RAF Jewish chaplain Jack Eisen permitted such a marriage after he himself had overseen the conversion and received written permission from the parents of the soldier that they would approve of their child marrying a convert to Judaism.[88] British Jewish chaplains similarly balked at interfaith marriages but sometimes allowed for conversion when they imagined that the potential spouse would affiliate Jewishly. In these cases, conversion not only prevented the soldier from leaving the Jewish community but also left open the possibility of gaining even more members once the couple had children.[89]

The American Jewish chaplaincy organization, CANRA, allowed for marriages between Jewish soldiers and converts to Judaism but insisted that no one be converted solely because of one's desire to wed.[90] Some American Jewish chaplains still expressed their willingness to oversee a conversion when they knew that the conversion request was tied to a desire to marry; others flatly refused.[91] This discussion was particularly contentious in occupied Germany, where chaplains such as Philip Pincus converted German Christian women in advance of their marriages, while chaplains like Mayer Abramowitz refused to do the same.[92] American Jewish chaplains outside of Germany were likewise divided on conversion for marriage's sake. One chaplain serving in the Middle East and North Africa, for example, recounted seeing five petitions weekly concerning conversion before marriage and worried that the differing practices of various Jewish chaplains would lead to an "awkward situation" among the military personnel.[93]

When investigating these and other cases, Jewish chaplains considered the degree to which the mass murder of European Jews and the chaos left in its wake had shifted their interpretation of Jewish law and practice. While separate from military priorities, their conversations and determinations became part of military inquiries. Many Jewish chaplains, for example, extended military regulations that prohibited couples from marrying if one of the parties had been previously married but lacked "proof" of being divorced or widowed. They reconsidered the Jewish legal mandate that a divorced person could only remarry if she or he could provide evidence of having received a *get* (divorce according to Jewish tradition). What if the *get* was lost and the members of the Jewish court (*bet din*) who had validated the divorce had been murdered? What if a Jewish civilian could rely only on hearsay that the Nazis and their collaborators had murdered his or her spouse? In their responses to these questions of religious law and practice, American, British, and Canadian Jewish chaplains revealed the disparate national contexts and denominations in which they were positioned.[94]

Coming from a background in which diverse denominational authorities could determine and implement radically dissimilar decisions around religious law, American Jewish chaplains agreed to respect "the various types of chaplains . . . and the various types of soldiers." In other words, American Jewish chaplains were to follow the couples' Jewish religious traditions; if that practice was at odds with the chaplain's beliefs and practices, he was to "adjust his service in conformity therewith." Providing only the examples of Orthodox and Reform petitioners, the responsa (ruling on a Jewish question) developed by CANRA established that in the case of a previous divorce without proof of a *get*, Jewish chaplains could approve the marriage petitions of Reform Jewish military personnel but disallow those of Orthodox Jewish servicemen. The former would accept proof of a civil divorce as sufficient, even if there was no *get*; the latter would not. On questions of confirmation of death, chaplains frequently were more lenient, permitting certain exceptions if enough witnesses could testify to the previous spouse's demise.[95]

When weighing these questions of religious law, British and Canadian Jewish chaplains articulated little interest in the denominational affiliation of their petitioners, a position consistent with Jewish religious life in both Britain and the independent dominion. British Jewish chaplains were responsible to Britain's chief rabbi, and ostensibly followed his Orthodox Jewish leanings, even if they themselves were not rabbinic representatives of Orthodox synagogues. In cases when either petitioner had been previously married, they tended to insist on a *get*. However, following the ruling of Britain's chief rabbi, they permitted, on a few occasions, an *agunah* (a married woman, no longer living with her husband, who did not undergo a Jewish divorce) to marry, provided there was sufficient documentation from other unaffiliated parties that the husband had been killed.[96] Canadian Jewish chaplains frequently followed their own denominational leanings and not those of the petitioners, leading to some cases when chaplains insisted on a *get* and in other cases when they did not.[97] However they ruled, their decision often became part of the military record: the petitioner was a member of the military personnel, and the adjudicator was a chaplain.

Religious practice also could influence the chaplains' evaluation of marriage petitions in another way. Following Jewish law, which prohibits Jewish weddings from taking place during the Jewish Sabbath (Saturday), the holidays of Rosh Hashanah, Sukkot, Passover, and Shavuot, and the fast days of Tishah be-Av and Yom Kippur, some chaplains restricted wedding ceremonies to certain days during the year.[98] Chaplaincy records suggest that American, British, and Canadian Jewish chaplains diverged in how they handled these restrictions, reflecting a tension between the demands of wartime and religious law. Canadian and British Jewish chaplains often looked to the Jewish calendar when evaluating marriage petitions. Many approved petitions but flatly prohibited Jewish weddings on Jewish holidays, with some even disallowing those dates barred by Jewish custom.[99] This became a matter of notice because there already existed a lag time between petition approval and marriage, and any additional obstacle could make the marriage on foreign soil impossible.

Unlike British and Canadian Jewish chaplains, American Jewish chaplains made little mention of the Jewish calendar in their evaluations. In practice, they did not officiate at weddings on days forbidden by Jewish law, such as the Jewish Sabbath, but they allowed marriages on days that had been prohibited by Jewish custom, such as the period between Passover and Shavuot (*omer*). CANRA stipulated that exceptions should be allowed for "marriages under special conditions of wartime" and they discouraged the practice once the chaplains resumed their pulpit positions in the United States.[100] These conversations were not taking place in a vacuum. As historians have shown, debates concerning marriage and family life were common among the DP and European rabbis who considered whether religious law could be fully followed in the postwar moment.[101]

Regardless of their positions on these and other questions, most Jewish chaplains expressed a degree of sympathy for the petitioning couple, particularly when both members of that unit were Jewish. In their view, the couples deserved to marry if they were found to be a good spousal match.[102] To define what they meant by this complementarity, chaplains drew on contemporary discourses of victimhood and morality.

Whether or not it was accurate, chaplains described many of the Jewish civilian-petitioners as "sole survivor[s]," insinuating that these civilians would remain alone if not permitted to marry.[103] At a time when understanding of victims and perpetrators was crucial to postwar occupation policy and daily life, these emphases were significant.[104] Jewish chaplains evaluated these marriage petitions just as military officials contested who should be considered displaced people and receive the benefits thereof. Occupation forces agreed that Nazi victims born outside of Germany deserved improved housing and food privileges, but, when evaluating those born in Germany, officials implemented disparate policies. Chaplains were familiar with these disputes, and it is possible that when they described the petitioners as orphans, sole survivors, camp victims, and survivors of death marches, they were claiming that these (mostly) women deserved access to unique privileges.[105]

Many family members of the military petitioners similarly linked the "right" to marry with a history of victimhood. When Teddy H. petitioned for the right to marry Marianne K., his father came to his aid when the couple faced a significant obstacle. Marianne's age dictated that parental approval for marriage was necessary, but her parents had been murdered by the Nazis and she had no immediate family members who could vouch for her. Her future father-in-law insisted that the young woman deserved pity and an opportunity for recovery. Imagining himself as best positioned to act in loco parentis, he sanctioned their marriage and promised that he would "care for her as if she was his own child."[106] Once he came to approve of their pending marriage, Daniel's father, Reuben, likewise invoked the murder of Clara's father (while overlooking her mother's survival) and expressed his hope that her union with Daniel would hasten Clara's recovery and make her feel as if she again belonged to a family unit.[107] These statements of parental approval, especially when such approbation was mandated, must have simultaneously— and paradoxically—reminded the survivors of their precariousness and fortune. On the one hand, when the family of their future spouses vouched for them, these actions made it more likely that they would be granted the right to marry. On the other, such interventions were necessary because the survivors lacked immediate family members who could appeal on their behalf.

Of course, not all parents were cooperative. Sidney K.'s mother refused to approve the engagement of her son to Sala. Not fully understanding the immigration laws of the time, she insisted that the couple wait and marry in New York City. Recognizing that Sala would not be able to immigrate to the United States unless she married him (or another GI), Sidney threatened to reenlist. Sala begged her future mother-in-law to reconsider, though she understood why Sidney's mother would refuse her consent. "It is possible that my parents would handle this the same way," she wrote to her future mother-in-law. "We don't really know each other. A child is everything to a mother, especially the youngest child."[108] It is likely that Sala's plea was not the deciding factor in the mother's consent; it was probably her son's threat to reenlist that pushed her to agree to the marriage. Over 900 miles away, Mort's parents similarly hesitated when they received word that their son required their consent before he married abroad. Though they (and Mort's commander) eventually approved the pending wedding, they initially worried that the couple's radically different backgrounds and their past traumas would make it difficult for their marriage to be successful.[109]

. . . .

After the couples received approvals from their chaplains and commanders and successfully submitted their paperwork—no small feat for the many survivors who lacked identification papers and faced difficulties passing a medical screening—they finalized their plans for solemnizing their vows.[110]

Much like acquiring permission to marry, the formal exchange of wedding vows was a complicated process. Couples had to determine who had the license to perform their wedding and what the wedding ritual ought to look like. For much of the war, chaplains had officiated nearly all the civilian-military weddings in enemy or occupied territory.[111] With the war's end, couples now would be required to follow both their military regulations and the local laws of those postwar countries whose legal jurisdiction the Allies recognized during and after the war. To further confound matters, different countries mandated disparate marriage calendars, prerequisites, ceremony locations, licensing laws, and officiants.

Which national laws mattered and who had the authority to officiate were thorny questions.[112] Several European governments returned to earlier prewar mandates that residents wed only in government-approved settings and in ceremonies led by authorized officiants. In both the Netherlands and in France, marriages between military personnel and local civilians had to take place in registrar-approved government buildings and be officiated by state-licensed registrars. So, when Clara and Daniel planned their wedding during the summer of 1945, they had to meet the requirements established by the city of Antwerp and the US military, including, but not limited to, obtaining commander approval, health screenings, birth certificates, and identity papers. The two spent weeks gathering the necessary paperwork, forms, and funds; once they had done so, they exchanged vows in Antwerp's Hôtel de Ville (city hall). Later that day, they hosted a second ceremony, this one officiated by a local rabbi.[113] When Bella and Ray married in Reims that same weekend, they first exchanged vows at City Hall with the local mayor as their officiant; the following day, they held a religious ceremony officiated by a local rabbi and a Jewish chaplain.[114]

While it was likely an unintended consequence, disparate European marriage laws allowed some couples to bypass their chaplains altogether. Ben O. and Phyllis R. exchanged vows at Antwerp's Hôtel de Ville and had no additional religious ceremony. The RCAF aircraftsman and his survivor fiancée married in June 1945, almost immediately after Canada acknowledged the sovereignty of Dutch marriage laws and permitted military-civilian marriages in the Netherlands. The couple married at the city hall, and archival records leave no indication of whether they did not want a religious ceremony or if they could not have one.[115] Having not forgiven Mort's chaplain for first refusing to permit their marriage on the grounds that they were too young, Mort and Helena gained his commander's permission to marry, received Mort's parents' consent, gathered the paperwork required by both the military and the city, and then arranged for a civil ceremony, exchanging vows at the semifunctioning city hall offices in Regensburg.[116] Because they were not married in a Jewish ceremony, traditional Jewish authorities considered these couples as "in a relationship . . . not sanctioned as marriage," and any children resulting from such a union would be considered illegitimate.[117] Observant military chaplains therefore urged their Jewish soldiers who wished, or were required, to marry in a civil ceremony also to participate in a religious one.[118]

Jewish chaplains (and military commanders) were also gravely concerned by couples who managed to wed in religious ceremonies that evaded both military and secular laws. In many cases, these weddings took place in parts of Europe that still lacked the infrastructure to regulate marriage, with the ensuing marriages not considered legal in the United States, Britain, or Canada. Marrying in a local religious ceremony wreaked havoc on the immigration plans of Friedl H., Canadian transport driver Sydney D.'s wife. Sydney's RCAF commander and chaplain had prohibited the couple from marrying on the grounds that Friedl's birth in Austria disqualified her from wedding a Canadian soldier.[119] The Canadian transport driver bypassed his chaplain and commander, briefly went AWOL to meet Friedl in Brussels, and illegally exchanged vows with her in a local synagogue. The Brussels rabbi was unconcerned about her place of birth or the city's marriage laws and married them (illegally) in a religious ceremony. It would take months to resolve the situation, and Friedl eventually came to Canada, albeit through the United Kingdom.[120] Judith S. and Sam, who had met in Germany, similarly married in a religious ceremony while in Prague searching for Judith's family. Having been told that they would not be allowed to marry in Germany, they decided it would be simpler to take advantage of a Czech rabbi who had the reputation of approving such marriages.[121] Judith faced real difficulties when trying to emigrate. "I had no [legal] paper," she remembered, "and I had to go through repeating my story over and over again."[122]

When they married in ceremonies separate from their chaplains, couples—sometimes unknowingly—intimated that local secular and religious powers outranked military authorities. For some Jewish chaplains, this was worrisome. New postwar diplomatic arrangements, which mandated state- or city-sanctioned ceremonies, were outside of a chaplain's control. Some fretted that they were being replaced by local civilian rabbis, which could have created tremendous excitement about the possibility of rebirth in the aftermath of genocide but did not. At a Canadian Jewish chaplains' conference as early as 1944, the attendees expressed their hope that army religious personnel would always have some involvement in marriage ceremonies that involved military personnel. They and their American counterparts suggested that military chaplains contact local rabbis or cantors to proactively reach a "gentleman's agreement."[123] In some communities, this became practice,[124] but in others, chaplains and local rabbis had difficulty reconciling their different Jewish cultural traditions and practices. The three officiating rabbis at Rachel and Mayer's Berlin wedding, for example, began arguing once the American Jewish chaplain started to read an opening prayer in English. The two other officiants, local rabbis living in the DP camp with the bride's family, refused to participate if English was uttered underneath the wedding canopy, and the ceremony continued in Hebrew (and Aramaic).[125]

While chaplains and local officiants sometimes debated who had the authority to officiate, Jewish chaplains performed many of the weddings between Jewish civilians and military personnel. Chaplaincy reports described hundreds of military-civilian marriages,[126] and sometimes the rabbis even officiated at several such weddings at once.[127] In his diary, American chaplain Ernst Mordechai Lorge frequently noted that he officiated at "soldier-DP" weddings, and Canadian chaplain Chaim Gevantman's monthly reports similarly listed performing civilian-military weddings alongside other obligations: counseling, organizing worship services, arranging compassionate leave, and officiating at funerals.[128]

. . . .

The wedding formalities, like the couples and officiants themselves, were diverse. They included disparate liturgy and readings, and took place at a wide range of military, religious, and cultural sites. American, British, and Canadian Jewish soldiers and officers often ignored the religious backgrounds of the Jewish survivors with whom they were involved and insisted on services that reflected their own denominational upbringing. As they did in other arenas, American Jewish chaplains often tried to conform to the couple's denominational affiliation.[129] When Harry and Flory started to plan their wedding, Harry insisted on including the traditional Jewish rites of a Ketubah (the wedding contract), Kiddushin (sanctification of the wedding), and the chanting of the seven wedding blessings, all witnessed by a quorum of ten Jewish adult men (*minyan*). Even though his Naples-based military chaplain had been licensed by a Reform seminary, the chaplain followed Harry's family's Orthodox traditions; Flory's Sephardic background and customs were ignored.[130] British and Canadian chaplains also often crafted ceremonies

Flory and Harry Jagoda cutting their wedding cake, June 1945.
United States Holocaust Memorial Museum,
courtesy of Flory Kabilio Jagoda.

with the military personnel's religious background and their own denominational leanings in mind.[131]

The ceremony and reception sites also differed, frequently reflecting the spaces to which the Jewish civilians and military personnel had access. Just as some first met in the DP camps, rebuilt synagogues, Jewish centers, and aid offices, couples also married there.[132] Weddings in such places offered the couples, their chaplains, and guests a sense of control at a moment marked by its absence.[133] For Norman and Gena, for example, it mattered that their exchange of vows took place at the Lübeck synagogue, which the Germans had vandalized and used as a stable. Theirs was supposedly the first wedding to take place in the synagogue that British military personnel had cleaned and helped to reopen.[134] Bella similarly insisted that her wedding to Ray was the first of its kind in the Reims synagogue.[135] Observers also delighted in those ceremonies that took place in spaces that once had been antisemitic or Nazi clubs, hotels that banned Jews, or places favored by Hitler and his inner circle. In their view, these weddings proved that the Nazi Reich had failed at its attempt to annihilate European Jews.[136]

Couples and their guests also invoked themes of Jewish resurgence and Allied victory when they looked to the weddings' attendees. With so many Jews murdered during the Holocaust, it seemed unlikely that many immediate family members or close friends would have survived to witness a couple's union. When ceremonies included parents, siblings, or other loved ones, observers saw in them both a "rare privilege" and evidence of the Nazis' failure.[137] Clara acutely felt the absences of her father and older brother when she married, but she also underscored her great fortune in having her mother, sister, brother, and Zionist friends and colleagues at her wedding. In her view, her wedding ceremony and reception brought multiple Jewish groups and factions together. The diverse guest list was evidenced in the desserts brought by many of those invited. "Everyone made a cake," she recalled. Some decorated their confections with the hammer and sickle; others used Jewish stars.[138] Daniel likewise recalled that it was a "party wedding . . . a wedding for all chalutzim [Zionist pioneers]."[139] Lala's wedding and reception similarly included a wide range of guests and officiants, though she emphasized their rank and status in her descriptions of the day. Her civil ceremony to Morris was officiated by the director of the Passau Standesamt and the religious exchange of vows was overseen by one of the best-known Jewish chaplains of the time;[140] the ceremonial sword used for the cake-cutting was borrowed from the army colonel who commanded the regional occupation forces; and the banquet was organized and catered by the director of UNRRA's food

Gena Turgel's parachute silk wedding dress, Belsen.
© Imperial War Museum (EPH 5546).

Lala and Morris Fishman on their wedding day in Passau, Germany, 1947.
United States Holocaust Memorial Museum,
courtesy of Morris and Lala Fishman.

service, not a "lesser mess captain." Though unlikely that "all of UNRRA" attended, Lala's description of her wedding and many guests allowed her to claim for herself a feeling of importance and inclusion, even when others had allegedly imagined her as "no one," "just a DP girl."[141]

Wedding ceremonies and banquets with sufficient drinks and food for dozens of guests offered a sharp contrast to a landscape of scarcity and hunger.[142] Lala remembered a wedding canopy composed of fresh flowers, a

WEDDING DINNER

HORS D'OEUVRE VARIE

*

OXTAIL SOUP

*

FILET OF VEAL
ASPARAGUS
CHOUX POTATOES

*

ROASTED GOOSE
APPLE SAUCE
PEAS
FRENCH FRIED POTATOES

*

ICE CREAM MERINGUE

*

COFFEE - WINE
CAKE

Lala and Morris Fishman's wedding dinner menu, 1947.
Morris and Lala Fishman Papers #1999.51_001_022_0003.
United States Holocaust Memorial Museum
Collection, gift of Morris and Lala Fishman.

"sumptuous banquet" with two entrees—goose and veal—and an enormous cake baked from "thirty-eight eggs. Thirty eggs!"[143] Her wedding, which included a "princess dress" and ice cream meringue, was more lavish than many of the other civilian-military weddings but was not unique in its offer of food, dessert, and music. To pay for their weddings, military personnel frequently relied on their rations, which they then bartered, and the underground economy. According to Lala, "The whole wedding cost Morris three boxes of Phillip Morris."[144] Daniel similarly bartered "booze and cigarettes" to obtain the food for the ceremony.[145] Of course, not all couples who received permission to marry could host such elaborate ceremonies and receptions. Gena and Norman, for example, married in the presence of only a handful of guests at the Lübeck synagogue in 1945, and Sala and Sidney wed in a civil ceremony with a small number of guests present.[146]

· ·

Some couples found themselves unable to formally solemnize their betrothal before their fiancé(e)s were demobilized or transferred. In some cases, they lacked sufficient time between receiving their permissions and when the soldier or officer needed to return home. Edith Festinger and Nathan Litvin became engaged in early 1946, for example, but Nathan had to leave Munich before they could marry. In other cases, the couple never received formal approval to marry. This occurred when Abe requested permission from his chaplain for him to marry Sala B. He discovered that Canadian soldiers could not marry civilians on German soil, whether or not the intended spouses had been victims of the Nazis. It took over a year for the two to determine how to reunite and marry. Edith and Nathan were more fortunate, marrying several months after Nathan's return to Detroit.[147]

Whether or not they married in Europe or North Africa, civilian-military couples found that with transfers and/or demobilization, their lives changed radically yet again. Couples went from seeing each other several times a week—sometimes even daily—to relying entirely on letter, telegram, and, if fortunate, the occasional phone call. Some even transitioned suddenly from the high of their wedding ceremony to the nadir of their separation. "On March 5, we got married, and that night he was on the train back to America," one war bride remembered.[148] While few separated so quickly after they wed, almost all couples faced extended periods of separation and uncertainty as they tried to determine how and when the war brides and fiancé(e)s would immigrate to the United States, Britain, or Canada.

4

Proving to Be a Headache

· ·

IMMIGRATION

Immediately after Clara and Daniel solemnized their wedding vows in July 1945, they underwent the laborious process of organizing Clara's immigration to the United States. Though in late September they were delighted to learn that Clara's paperwork had been approved, they soon discovered that Clara's departure date remained uncertain. Daniel would be demobilized and sent to Philadelphia, while Clara would have to wait her turn until she could embark on the transatlantic voyage. Immigration services would contact her "as to when and where to report for transportation." The best estimates were that she would depart Antwerp sometime between March and June 1946. But no one was sure. There was "nothing definite" about when she might leave, only that the American authorities had assured her that *one day* she would immigrate to the United States and reunite with her husband.[1]

In the immediate postwar period, countless numbers of people wished to make their way to the United States, Britain, and Canada. As the war ended, military officials began the daunting process of moving personnel and returning veterans home while concomitantly welcoming select immigrants and "repatriating" foreign-born spouses and fiancé(e)s.[2] In late 1945, US officials anticipated that so many spouses and dependents were waiting to immigrate that, once the gates opened, they would likely see more than 10,000 war brides enter per month.[3] Canadian immigration spokespeople imagined proportional increases, estimating that within the year they would see the immigration of over 10,000 spouses and their dependents.[4]

Despite the many accusations to the contrary, governments in the United States, Britain, and Canada prioritized returning military personnel home over transporting fiancé(e)s and spouses.[5] In November 1945, the US War Department denied a report that the *Queen Mary* would be used to bring over thousands of brides and children, insisting instead that it would convey troops home.[6] The backlog of war brides waiting to enter North America was so significant that the undersecretary of the US Navy reported that the "transportation outlook" for these women (and some men) would remain bleak for some time.[7] The "matrimonial entanglements" of soldiers, complained a second official, was proving to be a "transportation headache."[8]

While they were unlikely to describe their marriages as "matrimonial entanglements," many spouses and fiancé(e)s complained about the bewildering, slow character of immigration. Like Clara, they found it difficult to plan their travels. They did not know when they would leave, how they would travel, whom they would journey with, what the voyage would be like, or who would greet them upon their arrival. Moreover, as they came in and out of contact with military officials, government bureaucrats, non-Jewish war brides, Jewish immigrants, and various volunteers, Jewish war brides and fiancé(e)s often found that those with whom they could communicate most easily—fellow travelers from similar places of origins—were governed by disparate immigration policies and practices. The immigration regulations concerning war brides celebrated veterans and their families; the policies concerning other aspiring immigrants treated those petitioners as suspect. The immigration process extended and intensified the Jewish war brides' sense of uncertainty and unbelonging.

. . . .

To arrange for their hoped-for reunions, couples often depended on letters and telegrams, which they found vexing.[9] Postwar Europe lacked the infrastructure for the postal system to resume quickly, and mail remained slow and uneven.[10] Until November 1945, many couples relied on airgraphs, pre-made forms that would be censored, scanned onto microfilm, transported, and reproduced as photo prints usually about a quarter the size of the original letter. They were difficult to read, and recipients complained that they could not understand the senders' questions or directions because of the small type and sometimes terrible handwriting.[11] Daniel frequently bemoaned Clara's and Ruby's use of the airgraph when discussing important matters concerning Clara's immigration, imploring them to write clearly and to spend the additional money on full-sized stationery and postage.[12] In some cases, couples were even prohibited from sending letters to one another. For much of 1945, for example, civilians in Britain and North America could not communicate by post with residents in Germany or Austria, even if the latter had been victims of the Nazis. This policy complicated Kurt's early communications with Gerda when he tried to bring her to the United States after his demobilization. He eventually circumvented this restriction by sending her letters via Munich-based military personnel he knew, but not all soldiers were so well connected.[13]

The linguistic challenges that had plagued some couples since their initial encounters further exacerbated the difficulties of coordinating their reunions by letter and telegram. Daniel could write to Clara in Yiddish, albeit imperfectly, but some men and women failed to understand one another's letters, airgraphs, or telegrams. Edith relied on a former Army buddy of Nathan L.'s to comprehend the detailed immigration information Nathan relayed in his telegrams and letters, as well as the instructions on the multiple forms and documents he sent to her.[14] Likewise, Lydia's cousin had served as an adequate translator for the couple in Oran, but her English was not sufficient to fully grasp Harold's written queries and directions, and Lydia sometimes needed to seek out help at the army base to decipher his communications.[15]

As irritated as couples may have been coordinating immigration plans by letter or telegram, they expressed relief that somewhat more lenient immigration regulations existed for war brides. Separated by thousands of miles after her husband's demobilization, one German-born Jewish bride in Manchester complained about the long wait until she could come to Montreal but also recognized that "at least," as a war bride, she could reunite—one day—with her husband. She knew many children or parents of individuals now living in Canada whose family reunification was uncertain.[16] Flory and Harry similarly worried about when they would reunite but were confident that the

Italian war bride would leave Bari before any of the Jewish DPs whom they knew also were petitioning to immigrate to the United States.[17]

Officials never guaranteed the reunions of war brides and their military spouses, but immigration policies crafted by the American, British, and Canadian governments came close to making such a promise. The war bride regulations were different than other immigration laws. While the latter positioned national security and the economy against inclusion,[18] war bride legislation assumed that foreign spouses already had been well vetted and were "race eligible."[19] The war bride policies were distinct from other immigration regulations in additional ways. Most aspiring immigrants were responsible for completing their own paperwork or seeking assistance from the appropriate aid agency to do so, obtaining their own passage, and waiting for their place in the queue of the relevant quota or non-quota visa.[20] "Wouldn't you think we would have priority to go out or to get out of Germany?" one Polish-born Jewish survivor asked. "But no. I had to wait three long years. There were quotas. There were always quotas."[21] In contrast, the war bride legislation circumvented preexisting quotas, rested on the military or veteran spouse to apply on their spouse's behalf, and often included travel subsidies, if not full coverage, for bringing spouses and their dependents from their (temporary) residences in Europe or North Africa to their new homes in the United States, Britain, or Canada. This was no small matter. A sea passage could cost more than US$145 (about $2,400 today).[22]

The Canadian government was the first to create a formal travel system for foreign spouses that bypassed the quotas. Between 1942 and 1946, the Canadian cabinet issued five Orders in Council, guaranteeing that the wives, widows, and children of Canadian personnel serving overseas would sidestep existing immigration quotas. The Canadian government also assured payment for ocean and rail transportation and offered spouses citizenship or domicile status to match the status of the individual in service. To receive their travel visas, the military personnel or veterans needed to submit application forms to the adjutant general and Canadian War Brides Bureau Repatriation Section.[23] There were no clear immigration or travel policies concerning fiancé(e)s, one of many issues that would complicate attempts to bring Sala B. to Montreal after Abe's demobilization.

Like Canada, the British government also intertwined immigration and travel policies during and immediately after the war. It too mandated that military personnel or veterans apply on their spouses' behalf and provided expedited entry for spouses and dependents.[24] Unlike the Commonwealth, the British government established a travel visa program specifically for fiancé(e)s. It did not fund their travel, but alien fiancé(e)s were permitted a visa to come to the United Kingdom for two months; if they did not marry within that time, they would be deported.[25]

The United States would eventually organize the largest of the war bride immigration systems, in part because between 1943 and 1946 it experienced the most significant spike in requests for marriage and immigration. As early as December 1943, the Office of Immigration and Naturalization Services (INS) reported it was receiving up to 300 immigration applications concerning foreign spouses daily. Most but not all came from military personnel serving in Britain and Australia.[26] By September 1945, the American embassy in Paris was receiving sixty inquiries daily. Requests arrived at embassy and consulate offices from places as far flung as Egypt, Iceland, Italy, and the British West Indies.[27]

Until the passage of war bride legislation in December 1945, the United States permitted foreign wives and dependents of American soldiers and officers to enter the country, but these civilians could only do so by relying on existing channels of immigration. This meant that American military personnel who wished to bring a foreign spouse to the United States first needed to apply for the spouse's nonquota status. Spouses would receive permission to immigrate once the soldier, officer, or veteran had submitted his or her evidence of citizenship, affidavits by two American citizens who had known the serviceman or servicewoman for at least one year, and proof of financial ability to support the beneficiary of the petition. Once nonquota status was granted, military servicemen and servicewomen needed to apply for their spouse's immigration visa. That application required submitting other pertinent documents such as a birth certificate, marriage certificate, police certificate, passport, and evidence that the military personnel had sufficient means to pay for the spouse's immigration. While officials first insisted that military personnel be entirely responsible for the transportation of their dependents,[28] the armed forces agreed in November 1944 that, if available, wives could travel on government transport, paying "only" a subsistence charge of $1.50 a day (approximately $24.70 today).[29]

Passage of US emergency war bride legislation in December 1945 changed matters considerably.[30] Per Public Law 271, alien spouses and children of US citizens who were serving in, or had an honorable discharge from, the US armed forces could be admitted into the United States as nonquota immigrants without visas for a period of three years. Priority would be based on the status of the military personnel-petitioner, with greater urgency given to foreign spouses whose partners were hospitalized.[31] This legislation was followed a year later by the Alien Fiancées and Fiancés Act (GI Fiancées Act), which similarly permitted intended brides and grooms to enter the country as nonimmigrants through December 31, 1947.[32] Both laws stipulated that the American government would arrange and fund the transport of these men, women, and children, though, much like the marriage policies, they also mandated that applications be "consistent with current immigration requirements." Partners of military personnel who were of a different race would be prohibited from immigrating if they had hoped to settle in states that prohibited such marriages.[33]

Even if their immigration was nearly secured, Jewish spouses and fiancé(e)s still encountered several obstacles when planning their reunions. Many found the regulations confusing and were frustrated with the responses they received from immigration branch offices, consular offices, and embassies. Much as they had done when they first petitioned to marry, couples depended on a wide range of networks and organizations as they worked through the possibilities for immigration. However, spouses immigrating to North America now also relied on government-organized bureaus responsible for their care and immigration.[34] The Canadian Wives Bureau, founded by the Canadian Army, coordinated the wives' and children's passage to Canada, cared for them before they set sail, provided welfare services, and helped with their acculturation. It also created dozens of war brides' clubs across the United Kingdom, which then connected spouses across the continent with advisers who managed their emigration.[35] The American Red Cross (ARC) began to assist military spouses as soon as the United States entered the war, but it took on a more formal role with foreign brides and grooms in 1943 when it joined a committee created by the Office of War Services to consider a wide range of issues related to the marriages of military personnel serving abroad.[36] While the ARC clarified that it would not financially support the transport of foreign wives to their husbands' homes as it had for domestic spouses, it agreed to send Home Service personnel abroad to facilitate the war brides' care, emigration, and acculturation. The ARC first established offices in Great Britain; by the end of 1945, it also sponsored Home Service personnel in Australia, France, Italy, Belgium, the Netherlands, Austria, and Germany.[37] Like the Canadian Wives Bureau, these Home Service workers assisted military personnel and veterans when they petitioned for immigration, referred them and their spouses to appropriate agencies, provided information concerning the changing governmental regulations, helped them apply for government benefits and family allowances, and offered counseling.[38]

Jewish war brides and their spouses depended on these organizations, as well as on the Jewish NGOs that focused on DP care and emigration. Certainly, the latter had far greater and more demanding matters of concern, but they still devoted hours to helping these couples consider the immigration process and its demands. In their letters, petitions, and telegrams, couples frequently mentioned relying on the Hebrew Immigrant Aid Society (HIAS) and the Jewish Joint Distribution Committee (JDC). Each had offices in Europe and North America and thus individuals on the ground who could offer assistance, even after demobilization. Even those organizations with a slightly smaller reach, such as the Canadian Jewish Immigrant Aid Society, the Refugee Ex-servicemen's Association, the Jewish Committee for Relief Abroad (JCRA), and the Association of Jewish Ex-servicemen, helped veterans with organizing the war brides' immigration.[39]

Many of these organizations featured prominently in the 1946 letters and telegrams exchanged between Edith and Nathan L. The couple was stymied over how to ensure Edith's immigration, since the United States had not yet passed regulations concerning war fiancées. With Edith in Munich and Nathan in Detroit, the couple separately pursued counsel. Nathan solicited help from the Detroit chapter of the ARC, his former military commander, his parents, and their political representatives in the US House and Senate. Edith approached the JDC and HIAS, both of which had offices in Munich. No one knew definitively how foreign fiancées could reunite with their American partners. Dismayed by the obstacles in her path and desperate to leave Germany, Edith considered joining her sister in Australia, but Nathan's parents offered to pay for their son's roundtrip travel to Paris. The American veteran reunited with Edith in France, married her, and, with the help of Jewish organizations in Paris and his parents, arranged to fly to Detroit with his new wife.[40]

Serviceman Dave B. and his fiancée Jeanine F. similarly reached out to a wide group of networks to determine how Jeanine might emigrate from Belgium to Canada. Upon learning that only spouses could bypass Canadian immigration laws, Dave requested permission to travel to Brussels and marry Jeanine there.[41] Once married, he again sought assistance from his chaplain, commander, fellow servicemen, family members, and the office of the Canadian Wives Bureau to determine how to secure Jeanine's transport from Brussels. It took several months and multiple networks to determine that Jeanine first would need to travel to England and emigrate from there; many more months passed before she received her final paperwork. "There's no speeding them up," Dave's chaplain explained to the frustrated now-veteran, "for it is a straight matter of first come first serve. They are having an awful time of it."[42]

Jewish war brides and military personnel also relied on these organizations and chaplains when they encountered an additional obstacle: the demand for more paperwork including, but not limited to, police reports, statements of support from parents, and additional forms of identification.[43] Like when they had petitioned to marry, couples found the process of authenticating their identity in the aftermath of genocide to be difficult and fraught. Especially if they had spent the war in hiding or passing, they panicked over whether their papers would suffice. Jewish war brides submitted whatever form of identification they could: religious wedding contracts, work permits, DP cards, and even papers from the Nazi years, which still had the "J" stamped on them.[44] For the nearly two years of their separation, Gerda and Kurt were preoccupied with locating and obtaining the papers necessary for Gerda's immigration. This was particularly tricky because they had been unable to marry before Kurt's demobilization. Like Nathan and Edith, they eventually reunited and married in Paris, but only after Gerda traveled there illegally. Before they could marry and Gerda immigrate, Gerda needed a Polish passport, a residency permit, and a police certificate, some of which she could obtain only with the assistance of the local office of the JDC and the legal counsel hired by her uncle.[45]

· ·

As they waited for their paperwork, and again as they made their way to their new homes, many Jewish war brides and fiancé(e)s simultaneously inhabited at least two separate communities: those of civilians married or engaged to military personnel and those of other aspiring Jewish immigrants. In Europe and North Africa, Jewish war brides continued to socialize, work, and sometimes live among the very individuals with whom they had survived the camps, hiding, or their exodus from the Soviet zone.[46] They frequented the same shops and markets, socialized at one other's residences, attended dances, engagement parties, and weddings, and traveled to visit friends and loved ones at more distant DP camps. They patronized the same *hachshara* meetings, met at a variety of cultural activities, mourned together, and attended synagogue services and events at newly built synagogue centers. In their letters, they described active Jewish social lives.[47] Pointing to a photograph of her mother and other DPs, one daughter of a Jewish war bride

GERMANY)
CITY OF MUNICH)
CONSULATE GENERAL OF THE)SS
UNITED STATES OF AMERICA)

Before me, Howard C. Goldsmith, a Vice Consul of
the United States of America at Munich, Germany, duly
commissioned and qualified, personally appeared
Morris FISHMAN, who deposes and states:

I, Morris Fishman, being duly sworn, declare that
I am a citizen of the United States of America; that
on November 22, 1947, I married Lala WEINTRAUB who was
born at Kamieniec Podolski, Poland, on November 17,
1922, and who is a citizen of Poland. I further state
that she is my wife, and that her present name is
Lala W. FISHMAN. I further state that her personal description is as follows:

Height : 5 ft 5 in.   Color of eyes: hazel
Weight : 125 lbs.   Color of hair: blond
Face : oval   Other means of
                       identification: none.

I further state that the photograph attached to this
affidavit is a photograph of my wife, and that her true
signature appears thereon.

Morris Fishman

Subscribed and sworn to before me this 30th day of
December A.D. 1947.

Howard C. Goldsmith
Vice Consul of the United
States of America

Service No. ..25122...
Tariff Item 38
No fee prescribed

**An affidavit with attached photo, dated December 30, 1947, written
by Morris Fishman asserting that he is married to Lala Weintraub.**
United States Holocaust Memorial Museum,
courtesy of Morris and Lala Fishman.

explained that this was a "group kind of coming back to life, literally holding on to each other for dear life."[48]

At the same time, Jewish war brides participated in activities specifically for spouses of military personnel. They accessed certain work and leisure spaces open only to military personnel and their families, such as private clubs, eating halls, sports fields, and swimming pools. They bought groceries alongside other war brides from the PX, benefited from jobs at military bases and NGO offices, accessed medical care intended for military personnel and their dependents, and profited from family allowances and portions of their spouses' salaries or pensions.[49] They also received an additional benefit available only to them: the possibility of government-paid transport to their new homes. Military couples had the "luxury"—or at least the pretense—of deciding whether they wished to pursue government-supported travel or to privately fund the voyage.[50]

A sizeable minority of the spouses, particularly those going to the United States, financed their own journeys. Air travel from Europe to North America, which had begun only months before World War II commenced, was the most expensive but fastest option.[51] By October 1945, war brides could take advantage of regularly scheduled commercial flights across the North Atlantic by American Export Airlines, Pan American Airlines, and Transcontinental & Western Airlines. Depending on one's point of origin, this form of travel could take only one or two days. Of course, such speed came with a cost.[52] Passengers paid about US$400 (the equivalent of $6,500 today) for a single flight across the Atlantic. The same journey by ship cost approximately $150 less, about $145–$160 (roughly $2,400 today) for a privately funded sea passage, which could take anywhere from five days to two weeks.[53]

Plane travel now circumvented the long wait for available space on private cruise liners and government-subsidized ships, but couples articulated several other reasons why self-funded voyages were worth the expense. After years of having no control over their movements, Bella and Ray wanted the agency to dictate when and how Bella would travel. Between the solemnization of their vows in July 1945 and the passage of the War Brides Act in December of that year, the couple was consistently told that no transport ship leaving France had an available berth for Bella. In January 1946, they learned that even though there now were war bride ships sailing to the United States, the waiting list was so long that it would be another six to nine months before she could travel. Frustrated with the wait and unable to locate space on a private vessel, Ray, now in Philadelphia, used the $500 (approximately

$8,000 today) that his mother had saved from his military allowance toward a plane ticket for his wife.[54]

Other couples pursued private travel because they had become stuck, stranded in cities to which they had gone hoping to process their paperwork more quickly. In no city was this a more common occurrence than in Paris. Just as there had been rumors that marriage laws in Paris were laxer than elsewhere on the continent, couples gossiped that Parisian consular officials would accelerate paperwork, procure earlier shipping dates, and provide transit visas. Mainstream military and civilian newspapers such as *Stars and Stripes*, the *Maple Leaf*, the *Gazette*, the *Globe and Mail*, the *Toronto Daily Star*, the *Chicago Tribune*, and the *New York Times* reported on brides flocking to Paris, causing "a headache" for NGO and military officials alike.[55] Rumors of French lenience and the presence of Jewish organizations in Paris prompted Edith and Nathan L., Gerda and Kurt, Sala B. and Abe, and Judith S. and Sam to go there. Judith and Sam drove to Paris after finding it impossible to arrange for Judith's emigration from Germany, where Sam was stationed. When they reached France, however, they failed to obtain space for Judith on any of the ships leaving Le Havre. With Sam's demobilization date looming, they ran out of time and options. With funds from the sale of his car and his prewar practice as a dentist, Sam purchased his new wife an airline ticket to fly to the United States.[56]

Some war brides and military personnel took advantage of private travel because of the serious—and very public—complications plaguing the war bride ships. Strikes, ship explosions, and broken parts delayed travelers on several of the government transport ships. In March 1946, newspapers reported on the first case of war brides needing to be rescued from a vessel that had run aground during a storm. There were no fatalities, but the waters off Scotland's Firth of Clyde had been so intense that they had broken the 7,176-ton *Bryon Darnton* in half.[57] The timing was auspicious. That month marked the largest transport of spouses and dependents to North America since the passage of the US War Brides Act, and the March shipwreck underscored concerns about the large number of war brides and the multiple cargo ships, specifically the Liberty ships, that transported them.[58] The Liberty ships, which had been developed during World War II as low-cost vessels that could be built quickly, often survived longer than the five years they were intended to be in use, and American officials used them in the immediate postwar period to transport veterans and their spouses and dependents.[59] Rumors circulated around these vessels. One war bride requested that her husband purchase her a ticket on a private cruise liner because her sister, also a war bride, had experienced a grueling crossing. According to her spouse, there was no need to spend their savings on private travel; his sister-in-law's troubles allegedly stemmed from the fact that she had traveled to the United States on "one of those liberty boats I told you about." He told his wife that the Canadian Air Force, unlike the US military, assigned war brides to large cruise liners, so she would have a safer transatlantic journey than her sister experienced. She was fortunate that she was going to Montreal and not to the United States.[60]

. . . .

Like the Canadian war bride who first had worried about the Liberty ships, most war brides took advantage of the government-sponsored programs. They were cheaper than civilian travel, easier to organize, and assumed responsibility for all segments of travel, including, but not limited to, ocean transportation and meals, train fares, baggage fees, berths and meals, as well as hospitalization en route if that was necessary. Tens of thousands of women, men, and children journeyed on these transport initiatives and, to keep up with the demand, American and Canadian War Shipping administrations assigned fast passenger liners to take cargo to the United Kingdom and Europe, and bring war brides and dependents back.[61] Those war brides who married Allied servicemen between 1939 and early 1945—or whose spouses were hospitalized—were assigned travel dates before those who had married after the war and/or whose spouses were healthy.[62] By August 1946, an estimated 46,000 brides and 12,000 of their children had entered the United States thanks to the war bride program; by the end of that year, 42,098 spouses and 19,979 children had arrived in Canada on the war bride ships.[63]

As part of the North American government transport programs, war brides first reported to special embarkation facilities, where they would remain until they were cleared for departure. Designed to physically separate military spouses and fiancé(e)s from their friends and families, other immigrants, and military personnel, these centers were accessible by rail or bus and close to the harbor.[64] Immigration officials gave the spouses only a few days' advance notice before they were to leave their current residence and arrive at the staging facilities, where they might reside for as little as a few days or as long as several weeks. Clara and her sister Freide learned less than a week before their departure from Antwerp that they were to make their way to a facility near Le Havre, a journey of about 250 miles.[65] Ruth B.

similarly had five days' warning before she needed to travel from Manchester to Southampton via London. It was difficult for these women to leave behind the few close relatives with whom they had survived the war, especially not knowing when they would see one another next, but "security" concerns meant that family members, friends, even spouses, were prohibited from entering these facilities.[66]

Ruth B. was sent to Tidworth, near Southampton, England, and Clara and Freide lived in the complex of "cigarette camps" near Le Havre, about 120 miles from Paris. The two facilities were among the largest war bride dormitories in Europe. Named after popular cigarette brands like Lucky Strike, the Le Havre cigarette camps resembled a small city with a medical clinic, place of worship, movie theater, post office, and supermarket.[67] Though Tidworth was just as large, with a mess hall, health screening spaces, immigration offices, and barracks where residents slept in bunkbeds and washed themselves (and their laundry) in rows of sinks, many war brides remembered it as "strictly military," "like going to a boarding school," and "a desultory type of place."[68] Both centers were filled to capacity, with anywhere from dozens to hundreds of spouses of different ages and nationalities, as well as their children.

Over the course of 1945 and 1946, officials expanded both large staging facilities while simultaneously building a few others and requisitioning nearly a dozen small hostels and hotels to serve as additional clearing centers.[69] The smallest of these sites only had room for a dozen spouses and their dependents and, because of their privacy and level of comfort, tended to be remembered more affectionately than the massive, utilitarian war bride camps. Flory spent time in such a small hotel when she prepared to emigrate from Italy. Weighed down with her suitcases and her beloved accordion, she traveled alone from Bari to Naples, 173 miles in total, and remembered feeling relieved when she located the boutique hotel that had been reserved for her and other war brides. She had been worried that her staging facility would resemble the DP camps in Bari. She was grateful to share meals and sleeping space with a small group of women with whom she would travel.[70]

Flory's experience was unlike that of many other Jewish war brides. Not only was she housed and processed in a small hotel before her voyage, but she also openly discussed her embarkation site. Many of the other Jewish survivors ignored the staging facilities in their interviews, letters, and memoirs, silences that may have been due to the ways these large barrack-based camps triggered their wartime traumas.[71] Sleeping in rows of bunk beds, living among individuals with whom they did not share a language, waiting

War Bride Processing Centers

on lines to be cleared, submitting ration books, being assigned numbers in lines, having their hand baggage inspected in the presence of others, and undergoing health screenings must have been hauntingly reminiscent of their wartime experiences.

Jewish war brides tended to speak about their experiences on the ships, but those reflections also were uneven. Like the staging facilities, the ships were enormous, carrying anywhere between several hundred and several thousand travelers. To accommodate such volume, the United States and Canada utilized a wide array of vessels, including Liberty ships, cargo ships, travel liners, and hospital ships, all of which were outfitted to transport large numbers of people and were staffed by a few dozen—and sometimes nearly a hundred—employees.[72] Cabins held twenty to forty women each, with two-tiered bunk beds, though women who traveled with their babies and infants roomed in slightly larger rooms with fewer adults but with bunk beds, cots, and cribs.[73] In their letters, diaries, and interviews, war brides complained bitterly about the cramped cabins. One woman grumbled about having to room with thirty-six women in a space that was about fifty by thirteen feet.[74] Despite how large the ship was, Flory likewise described the *Algonquin* as "stuffed with war brides," many of whom were physically on top of one another because of the lack of space in their cabins.[75]

At both the staging facilities and on the ships, Jewish war brides and fiancé(e)s journeyed alongside military transport authorities, returning military personnel, Jewish and non-Jewish immigrants, and other war brides and their dependents. Travelers were "from all over," and included spouses from England, France, Belgium, Austria, Germany, Russia, Poland, Italy, the Netherlands, Tunisia, and Morocco.[76] Writing in her journal, one woman noted that on her American-bound ship, she traveled with 300 brides and 45 children, mostly but not exclusively from the United Kingdom, 43 GI and Navy personnel returning home, 33 Army transport authorities, and a crew of 100.[77] On the *Algonquin*, Flory was among hundreds of Italian, Austrian, and French brides, large groups of American soldiers, several Jewish DPs, and a handful of Jewish spouses also from Italy, France, and Austria.[78] Registries from the staging facilities and ships did not always indicate religion, but when they did, they confirmed that Jewish war brides composed a minority of the passengers. One ship bound for Canada, for example, had one Jewish war bride among the sixty-six military dependents.[79] Some non-Jewish war brides recalled the small number of Jewish women among them, noting the presence of those who had been liberated by their future spouses.[80] Their invocation of these triumphalist tropes suggested both that the non-Jewish war brides were aware of their own diversity and that they had begun, early on, to invoke themes of chivalrous military personnel who had "saved" women by liberating and then marrying them. At the same time, while these recollections affirmed the presence of Jewish women among the larger war bride population, none of the non-Jewish brides mentioned creating relationships—or even mingling socially—with the Jewish women on their ships. Several Jewish war brides recalled exchanging niceties with other war brides but did not remember establishing any friendships, certainly none that were lasting.[81]

The lack of deep social interaction among the spouses may have been due, in part, to linguistic challenges. Several Jewish war brides were not conversant in English, French, or German, the languages spoken by most of the spouses and staff at the staging facilities and on the ships.[82] Unless one was like Flory, who communicated with fellow passengers in Italian, or Ruth B., who spoke with her fellow war brides in English, immigration could be a deeply lonesome experience. Not speaking either English or French comfortably enough to communicate with the war brides with whom she resided at the Le Havre cigarette camps, Arlene J. focused on her son, with whom she chatted in Czech and Slovak. She had difficulty understanding the announcements made at the staging facilities and again during her voyage, and frequently worried about missing important instructions or directions.[83] Likewise, while the staff on the *Aquitania* made announcements in Dutch, English, and French, individuals who did not speak those languages did not benefit.[84]

The Jewish war brides who could communicate with others remembered their time together more affectionately, focusing on their shared deprivations: the lack of space, the cold bathing water, the seasickness, the endless number of programs that demanded their attention, and the chaos that ensued on board when they arrived in New York or Halifax. Flory described a convivial spirit among the women, who counseled one another on how to accommodate seasickness, the lack of warm water, and the rich food. Even though "half of them were laying down sick," she said they all rushed up to the deck when it rained to wash each other's hair, "just like in a Broadway play."[85] One daughter recalled that her mother's stories of the war brides centered on them as "jolly when they weren't throwing up," but that her mother could not recall any of the women she met. Clara, too, remembered a comradery among the war brides on the *Goethals* but a sense of lonesomeness when she could not be with her sister or spend time with the others with whom she shared several commonalties, namely other Jewish immigrants.[86]

Clara could have spoken with some of the former DPs at the clearing centers and on the ship, since she most comfortable speaking in Yiddish and had long been involved in community building. However, she likely found few opportunities to do so. Government, ARC, and Canadian Wives Bureau officials kept the war brides separate from other immigrants, and while Jewish war brides knew other Jewish travelers were among them, they had to seek them out. Sometimes, that was impossible. At Clara's cigarette camp, the war brides occupied a separate set of barracks and ate, underwent medical screenings, and had their paperwork processed apart from the other aspiring immigrants. On the *Goethals*, she and other war brides slept, ate, and attended programs only with one another.[87] One JDC representative described a similar situation at the clearing center in Bremen, which housed several hundred war brides—representing multiple nationalities and including some

Jews—as well as 140 European Jewish DPs. Staff independently cleared the DPs and military spouses and assigned them separate cabins on the *Ernie Pyle*.[88]

Officials even conducted separate health screenings of foreign spouses and immigrants. Health policies concerning the war brides intertwined concerns about sexual disease with moral character, focusing on sexual, gynecological, and maternal health; regulations concerning the DPs zeroed in on tuberculosis (TB) and illnesses associated with poverty and forced incarceration, as well as wartime diseases.[89] War brides had to demonstrate that they were free from syphilis and gonorrhea at least twice, first upon petitioning to marry and then again immediately before departure. Women who arrived in the United States or Canada with children underwent a third screening at their port of entry. "Immigration was stringent," one non-Jewish war bride remembered of Tidworth. "They were trying to make sure that they kept out anyone who had a disease. . . . We were checked thoroughly."[90]

Health officials treated war brides and immigrants differently when considering pregnancy and childcare. War bride policies focused on the spouses as mothers, recognizing (if not embracing) that some of them would be pregnant and/or have dependents in tow. Disability and pregnancy were grounds for refusal of entry under general US and Canadian immigration legislation, but war bride regulations permitted spouses with disabilities and pregnant women to immigrate if they cleared all other hurdles.[91] Health authorities mandated that clearing centers and ships be stocked with cots and cribs for young children and infants, special foods and formula, and diapers. They also were supposed to be staffed by nurses who could attend to the specific health needs of the youngest on board. This was especially crucial between May and October 1946, when over a dozen infants died at sea or upon arrival in New York from respiratory and gastrointestinal diseases. The largest number of fatalities took place on the SS *Zebulon B. Vance*, a Liberty ship that sailed to New York three times during that period: from Le Havre in May, Southampton in June, and Bremerhaven in July.[92]

Public media sources covered the children's gastrointestinal and respiratory illnesses in detail, and medical officials took note, prohibiting infants younger than six months from traveling on the war bride ships and demanding certain behaviors of the foreign mothers.[93] Despite the fact these illnesses were likely due to overcrowding, unsanitary conditions, and lack of formula and water for infants, health officials (and the North American public) placed blame squarely on the war brides.[94] When the Army and the New York City Health Department launched formal investigations into the first of the *Vance* deaths, they attributed the spread of disease to "the improper hygiene practiced by the mothers." Dr. Henry M. Friedman of the US Public Health Service reported that he had found food thrown under the bunks on the *Vance* and that war brides used unsterile pacifiers, nipples, and bottles and gave their infants a mixture of sugar and water to drink. According to Friedman, army personnel and attending nurses forbade these behaviors.[95] These sentiments reflected the widespread xenophobia of the era and the general ambivalence over foreign World War II brides. Especially in the United States and Canada, which received large numbers of foreign brides, critics had long worried that war brides would fail as mothers and helpmeets once they arrived in their new homes.[96]

Jewish war brides tended not to be forthcoming about the medical screenings or the childhood illnesses on board, only affirming—when explicitly asked—that they had been subjected to comprehensive examinations or that they had known of the sicknesses ravaging the ship.[97] Their silences are noteworthy, especially as many reflected on their medical care at other touchpoints, particularly when settling into their new homes in the United States, Canada, and Britain.[98] Medical checks, as well as ship or center illnesses and fatalities, likely triggered wartime traumas of war brides who had survived concentration camps or lived in hiding. Indeed, these populations found themselves disproportionately targeted for specific medical examinations. Women and men who had been imprisoned in Nazi camps or who had come from locations with high rates of TB, such as a DP camp, had to undergo additional screenings for TB, typhus, and typhoid. Contagious illnesses like these would have been scourges at the clearing centers and on the ships, but they also were seen as evidence of poverty and filth. Since so many of the Jewish war brides had been in the camps and/or had lived among groups of DPs, they would have undergone these additional tests. Their fellow travelers often knew who was being tested for what. War brides attended the medical evaluations in large groups, frequently lining up in spacious anterooms until their names or numbers were called and, in some cases, changing into medical gowns in the presence of other war brides, staff, and volunteers. In these loud and chaotic spaces, those being screened could hear noises and test results across the partitions.[99] Such a scene could have been difficult enough, but several of the clearing centers also required gynecological exams. Some war brides had never undergone pelvic screenings, and some had not experienced vaginal exams since their imprisonment in Nazi camps. Scholars have written about the ways gynecological exams and giving birth can trigger posttraumatic stress disorder. For survivors of sexual assault and violence, the clearing centers and ships might similarly have served as sites in which Jewish war brides relived parts of their horrific pasts.[100]

Jewish war brides also expressed ambivalence about the acculturation programs at the staging facilities and on the ships. Created by immigration officials and volunteers, these activities and publications were intended to prepare the war brides for their lives as wives and mothers in North America. Canadian Wives Bureau and ARC workers distributed pamphlets with titles such as "Welcome Warbrides!" "Canada Cookbook for British Brides," and "Make Do and Mend."[101] They offered lessons about American and Canadian currency, the different items sold in North American stores, and the hours stores were open. War brides and fiancé(e)s played "American" or "Canadian" games; they learned how to dress in their new homes, paying specific attention to diverse settings: dinners with the husband's supervisor, a tea with friends in the neighborhood, or a quiet supper at home with one's husband.[102] They took part in cooking lessons and were introduced to foods they would likely eat in North America, such as "pancakes for breakfast . . . slopping in syrup."[103] Many of the clearing centers and ships also provided yarn for knitting, showed films, and stocked libraries with popular books and magazines.[104] Several organized newsletters that featured the war brides' writings, discussed seasickness, provided light news (usually about entertainment), and included trivia about the countries that these (mostly) women would soon call home. Some ran a variety of contests, such as "Mrs. GI," "Mrs. *Goethals*," and "Mrs. *Algonquin*."[105]

Even if they could adjust to the pancakes with syrup or loved to knit, many of the Jewish war brides found that the materials and presentations were not crafted with them in mind. Not surprisingly, most of the programs promoted a white, middle-class, Christian image of the wife and mother.[106] The pamphlets were intended for English-speaking (if not specifically British) audiences, and images displayed inside them included blonde-haired, blue-eyed, plump, rosy-cheeked women and their infants. Not only would these portraits have been foreign to many Jewish war brides, but many of the acculturation lessons were not (yet) salient or understandable.[107] The fashion shows and classes concerning store hours were impractical for those (mostly) women who "came with nothing." Few had wardrobes extensive enough to be utilized for the different settings envisioned by ARC and Canadian Wives Bureau programmers. Bella, for example, had lost so many of her possessions during the war that she arrived with only "a little suitcase, and all it had inside was a towel."[108] And those still battling gastrointestinal symptoms associated with years of incarceration and deprivation became sick from the rich food.

Afraid that they would be sent back if they were excessively ill on board, some avoided meals. Finally, if they did not share a language with their fellow travelers or staff, the films, workshops, and newspapers would have had little influence on them. They could attend these programs, but they did not understand them. One former war bride remembered that she had remained in a state of unease throughout her voyage in part because she simply could not comprehend her surroundings. Once they approached Halifax, however, her unease dissipated slightly. She was eager to be reunited with her spouse after several months' separation.[109]

· ·

Once their ships entered the harbor (or their flights landed), war brides would again be formally separated from other travelers, possibly undergo another medical screening, have their paperwork checked, and then be permitted to reunite with their spouses or their spouses' families. Arrival narratives differed slightly between non-Jewish and Jewish spouses. In their reunion stories, non-Jewish British and Australian women dwelled on their husbands' appearance out of uniform and on introducing their spouses to the children born in the men's absences.[110] Jewish war brides usually had not been separated from their spouse for as long, nor were they likely to have given birth to infants while waiting to have their visas approved. They tended to fixate on their initial, often uncomfortable, encounters with their spouses' families, something that foretold how they would remember their early lives in their new homes.[111]

Several of the families came to the ports of entry to meet the new brides.[112] Family members journeyed to New York, Montreal, Chicago, London, and elsewhere to demonstrate their welcome and satiate their curiosity. Harry's siblings and father had been eager to meet Flory when she disembarked from the *Algonquin*, and he and his family drove from Ohio to New York. "The whole family came to see what Herschel brought home," Flory recalled, referring to Harry by the Yiddish name her in-laws used for him and to herself as an object or possession.[113] Ray's mother and sisters similarly accompanied him to La Guardia to meet Bella. They desperately wished to meet her, but they also had not been to an airport before and were curious to see what it was like.[114] Other family members met the spouses and fiancées at their ports of entry because the men, still in military service, were unable to greet them in person. Lydia arrived in the United States in November 1945 while Harold still was in Europe; Harold's parents, Abraham and Goldie, met her soon after she disembarked from the *Mingo Seam*.[115] Nearly four months later, Hetty V. was collected by her husband's parents at the train station in Montreal. Her husband, an RAF pilot, was at the base in Picton, Ontario. It would be several more weeks before she would see her spouse and several more months before she could reside with him.[116]

These initial family encounters exaggerated feelings of strangeness and worries about integration. In addition to the emotional stresses of disembarking, then meeting an entirely new family that would become one's own, several war brides found that they simply could not understand the conversations being directed to or around them. Lydia was unable to communicate with Harold's parents. They spoke English and Yiddish. She spoke French, and some Ladino and Arabic. Indeed, she required a translator, provided by HIAS, to find her now-in-laws.[117] Flory, too, had been surprised when she overheard Harry's family chatting in Yiddish. She had learned some English during her time in Bari, but she knew no Yiddish. Flory remembered, "Nobody speaks English. They're all speaking Yiddish. That was a shock in my life." It was particularly jarring, she recalled, because she had been able to communicate with the Italian brides on the ship. Now she was in the United States and physically separated from the women with whom she had traveled and socialized. She felt lonesome.[118]

Other cultural differences abounded. When she disembarked, Sala K. found herself immediately surrounded by an extended family, whom she was not yet prepared to meet. They all seemed to speak at the same time, and she found everyone's dress and carriage intimidating. She worried about her ability to fit into her new husband's family.[119] In contrast to Sala, who was awed by her brothers- and sisters-in-law, German-born Dorothea Brander was alarmed by her husband's parents' parochialism. Upon disembarking from the train in Glasgow, Dorothea, who had studied English in Ankara, understood the conversations around her, but she was struck by the "completely different" way in which Donald's parents presented themselves.[120] Lala, too, compared herself with the staid, old-fashioned demeanor of her mother-in-law. "She looked like an old lady to me," she remembered.[121] Those first impressions only intensified their anxieties about their abilities to settle in their husbands' childhood homes.

. . . .

As she waited to clear immigration on board the *Comfort*, Ellen Knauff, a German-born Jewish war bride, similarly worried about meeting her husband's family. Kurt Knauff had applied for Ellen's travel papers in 1948, even though he knew that he would have to remain in Germany to continue his work with the American military authorities there. He and Ellen wanted to take advantage of the war bride transport program before it expired in December 1948 and have her seek medical care in New York; so, like Lydia and Hetty, Ellen underwent the immigration process while knowing that she would be greeted by a family she had never met. When the *Comfort* docked on August 18, 1948, she prepared herself to meet Kurt's family. She did not know whether she would like her in-laws, when she would be reunited with her husband, or what her new life would be like.[122]

Soon those worries would seem inconsequential. After making her way to the main clearing area, Ellen discovered that she was prohibited from entering the United States. Why would a war bride be prevented from setting foot on American soil, especially after she had received permission to immigrate on a war bride ship? While unusual, there were some war brides, like Ellen, who were barred from entry. Their stories, too, also offered ways of thinking about recovery and reconstruction after World War II and served as touchstones for the most contested issues of the day.

5

Who Deserves More Rights than a Jewish Girl?

· ·

EXCLUSION

By the end of January 1948, Friedel Rosenthal, a survivor of several ghettos, camps, and the death march, realized that she was going to be unable to leave Germany and join her fiancé in the United States as she had hoped. She had met James Bilotta over two years earlier, less than twenty-four hours after the American forces had liberated her and her sister from Turkheim, a subsidiary camp of Dachau. The survivor and former infantryman were engaged early in 1946, and Friedel gave birth to their daughter Valerie that spring.[1] James returned to Boston a few months later and immediately tried to bring his fiancée and daughter to the United States.[2]

Friedel's case was complicated. Not only had James been married to someone else when the couple first met, but the former infantryman and clerk-typist also had left Germany involuntarily, and under dubious circumstances. He had been discharged from his civilian position with the US Army because of his affiliation with the Communist Party and his alleged political activities in Frankfurt, where he had last been stationed and then worked. James was a "person of interest." Since 1943, apart from the period during which he served in the military, he had been under FBI surveillance.[3] However, for much of 1946 and 1947, military officials and relief workers were ignorant of the allegations lodged against him. They pitied Friedel and assumed that James had served honorably. In November 1947, after receiving copies of the divorce papers from James's first wife, the US consulate in Frankfurt began to process Friedel's paperwork; Hebrew Immigrant Aid Society officials in Frankfurt, Boston, and Paris each forecast that Friedel would travel to the United States sometime between mid-December and mid-February.[4] But the FBI pushed the State Department to deny Friedel's request, and the State Department concurred.[5]

Not welcome in the United States, Friedel pursued other immigration options. She did not wish to remain in Germany. Not only did Frankfurt remind her of her wartime traumas, but she also wanted assistance raising her young daughter. HIAS officials to whom she turned for advice agreed that her best course of action would be to immigrate to England, where she had a sister willing to serve as her sponsor and help with childcare.[6] They hoped that, from there, mother and daughter could move to the United States, but, after Friedel settled with her sister, the US consulate in London denied her permission to travel to Boston. It seemed that if James wished to reunite with his fiancée and daughter, he would have to go to the United Kingdom, which he did in February 1949. Within a week of his arrival, the couple was married.[7] But when James requested permission to bring his now-wife to Boston, he was rejected and the two remained in England.[8]

Friedel's story stands in stark contrast to most war bride narratives that focus on the reunions of military personnel and their foreign-born spouses and fiancé(e)s. Despite the very real ambivalence concerning the war brides and these "hasty marriages," postwar North American newspapers and newsreels celebrated their countries' supposed generosity and hospitality by capturing and promoting the successful immigration of foreign spouses and fiancé(e)s to their new homes.[9] Even when couples initially faced difficulty reuniting, their long-delayed, but ultimately triumphant, reunions took a prominent place in contemporary newspaper coverage.[10] In contrast, Friedel and a small number of other war brides and fiancé(e)s could not settle in their spouses' home countries. Unlike those who successfully immigrated, these war brides were excluded. Some were immediately refused admission. Others, like Friedel, received initial approval to immigrate but then had that permission revoked. Some were deported after arrival, while others were detained upon disembarkation. One of the most prominent war bride detention cases was that of Ellen Knauff, the German Jewish war bride introduced briefly in the last chapter. Ellen's case, which would reach the US Supreme Court, is still cited today when considering the "rights" of immigrants detained at the US border and the authority of the executive branch in matters of exclusion.[11]

Ellen arrived in the United States on August 18, 1948. After making her way to the main clearing area, an immigration official pulled her aside and began asking her pressing questions concerning her identity and place of origin. Why would it matter, she wondered, whether she had been previously married? Or whether she once had lived and worked in Prague? After what seemed to her like an interminable amount of time, the officer informed her that she needed to remain on Ellis Island. For reasons not disclosed to her then, she was forbidden from entering the United States.

In response, Ellen's husband, a US citizen, submitted a habeas petition, insisting that Ellen deserved the right to discover why she was being detained and refused entry. A federal district court dismissed the petition, setting out that aliens—even those married to current or former American military personnel—living outside of the United States lacked the right to a fair trial. The US Court of Appeals for the Second Circuit upheld the federal decision. Kurt Knauff appealed, and in January 1950, the Supreme Court affirmed the US Court of Appeals decision, reinforcing that the government had "absolute and unreviewable authority in exclusion matters."[12] Several American politicians attempted to prevent Ellen's deportation and circumvent the Supreme Court ruling; they introduced congressional bills that would have permitted the war bride entry. However, before Congress could act on the proposed legislation, an Immigration Appeals Board determined that there was not sufficient evidence to justify Ellen's exclusion and mandated that she be admitted for permanent residence.[13]

Ellen and Friedel each became a cause célèbre, with immigrant advocacy and opposition groups, self-defense organizations, local, state, and national governments, and legal defense funds paying attention to their woes. Local and national offices of the American Civil Liberties Union (ACLU) issued dozens of press releases concerning Ellen, filed legal papers on her behalf, lobbied for her entry, and worked with several newspaper editors. They saw their involvement as a way to promote democracy while warning of authoritarianism coming to the United States.[14] HIAS, the Jewish Telegraph Agency (JTA), the American Committee for the Protection of the Foreign Born

(ACPFB), and local and national communist groups expressed interest in Friedel's case. They envisioned Friedel's exclusion as threatening immigrants, Holocaust survivors, so-called political undesirables, and veterans.[15] Reporters and editors at mainstream newspapers such as the *New York Times, New York Post, Evening Star,* and *Cleveland Plain Dealer,* left-leaning newspapers such as the *St. Louis Post-Dispatch,* and Jewish periodicals such as the *Jewish Advocate,* kept the Knauff case in the public arena between 1950, when the Supreme Court announced its intention to hear the case, and 1952, when Ellen published a memoir a few months after her release. On some days multiple articles were published about her detention, including photographs of her and her husband, editorials concerning her case, and interviews with her legal team.[16] Friedel's case generated less national attention, in part because of James's communist background and in part because she never reached American soil. Yet it too was featured frequently in mainstream newspapers, the communist press, and in local and national Jewish newspapers and magazines.[17]

Why was the American public attracted to these exclusion cases? Friedel and Ellen were caught in the crossfire as the US, Canadian, and British governments shifted from envisioning the Nazis as the enemy to now considering the Soviets as the epitome of evil. Invoking long-standing anxieties about women, Jews, Germans, foreigners, and political deviants, discussions about Friedel and Ellen offered one touchstone for considering what the nation's responsibility was toward survivors and former military personnel; whether the family endangered or strengthened the nation-state; and whether spousal reunification was a "right" or a "privilege." During a period in which governments sought to define who was a political enemy, got caught up in the spy paranoia of the looming Cold War, and debated their countries' commitment to survivors of Nazi atrocities, reflections of Friedel and Ellen juggled multiple pressures: the wish to assist former Nazi victims, the patriotic desire to reward military service, the value of family reunification, and the threat of communism.

. . . .

Of course, British and North American histories of exclusion, detention, and deportation long preceded Ellen and Friedel. During the First World War, governmental incarceration and expulsion of enemy aliens, ethnic outsiders, and internal enemies became "internationally accepted."[18] In Britain, the Aliens Restriction Act and the British Nationality and Status of Aliens Act, both of 1914, paved the way for the government to intern and expel aliens living in England and allowed the home secretary to implement policies concerning the foreign-born without parliamentary oversight.[19] The British home secretary continued to implement these kinds of policies and, in May 1940, introduced Regulation 18B of the Wartime Defence (General) Regulations, which empowered the executive to detain those believed to pose a danger to national security.[20] Canadian policies were similar. Shortly after the outbreak of World War I, its federal government passed the War Measures Act, which, among other things, allowed its cabinet to arrest, detain, exclude, and deport. Over a quarter century later, it again paved the way for the internment of enemy aliens. In 1940, when Great Britain deported to Canada 2,500 enemy aliens—mostly German and Austrian nationals (including many Jews)—the Commonwealth regarded them as a security risk, denying them refugee status and interning them.[21]

The United States also excluded and detained those deemed a threat to national security. During World War I, President Woodrow Wilson relied on the Alien Enemies Act and the Alien Friends Act (1798), which permitted the government to arrest and deport male citizens of an "enemy nation" and to deport any noncitizen suspected of plotting against the government. In April and November 1917, the executive branch imposed numerous restrictions on German-born male residents over the age of fourteen; during the war, the Department of Justice interned approximately 2,000 German-born residents in two large internment camps.[22] Over two decades later, in 1940, the US government implemented the Smith Act (Alien Registration Act), which both required that all aliens be registered and fingerprinted and added new classes of aliens subject to deportation. One month before the United States entered the Second World War, Franklin D. Roosevelt issued Presidential Proclamation 2523. This authorized the secretary of state and attorney general to exclude aliens whose entry they deemed to be "prejudicial to the interests of the United States during a 'national emergency.'" The reason for exclusion could be kept secret.[23]

Once the war broke out, Congress gave the president even greater powers to exclude and intern those deemed a national security risk. In June 1941, it permitted the executive branch to impose additional restrictions on the entry or departure of aliens during a period of war and/or national emergency. Less than a year later, in February 1942, the president issued Executive Order 9066, which, among other things, designated significant portions of the western United States as military areas of exclusion and created "relocation centers" in the West. This order eventually allowed for the involuntary incarceration of 120,000 people of Japanese descent, including over 70,000 US citizens.[24] In 1946, envisioning the looming Cold War as a serious threat to national security, President Truman continued the state of emergency. Reflecting earlier bouts of xenophobia, he and his advisers pushed to maintain policies that prevented "undesirables" from settling and remaining in the United States. It would be this power that would be cited when justifying the exclusion of some war brides.

Anglo-American operatives and observers identified war brides and fiancé(e)s among the groups of potential immigrants who posed serious political threats. They worried that it was relatively "simple" for undercover agents and communist sympathizers—masking as war brides—to immigrate to the United States, Canada, or Britain. They warned that women could easily infiltrate any of these countries at the Soviet Union's behest. Like earlier charges that women used their sexuality to seduce innocent soldiers into providing them with food, better living conditions, and/or immigration papers, some officials and pundits now claimed that the brides and fiancées of soldiers and officers were foreign agents in disguise. Russian war brides, one anticommunist protester in Britain explained, were "spies and saboteurs."[25] In the United States, the FBI similarly warned of a "probable infiltration of Soviet Agents into the United States." In their view, Soviet officials "instructed" female Russian nationals to seek out American military husbands "by any means" possible.[26]

Canadian and British authorities were less likely to exclude white spouses of former or current military personnel, but US officials barred, detained, and deported some non-Jewish and Jewish military spouses based on fears of communism. In 1948, the INS detained "White Russian" Valentina Gardner, who had been born in northeast China and arrived in the United States from Japan with her new husband and a Soviet passport, for nearly thirteen months.[27] Six years later, the United States deported thirty-three-year-old British-born Mary Esther Gebhart back to England. Mary had met and married her husband Joe in London and, after the war, immigrated to Schenectady, New York, to join him there. A two-day hearing found the mother guilty of actively participating in communist activities. Afterward, US attorney general Herbert Brownwell Jr. lauded the Department of Justice for keeping America safe. "This woman . . . this alien," he reminded them, had posed a serious danger.[28]

Within this charged landscape, immigration officials denied Friedel and Ellen entry. While they refused to tell the women why they were excluded, archival records indicate that Friedel and Ellen were prohibited entry to the

United States because of their alleged political beliefs, their associations with men whose political activities were supposedly seditious, their sexual and marital pasts, and their foreignness.[29] At a time when many contemporaries imagined that a woman shared her husband's, fiancé's, or employer's predisposition to loyalty or disloyalty,[30] the suspected political beliefs and activities of James, Kurt, and Vaclav Victor Podhora, the Czechoslovakian consul general in Frankfurt, posed obstacles for Friedel's and Ellen's inclusion. James's record included a string of alleged transgressions: he was a member of the Communist Party; he had petitioned the governor of New York to pardon a Communist Party member of perjury; he spoke at Communist Party press conferences; he subscribed to a communist newspaper; he wrote letters to newspaper editors that included antifascist, if not communist, sentiments; and in October 1946, he published a letter in the *Boston Evening Traveler* that criticized German-US relations.[31] For much of 1946 and 1947, the FBI seemed absorbed with James alone, but in early 1948 J. Edgar Hoover's office expressed interest in Friedel and her brother Max, who also was in Germany at this time. Hoover reported to the State Department that Max was a leader of the German Communist Party and involved in communist work along the Danish border. Moreover, according to the FBI, Friedel herself was promoting communist activities across Germany.[32] Not all administrators agreed that Friedel was a "full-fledged party member," but they believed that her relationship with James and Max implied that she was sympathetic to the "Communist cause." This was sufficient to deny her entry.[33]

The paranoia of the postwar era similarly shaped questions about Ellen's loyalty, which also rested on her supposed political beliefs, seditious activities, and male influences. Charges that Ellen had provided secret information to the Czech government when she was employed by the US Civil Censorship Division in Frankfurt emerged—without her knowledge—in the winter and spring of 1948. When Kurt filed Ellen's war bride immigration paperwork, the US Army's Counter Intelligence Corps (CIC) in Germany recommended that Ellen's application be denied because she had (supposedly) imparted confidential security information to the Czechoslovakian consul general in Frankfurt.[34] Officers at the European Command headquarters dismissed this claim and approved Ellen's immigration petition.[35] Not knowing that there had been an investigation into her worthiness for admission, Ellen departed Germany, setting sail during the summer of 1948 on the *Comfort*. As she made her way to New York, the Intelligence Division of the War Department, which had disputed the findings of the European Command Headquarters, alerted the FBI and the State Department of Ellen's imminent arrival and the danger she posed.[36] When she reached Ellis Island in August 1948, Attorney General Tom Clark clarified in a letter that the war bride could not be allowed settle in the United States.[37]

Ellen came to the attention of the CIC as Czechoslovakia was undergoing its communist coup in February 1948. The first accusations against her focused on her *general* disloyalty to the United States. As Czechoslovakia became named as part of the Soviet bloc, allegations against Ellen intensified in tone and content. Increasingly, FBI and immigration officials promoted claims that Ellen embraced communist beliefs, located witnesses who testified seeing Ellen in Victor's office, and offered further reports that she had visited the German Communist Party headquarters in Frankfurt, ironically the same place Friedel and James purportedly frequented.[38]

Just as US officials found it difficult to imagine Friedel as a "subversive" without male influence, Ellen's critics repeatedly drew a link between her and the "seditious" men in her life. Contemporaries focused on Ellen's interactions with the Czechoslovakian consul general, whose "very effective penetration" of the Civil Censorship Office ostensibly relied on Ellen's subversive activities.[39] Even when some witnesses contended that Ellen had met Victor only casually and in public places, her associations with him and other men were sufficient to cast aspersions on her integrity and worthiness as a future US citizen. The FBI continued to try to find evidence of the two together.[40] In the spring of 1951, as the case was looking quite shaky, INS agents suddenly procured additional testimony from recent Central European émigrés that Ellen had indeed visited the consul general's office.[41] Meanwhile, FBI and INS officials highlighted Ellen's relationships with other questionable men to cast doubt on her trustworthiness. They linked her with Frederick Emil Bauer, a German refugee soldier who had served in the United States military and had recently been deported from the United States for espionage; her current spouse, Kurt, a German-born American soldier, whose patriotism they also questioned; and her first husband, with whom she had lost contact after their divorce.[42]

Discussions about both Ellen and Friedel emphasized their "suspect marriages." Ellen frequently had to explain her first marriage to a man with whom she no longer communicated; during her 1950 congressional hearing, congressmen asked her twice about her first husband, as did immigration officials and journalists.[43] FBI and immigration files similarly described Friedel as a "paramour," "girlfriend," and "fraulein," underscoring that Friedel had become pregnant while James was still married to his first wife.[44] These accusations were consistent with contemporary anxieties about marriage. As historian Andrea Friedman has argued, during the Cold War, many Americans imagined strong marriages as bulwarks that defended the United States against the Soviet Union and weak marital unions as capable of undermining the stability of local homes, neighborhoods, and schools. In the late 1940s and 1950s, critics of the war bride transport program pointed to examples of marital fraud, divorce, and alleged polygamy among foreign women who married American military personnel.[45] Even as they celebrated the reunion of some war brides with their spouses, North American newspapers began to scandalize readers with tales of other brides and fiancées who entered the United States under suspicious conditions or became involved with other men.[46] A previous divorce on a woman's record might slow down her paperwork or cause hesitation among the bureaucrats involved, particularly when immigration officials imagined that the woman in question had some link with the Soviet Union. As early as 1946, for example, American Jewish chaplain Joseph Messing complained that his wife Maria Michalovskis faced two obstacles concerning her immigration: she originated from Latvia and she had been previously married.[47]

The accusation that foreign women (and to a lesser degree, men) might use marriage to sneak into the country was hardly a new trope; throughout World War I and World War II there existed deep concern about German women trying to trick American soldiers into marriage and the presence of German spies hidden among the American populace. Even as the Soviet Union eclipsed Germany as principal bogeyman, Ellen's and Friedel's alleged Germanness invoked enemy-alien status, deviant morals, and sexualized character.[48] Immigration officials and contemporary critics emphasized these women's Germanness, even though their German citizenship was anything but certain.[49] In her memoir, Ellen recalled that the first official with whom she interacted on Ellis Island insisted on her "Germanness." When she countered that she was stateless, he supposedly responded that she had been "born in Germany and that makes you a German."[50] Newspaper reports, subcommittee testimonies, and legal arguments also reified her Germanness, frequently referring to her as a "German war bride" who had married a "German-born" US veteran.[51]

Friedel's immigration and FBI reports likewise emphasized her German nationality while simultaneously casting suspicion on her attempt to be classified as a DP.[52] The latter concern was part of a general anxiety that survivors in Germany relied on illegal means to finagle their way into the United States, Canada, or Britain; that they were culturally and economically unassimilable; that they were communist spies in disguise; and that they were disproportionately involved in the black market.[53] Relying on enduring anxieties about Germans, Jews, foreigners, political subversives, and women, FBI and immigration reports continued to label Friedel as a "German black marketeer." James's frequent packages to Friedel only seemed to confirm that perception.[54] A 1948 surveillance report detailed that James regularly sent large quantities of "canned foods, coffee, sugar, oil, margarine, cocoa," which Friedel allegedly used "for her own personal consumption and for bartering purposes."[55]

. . . .

In contrast, Friedel's and Ellen's advocates looked to their foreign status to insist on their worthiness for admission. Consistent with contemporary language that pushed for the inclusion of Holocaust survivors more generally, they insisted that the United States had a particular obligation toward those who had suffered during the war and an even more compelling responsibility toward victims who married or were engaged to current and former US military personnel.

James was the first to publicly promote Friedel's victimhood as justification for immigration. As early as 1945, he detailed her horrific story in the American Jewish press, emphasizing how the Nazis had exterminated her entire family and destroyed her home and health.[56] Over the course of the late 1940s, he and Friedel's other champions suggested a kind of hierarchy of victimhood and described her as having "a spotless record as a Nazi victim."[57] They unfailingly returned to the loss of her adolescence, family, and material possessions in the Holocaust. She had "lived seven starved, louse-ridden nightmarish years" in some form of incarceration, said writer and former *Daily Worker* journalist George Marion.[58] Friedel "looked like a small, starved child," lamented the feminist *Daily Worker* writer Elizabeth Gurley Flynn, "sick and emaciated."[59] For these advocates Friedel's traumatic past was sufficient argument for admission into the United States. Humanitarian grounds should determine her emigration. "She has hardly know [sic] happiness for the past ten years," James pleaded to Abner Green, the executive secretary of the ACPFB. "Isn't there room for her in our country—this asylum of mankind?"[60] A year later, in 1949, he cited not just her past traumas but her worsening health as grounds for admitting her to the United States. Four years after her liberation, she still was desperate for proper care, "near death in a London hospital . . . collapsed into a coma."[61] "I am asking you to save my fiancée," James appealed to one journalist. "I know that as surely as night follows day that she will succumb."[62]

Ellen and her supporters cast her also as a victim of Nazi persecution deserving kindness and courtesy, if not also some kind of retribution. Although she successfully escaped Nazi Germany in 1934 and Czechoslovakia in 1938, many of Ellen's accounts focused on her status as an orphan whose entire biological family had been murdered by the Nazis.[63] "My whole family had been exterminated in an extermination camp near Riga, in 1941," Ellen told the House Judiciary subcommittee in 1950. "I have no family left."[64] The *St. Louis Post-Dispatch* likewise insisted that Ellen's status as a victim of the Nazis was one of the many reasons why she deserved consideration for admission. Reporter Edward A. Harris concluded one of his sympathetic articles with a reminder that Ellen's "entire family was killed by the Nazis in a concentration camp."[65] Others weighed in similarly, invoking an image of a large, uncaring United States, positioned against a diminutive victim of Nazism. "The question is," one editor opined, "under the Bill of Rights, which protects aliens as well as citizens, does not this little woman, many of whose relatives were killed in Hitler's persecution of Jews, deserve to know the specific charge against her?"[66]

For many writers, cases like Ellen's and Friedel's underscored the need for the United States to permit entry to more Jewish victims of the Nazis, to open its gates to immigrants more generally, and to curb the growing authority and power of the Department of Justice. These women "personified millions of Jewish victims of the Nazis" who deserved sanctuary but could not find a home that would welcome them.[67] According to Gurley Flynn, Friedel's case "is a terrible reminder of 3 [sic] million murdered Jewish people. America needs such reminders. Jewish refugees are being deliberately excluded from our country."[68]

In fact, Friedel's story followed the immediate postwar timeline of the immigration debates. In December 1945, as James requested that American Jews assist Friedel in her quest to immigrate, the American public and its immigration officials continued to support prewar immigration restrictions based on quotas. A Gallup poll released that same month revealed that only 5 percent of Americans were willing to accept more European immigrants than the United States had permitted before the war began. Even when President Truman issued his directive that year calling for DPs to receive priority for US visas within the existing quota system, overall immigration did not increase. Three years later, in 1948, when Friedel and Ellen learned of their inadmissibility, Jewish DPs still found themselves frustrated by US immigration laws. Congress had passed new immigration legislation authorizing 200,000 DPs to enter the United States, but the bill disfavored Jewish DPs because it restricted eligibility to those who had entered Italy, Austria, or Germany before December 22, 1945.[69] In 1950, as Friedel settled into her new life in London and Ellen's case occupied the attention of the US judicial, executive, and legislative branches, Congress authorized additional visas for DPs and removed the chronological and geographical restrictions.[70] The following year, as Ellen received permission to stay in the United States, though not as a citizen, and as Friedel was refused permission to enter the United States, even as James's wife, the US government opted against signing the Convention Relating to the Status of Refugees, which the United Nations had just ratified. For many of Ellen's and Friedel's advocates, their stories were part of a larger narrative of a United States that should—but did not—welcome immigrants to its shores. In their view, American immigration policies were "undemocratic and anti-Semitic" and required change.[71] "One of the great traditions of this free Nation is symbolized by the lady with the lamp held high in New York Harbor," wrote writer Marquis Childs. "If that tradition of refuge to those who have stood up against autocracy, as Ellen Knauff and her husband did, is broken off, we shall all be the poorer for it."[72]

The US government's concomitant admission of some German non-Jewish war brides seemed to throw into relief the inequity underlying US immigration laws and practices. "A screening process that lets former Nazis and their sympathizers into the United States while excluding Hitler's victims is a danger and disgrace to the country for which we GI's fought," complained James. "I expect my Jewish fiancée who has suffered incalculable horrors under American's German enemies to be treated with as much respect as that given German *frauleins* coming to this country."[73] In York, Pennsylvania, the editor of the *Gazette and Daily* imagined swarms of German men and women coming to the United States while women like Friedel were being rejected and detained.[74]

While Ellen's mainstream defenses tended not to bemoan the entry of German war brides, favorable articles about her in the Jewish press were more likely to label Ellen as a Jew and juxtapose her difficulties with the supposedly relaxed immigration experiences of non-Jewish German brides. According to writer Estelle Brand, "While this Jewess was confined at Ellis Island . . . , hundreds of German girls, brides of GIs, arrived in the country. Nobody said much about any past Nazi affiliations these girls might have had."[75] For Brand, Ellen was a victim of a vindictive government that embraced its former enemies and punished Holocaust survivors.

Positioning "the little" war brides against the US government, Ellen's and Friedel's supporters insisted that the women had been victimized by both the Nazis and the Departments of State and Justice. Ellen, her advocates, and her legal team criticized the government for preventing her reunion with Kurt on the basis of evidence already known to be flawed.[76] Describing her as a victim of "gross injustice" at the hands of "powerful" immigration officials,[77] they pointed to the fact that the military and CIC had vetted the Knauff marriage; if there had been real security concerns, those earlier worries would have been sufficient to prohibit the betrothal, which then would have made her immigration as a war bride moot. Kurt's marriage "was cleared by seven agencies, including Army Intelligence," opined one reporter, but when he sought to discover the justification for Ellen's exclusion, "he immediately found himself in a maze of buck-passing, stalls, and delays."[78] The chairman of the House Judiciary Subcommittee, Francis E. Walter, similarly maintained that Ellen's exclusion was "perfectly outrageous." In his view, "Some clerk somewhere has made a mistake which no one had the courage to admit."[79] A 1951 editorial in the *Salt Lake Tribune* likewise asserted that the attorney general "is merely trying to cover up a blunder—or serious case of vindictiveness of the immigration service."[80] "There is something very funny about the way her case has been handled," opined the editors of the *Indianapolis Star*. "Congress should force a thorough shakeup in the immigration service and the Justice Department."[81]

Friedel's supporters also described her as a vulnerable victim of a cruel bureaucracy. Reporter George Marion bemoaned that Friedel had undergone a "a two-year run around." According to the writer, "She was cleared for passage and then the passage was canceled. Dates for sailing were set and mysteriously postponed. Her papers were submitted and resubmitted a dozen times."[82] Marion and others sharply criticized officials for allegedly harassing Friedel, interrogating her for hours, hinting at James's infidelities, and allowing for a German non-Jewish woman to interview her.[83] Calling upon President Truman to intervene, leaders at the national office of the ACPFB and the Boston chapter of the ACLU expressed dismay at "the treatment" she and James suffered.[84] This was an issue of human rights and justice. "I am not asking [for] any favors or political patronage," insisted James. "I believe a basic question of justice and human rights is involved. The arrogant treatment accorded my beloved fiancée is a betrayal of all that America stands for."[85] Erasing Friedel's agency, James complained that questioning her about communist activities in Germany "was like prodding a baby with questions about Hailey's [sic] Comet."[86] Unlike those critics who exaggerated Friedel's negative sway, James and other supporters of both women stripped them of their power and influence.[87]

Advocates generated these complaints during a moment in US history when the power of the Department of Justice was on the rise. The INS, which was so heavily involved in Ellen's case, had increased its authority dramatically since its creation in 1933. Originally controlled by the Department of Labor, in 1940, just one year before the United States entered the war, President Roosevelt moved the INS to the Department of Justice, citing a need to control aliens more effectively. The powers given it the following year to supervise the internment of enemy aliens arrested by the FBI did not diminish with the war's end. Instead, when Truman declared that the Cold War still constituted a national security emergency, the INS continued to intern and deport aliens, identifying its protection of the nation's borders as its priority and began rounding up foreign-born radicals for deportation.[88] The FBI, also an agency under the supervision of the Department of Justice, expanded during this time, growing from a few thousand employees in 1940 to over 10,000 by the war's end. It enjoyed a seemingly unlimited budget along with widespread support and access to an array of new technologies and intelligences.

Critics warned that the unfettered growth of these agencies threatened the very democracy being endangered by the emerging Cold War. Painting a slippery slope between withholding a hearing and allowing inroads toward totalitarianism, ACLU officials and Ellen's legal team worried about the possibility of authoritarian trends taking root in the United States.[89] In his dissenting opinion in *United States ex rel. Knauff v. Shaughnessy*, Supreme Court justice Robert H. Jackson warned against the United States embracing the same demonic forms of detention employed by both Nazi Germany and Stalinist Russia.[90] "The menace to the security of this country, be it great as it may, from this girl's admission is as nothing compared to the menace to free institutions inherent in procedures of this pattern," he wrote, juxtaposing Ellen's security risk—if existent—with the dangers of a nation-state that ignored its underlying principles in the name of defense. "In the name of security, the police state justifies its arbitrary oppressions on evidence that is secret. . . . The plea that evidence of guilt must be secret is abhorrent to free men, because it provides a cloak for the malevolent, the misinformed, the meddlesome, and the corrupt to play the role of informer undetected and uncorrected."[91] New York congressman Franklin D. Roosevelt Jr. agreed. Ellen's situation dramatically "spotlights a fundamental principle in our democratic way of life . . . the right to be heard before being adjudged guilty."[92] Moreover, others worried that Ellen's exclusion, detention, and lack of hearing jeopardized the very tentative support the United States received from those countries "pressured" by communism. Ellen's case mocked "the very due process which we say democracy holds out to the depressed peoples of Europe and Asia."[93] For ACLU officials, withholding Ellen's right to due process would only encourage communists at home and abroad to call American democracy into question. When Ellen was finally released, the ACLU national office touted that "today's action . . . refutes Communist propaganda charges that our due process is a sham."[94]

Ellen and Friedel's supporters also painted the growing US immigration and judicial bureaucracies as knowingly keeping families apart and intentionally overlooking the "rights" of military personnel. Family reunification—like democracy—they argued, was a foundation of US society and culture and distinguished it from the Soviet Union.[95] According to the editors of the *Washington Post*, the Department to Justice had a "clear duty" to abolish "the system that may keep veterans and their wives in separate countries," not to defend it.[96] In his dissenting opinion, Justice Jackson similarly criticized governments that allowed for familial division, bemoaning a Congress that "authorized an administrative officer to break up the family of an American citizen or force him to keep his wife by becoming an exile."[97] Reviewing the case, the ACLU expressed deep disdain for a government that forced Kurt to decide between "living in the United States and abandoning his wife, or of living in exile with his wife."[98] Such a choice, added the ACLU, was particularly problematic because if Kurt returned to Germany with his wife, he could lose his citizenship. He was a naturalized citizen and only lived outside of the United States because he was serving as an employee of the US military.[99] Abner Green similarly described the "enforced separation" of Friedel from James as "cruel, inhuman, and sadistic."[100]

Depictions of family reunification rested on images of loving families supported by traditional gender hierarchies,[101] and Ellen's and Friedel's advocates cast the couples as great American romances. In pushing for Friedel's inclusion, journalists described a deep and passionate love that "blossomed amid the horrors of war and concentration camps."[102] In their public campaign to gain sympathy for Friedel's plight, they always omitted the fact that the US veteran had been married to his first wife during liberation. Perhaps to compensate for his first marriage, some of these narratives changed the courtship's chronology, making it "clear" that James only fell in love with Friedel after she had recovered, and he had divorced. According to one source, it was only after "months of kindness" that "Jim fell in love."[103] In fact, the FBI had become so frustrated by James's success in rewriting the couple's chronology that it tried to work with the city editor of the *Boston American* (supposedly an FBI source) to feature a story that included photographs of James's first wife and children. Such an article, they hoped, would counteract the "favorable publicity" James and Friedel received.[104]

Ellen's case for admission also cast their story as a gripping romance. Kurt was loving and devoted, someone who sent his wife roses frequently and called and wrote as often as possible. She defended her relationship as "romantic," "wonderful," and exclusive, noting that Kurt's appeal and attractiveness had led some women—whose advances to her husband had been thwarted—to lay false claims against her.[105] In her description of their 1951 reunion, she insisted that their relationship was so solid that their estrangement had not negatively affected their marriage. "The moment I was in Kurt's arms," she recalled, "I knew that everything between us was all right."[106] Later, when she was released from Ellis Island, she revealed to reporters that the very first thing she wished to do was to reach out to her husband and spend time with him.[107]

Just as critics had exaggerated Ellen and Friedel's influence, their supporters downplayed the women's agency. In their appeals to gain the women entry, advocates cast Kurt and James as active protagonists and rescuers. Kurt was a war veteran who, despite (or, perhaps, in spite of) his German origins, had returned to Germany to fight against the country of his birth with honor.[108] Kurt had saved democracy from Hitler's fascism and had rescued his wife. Intimating that without his active role Ellen would remain on Ellis Island, Ellen's advocates placed Kurt at the center of her narrative.[109] In its laudatory editorials, the *St. Louis Post-Dispatch* consistently praised Kurt for his gumption. When immigration officers detained Ellen at Ellis Island, "he went to Washington to find out why."[110] When, in 1951, Kurt returned to the United States to meet with the attorney general, ACLU press releases credited Kurt's "personal intervention"[111] with "saving" Ellen "from deportation."[112]

James, too, had taken part in "savage fighting," rescuing "thousands of Jewish victims of the Nazi regime," supposedly including Friedel.[113] In fact, in a 1948 letter to the ACPFB, James himself insisted that Friedel would have perished if he and his fellow infantrymen had not been in Turkheim. The *Boston Globe* even claimed that James personally saved Friedel from the death camps, falsely asserting that he had encountered Friedel as "she was being marched to the Dachau Concentration Camp to be another victim of the gas ovens."[114] Now, according to some, just as James had rescued Friedel at liberation, he was prevailing over her immigration obstacles and saving her from the depression that threatened to undo her. "For a time," one reporter wrote, "it seemed that Friedel Rosenthal would die.... She recovered only when her fiancée [sic]—Jim Bilotta, the GI with whom she fell in love in 1945—managed to fly to London to be with her."[115] Even his detractors commented upon the time, funds, and energy James dedicated to Friedel's release; like Kurt, James supposedly wrote six letters a week to his fiancée and "continuously fought to obtain a visa for her."[116]

Of course, these formulations made political sense. The admission of both women rested on their marriages. As Representative Francis Walter made clear at the beginning of the March 1950 House Judiciary Subcommittee hearing concerning the private bill he had introduced to allow for Ellen's inclusion, the "War Brides Act was adopted not for the benefit of any alien but for the benefit of American soldiers."[117]

Central to this notion of the rescued woman was that of the wife worthy of being saved. During a time when there was real worry about immigrants' unworthiness, defenses of Ellen and Friedel highlighted their vulnerabilities and attractiveness. Reminiscent of the rhetorical work that determined why some Asian wives were assimilable while others were not,[118] advocates portrayed Ellen and Friedel as physically appealing, diminutive, and vulnerable. Newspaper reporters described Ellen as "petite, grey-eyed," "curvesome," "comely," and "small."[119] She was a "girl," a "lady in distress."[120] Friedel's photographs captured her soulful eyes, wavy hair, and pretty face. In his appeal for Friedel's inclusion, one *Boston Globe* reporter insisted on the way her exclusion had detracted from her comeliness. Highlighting her physical appeal and her helplessness, he stressed that the first photograph, taken in November 1946, showed Friedel "as an attractive young girl, restored to health"; in contrast, the 1948 photograph "shows her much thinner, her face etched by lines of anxiety."[121]

· ·

Just a few months after editors of the *St. Louis Post-Dispatch* opined in 1950 that "the great and powerful United States Government" was about to deport "little Ellen Knauff,"[122] Justice Jackson issued a stay, temporarily preventing

"Free to Become Citizen," Ellen Knauff.
Bettmann Archive via Getty Images.

her deportation. Pundits quickly and enthusiastically forecast that "Mrs. Knauff's cherished dream of becoming a citizen was closer to fulfillment."[123] They were mistaken. It would be another year until an Immigration Appeals Board determined that there lacked sufficient evidence to justify Ellen's continued detention or deportation, and it would take another decade before she could become a US citizen.

Nevertheless, Ellen continued to promote her love for—and allegiance to—the United States. In her view, she "could not and would not blame the United States for the injustice" she had faced. Instead, her exclusion was the fault of those who "flirt with what they have learned of totalitarian methods, Fascist and Communist." For Ellen, if not checked in time, these individuals "could pull this country down to the level of dictatorship."[124] Ellen knew of the dangers of totalitarianism; she had experienced Nazi and communist dictatorships firsthand. She had witnessed the Hitler Youth "marching past our house, shouting their songs about Teutonic supermen, and blindly following their hideous flag"; later, she would hear and see "the songs of the Russian Revolution . . . the same goose step, the same drumming march rhythm, the same fanatical hysteria in young throats."[125] Both forms of authoritarianism threatened democracy, and Ellen positioned herself as an ideal citizen who would be vigilant in her support of the United States.

Unlike Ellen, Friedel never received permission to immigrate to the United States and a few organizations dropped their support of her. As early as 1949, James lamented that "HIAS is not handling the case anymore." There is no clear archival evidence as to why HIAS dropped the case (or if it really did), but there are some strong suggestions as to why it and other organizations may have stopped involving themselves in Friedel's exclusion case. James had become increasingly vocal about his own politics and his story. In the increasingly electric atmosphere of the Cold War, HIAS and ACLU officials might not have wanted the taint.[126] James and Friedel never immigrated to the United States. The couple settled in Britain, where they remained until their deaths.

. . . .

The cases of Friedel Rosenthal and Ellen Knauff allowed contemporaries to think about the US responsibility toward survivors and former military personnel; whether the family risked or fortified the United States; and whether spousal reunification was a "privilege" or a "right." Just as notions of victimhood, military service, and strong families shaped the conception and treatment of those refused admission, these themes also influenced how war brides would be imagined as they settled in their new homes. As new immigrants, these women and men would be caught among multiple expectations and communities. They would find that the simultaneous sense of belonging—and not belonging—in several circles and networks would follow them as they created new lives in the United States, Britain, and Canada.

6

A Home of One's Own

∙∙

THE EARLY YEARS

When Lala and Morris stepped off the DC-4 airplane at LaGuardia Airport on September 21, 1948, they were met by his parents, Bessie and Albert Fishman. Now that Morris had completed his service at the German displaced persons camps, he and Lala went to Brooklyn, where they moved into the Fishman family home. Like so many other returning military personnel, Morris did not have a place of his own where he and his new wife could settle.[1]

The newlyweds were exhausted after their nearly seventeen-hour journey from London to La Guardia. Despite her fatigue, when she and Morris deplaned, Lala appeared glamorous to the outside observer. Wearing the new suit that the couple had purchased in Paris and sporting a French haircut, Lala's chic blonde hair, hazel eyes, and fashionable dress were at odds with Morris's parents and, likely in contrast to their perception of what a Nazi victim looked like. According to Lala's recollections, in the taxi ride to the Fishman home, Bessie leaned over and set the stage for the emotional dynamics that would play out over the next few years. "You must be a very smart girl," she whispered in Yiddish to Lala. "You took my Morris for your husband, you must be very, very smart."[2]

Lala remembered her mother-in-law as possessive and antagonistic at first, and the war bride did not find it easy to share an apartment with her. Lala, Morris, Bessie, and Albert represented different generations, lifestyles, and wartime experiences. The younger couple strongly affiliated with Jewish tradition and culture but embraced a more liberal interpretation of religious observance than did Morris's parents. Lala had witnessed horrors, suffered losses, faced experiences, and seen things that her husband's parents, who had spent the war years in Brooklyn, could not fully comprehend. Moreover, Lala and Morris's interest in travel and new adventures was at odds with Albert's and Bessie's pursuits. Morris's mother infrequently left Brooklyn, and his father was occupied with work. With no friends nearby and no employment to fill her days, Lala quickly became bored. She took long walks to escape. She window-shopped, studied English by reading the newspaper, and, upon becoming pregnant with their eldest child, enrolled in a war bride infant care class. When Morris assumed the directorship of the Hillel Jewish student organization at the University of Missouri and moved the family to Columbia, Lala finally began to feel as if she was emerging from her war years. She now had "a home" of her own.[3]

Over 3,000 miles away, Gena found herself in similar straights. Once she married Norman in October 1945, she became a British subject, and British military regulations prohibited her from remaining in Germany. Though Norman would not be demobilized for several more months, he had no choice but to arrange for her to travel from Bergen-Belsen to northwest London to reside with his parents.

Gena found Hendon stifling. Her mother-in-law did not fully approve of the match, and northwest London offered Gena little social support. Gena was lonely and desperately missed her mother, whom she had left behind in the DP camp. She initially had trouble making new friends in part because she lacked a shared language with those around her. Norman's parents and their neighbors all spoke English; Gena only knew a few words of the language. Hendon was removed from the neighborhoods where Polish Jewish survivors had begun to move. Like Lala, Gena spent her days working tirelessly on learning the English language and avoiding her mother-in-law. A few years later, when she and Norman left the Turgel family apartment, Gena finally felt a sense of stability and belonging.[4]

In interviews and published memoirs, Gena and Lala offered ambivalent portraits of their early years in their new homes. On the one hand, they highlighted the nearly suffocating presence of their husbands' families, their feelings of foreignness, their desperate longing for their murdered family members, and the unprecedented physical and emotional marks left by the Holocaust. On the other hand, as spouses of current or former military personnel, they had access to unique assimilatory educational opportunities and support systems. They faced fewer difficulties becoming naturalized and more easily arranged for family members' sponsorship and emigration. They had opportunities to meet other spouses of military personnel and participate in programming intended only for war brides. Much like in North Africa and Europe, these spouses found that their early lives in America, Britain, or Britain did not compare neatly to the acculturation and integration processes experienced by their fellow non-Jewish war brides or the Jewish survivors who were embarking on their own immigration.

· ·

Whether they arrived in Brooklyn, Hendon, or Montreal, war brides usually settled with their spouses' families. Soldiers returning from the war found that housing across the United States, Britain, and Canada was in short—if not in the shortest—supply of all essential commodities. Because of material shortages and wartime controls, only 236,000 dwellings were constructed in the United States in 1945 as compared to over 1,000,000 in 1941.[5] Enemy action in Britain, which resulted in the destruction of over 200,000 homes and damage of 3.5 million more, had made housing there even scarcer.[6] Millions were living with relatives and/or in squalid temporary housing. Into 1948, local and national newspapers in the United States, Canada, and Britain called for governments to devote resources to solving the housing crises and to guarantee that veterans of World War II had houses of their own.[7]

In apartments, small townhouses, and larger homes, the "greatest generation" shared bathrooms, cooking spaces, and living areas with older and younger generations.[8] Cohabitation was difficult, and postwar films, plays, newspaper articles, and novels captured the strain that resulted from these claustrophobic living arrangements.[9] In such conditions, returning war veterans and their spouses, family members, neighbors, and friends were exposed to one another's habits, mores, peccadillos, and sex lives. Tensions were high generally, but those between parents and their grown children now returning from war were particularly contentious. This led the pathbreaking sociologist

Evelyn Millis Duvall to develop an explanation of kin-conflict that pushed for sons to remove themselves and their new wives from their parents' home as quickly as possible. Building her theories upon existing concerns about the reintegration of military veterans into "peaceful" life and developing notions of "momism," the belief that mothers were predisposed to keeping their children unnecessarily close, Duvall argued that living with one's parents engendered intergenerational conflict. Married couples, she argued, needed to build sufficient autonomy to create their own successful family units.[10] Six years earlier the British writer Jean Bird similarly had bemoaned that "every woman knows by instinct that a happy family life is impossible without a home of one's own."[11]

The quest for a new normalcy in postwar homes could be combative and recently arrived Jewish spouses struggled to settle into these conditions. Memoirs, interviews, and letters emphasized feeling isolated while simultaneously finding it draining to live within close quarters with strangers who now were to be considered family. For Sala B., postwar life in Montreal was arduous. When she and Abe arrived in Canada, several years after her illegal emigration out of Germany, the couple settled with Abe's mother in her small Montreal home. Sala knew little English, "had three children, a mother-in-law, and worked full time." The chaos was overwhelming. "I felt I needed the peace and quiet," she explained to her interviewer.[12] When she immigrated to the United States, Sala K. similarly moved with her husband Sidney into the tiny New York City apartment of her husband's mother, located near the family store. The space did not feel large enough for all of those living there. Sala, who had been apart from her husband since almost immediately after their wedding, was desperate for some time and space for just her and Sidney. But her mother-in-law—or one of Sidney's siblings or cousins—always seemed to be underfoot.[13]

It was particularly difficult to reside with parents who resented their children's decision to marry abroad. Sidney's mother had expressed her displeasure months earlier when she had tried to prevent her son's wedding from taking place in Germany. Not surprisingly, Sala K. found cohabiting with "the Jewish mama of all Jewish mamas" uncomfortable.[14] Clara similarly depicted a fraught relationship with her mother-in-law, who had opposed Daniel's engagement. Daniel's father had come to accept Clara, making amends when she still lived in Antwerp by writing her "love letters." "His mother I never got a letter from," Clara remembered. Once Clara arrived in Philadelphia to settle with her in-laws, her discomfort grew and festered.[15]

Of course, contentious relationships between mothers and daughters-in-law were nothing new. Many of the spouses knew nothing about the films, card games, foods, or clothing that were so important to the daily lives of the households they found themselves in. Even Lala, who had self-presented as a woman of the world, was embarrassed when she compared herself to her sister-in-law, who possessed dresses and an innate understanding of what to wear when. During those early days, she felt lonely and ostracized by her neighbors. "I had no friends," she remembered.[16] Similarly, while Bella found that the Ostroff family apartment was like that of her mother's boisterous, crowded, working-class household, she felt overwhelmed by the American codes of behavior, which seemed entirely foreign. Like Lala, she recalled comparing herself to her American sisters-in-law, who appeared poised, well dressed, and able to navigate the multiple worlds in which they moved.[17]

Many resided in households whose languages or culture they did not share, and a lack of familiarity with English made coexistence challenging. "They used to stare at me a lot," Gina, who moved into the Turgel family home without Norman, remembered. "Although my knowledge of English was limited, I sensed that they were talking about me."[18] The existence of multilingual Yiddish/English households did not necessarily offer much solace. In the Kirschner family, Sidney, his siblings, and their families conversed with one another almost entirely in English, and Sala was hyperaware of her status as an outsider. When Sidney's siblings and their families gathered in his mother's small apartment, Sala could understand nothing. As her rowdy brother-in-law shouted to be heard above the din, she imagined that he was "hollering about me and I just wanted to kill myself. What am I doing in here? I don't understand what they are saying."[19] Sala felt unwanted and judged, sentiments that became exaggerated in these intimate, foreign spaces.

Some Jewish spouses shared a language with their new family members. Gerda and her German-born husband, Kurt Klein, first settled close by Kurt's sister, her husband, and their children. While Kurt and his siblings strove to speak in English, they reverted to German when Gerda struggled with comprehending her surroundings.[20] The same could be true of spouses who married American-, British-, and Canadian-born veterans who had been raised in Yiddish-speaking households. For Bella, her in-laws' ability to speak with her in Yiddish was reassuring. She imagined that she "picked up a lot of things real quick" because Ray's sisters and mother switched to Yiddish when she failed to understand what they were trying to convey in English.[21] By the time she arrived in Montreal, Sala B. had learned some English, but her mother-in-law's familiarity with Yiddish provided her with a minimal sense of belonging in this foreign landscape.[22] Even when remembering that horrific first day in her mother-in-law's apartment, Sala K. recalled with fondness—and some desperation—Sidney's cousin who attempted to speak with her in Yiddish.[23] Of course, a family's knowledge of Yiddish did not necessarily mean that their son- or daughter-in-law spoke that language. Neither Lydia nor Flory grew up in Yiddish-speaking homes, and when they arrived in their in-laws' Yiddish-speaking households, they could not understand their surroundings.

Lydia and Flory also were unfamiliar with the Ashkenazic traditions and practices embraced in their husbands' homes.[24] Lydia had grown up in a traditional, religiously observant Sephardic environment. Her parents hosted enormous weekly Friday night dinners that included extended family members, synagogue attendees, and Jewish visitors, and Harold had been one of those guests. In contrast to her parents, the Ashkenazic Servetnicks were less ritually observant. They tended not to organize large Friday night or holiday gatherings, and it was difficult for Lydia to adjust to the smaller Servetnick household.[25] Flory also found the Jagodas' Ashkenazic home unfamiliar, with different foods, customs, and music. For the musician, the latter was particularly challenging. "Songs were different," she remembered, "and I missed my father's songs. Tunes were very different. . . . It's a change of life. A whole life."[26]

Ashkenazic families also witnessed these cultural disparities. Gena experienced the modern Orthodoxy of London Jewry—and its notions of decorum—as foreign to what she remembered of her Jewish childhood in Poland.[27] Sala K., who married into a family that had originated from a region in Poland that was close to where she had been born, still found some of their Jewish customs unfamiliar, owing to both the Americanization of Jewish rites and the fact that she had been robbed of opportunities to experience Jewish observance as an adolescent and young adult. When she and Sidney married (again) in a Jewish ceremony two weeks after her immigration, she was horrified that wedding guests gifted her with money. She thought they felt sorry for her, that the gifts were a form of charity "because I was an orphan." "So," she recalled, "I ran away and I started crying."[28]

Sala and Sidney were not the only couple to undergo a second ceremony upon the survivor's arrival in the United States. This was particularly common among couples who had celebrated a civil marriage abroad. Sala and Sidney married in New York because they had exchanged vows only in a secular ceremony in Germany. In the eyes of observant Jews, the absence of a religious wedding ceremony meant, among other things, that any child of such a union would be considered illegitimate. Morton's parents similarly asserted that because their son and Halina had married in a civil wedding in Regensburg, the young couple was not considered married within Jewish tradition. His parents planned a wedding for him and Halina to be held immediately after the war bride immigrated to the United States. They did not want the couple spending an evening together on American soil unless they were legally wed in a Jewish religious ceremony. When a shipping strike prevented Halina's boat from docking on the originally scheduled date, Morton's parents planned a second religious wedding ceremony to take place when she finally disembarked.[29] Edith and Nathan L. likewise married in a religious ceremony soon after they arrived in Detroit, though it was her religious observance—not that of Nathan's parents—that prevented the couple from consummating their European secular marriage: "Nate had brought me a gorgeous nightgown and a matching robe, you know, for our wedding night. . . . Nothing happened . . . because I was brought up that if you don't have a *Chupa*, a regular Jewish wedding, and break a glass, then I'm not considered married. I personally didn't consider that I was actually married. . . . I didn't [sleep with Nathan] until we . . . celebrated our wedding."[30]

Like Jewish spouses who found themselves participating in a second wedding, engaged couples also married quickly after the fiancé(e)s arrived in the United States, Britain, or Canada. In these cases, the rapid timetable was due to policies concerning fiancée or travel visas.[31] Alice R. and Meyer "Chesty" L. married in a Jewish ceremony just days after Alice's arrival in Pittsburgh from Cairo. The couple had been unable to wed in Egypt before Chesty's demobilization. Chesty organized Alice's travel papers, and they had to marry relatively quickly for her to remain in the United States. As Chesty filed the paperwork, his mother planned the wedding ceremony and reception.[32] A few months later, Leesha disembarked in Ottawa and found herself swept up in plans for a wedding ceremony and celebration. Leesha had successfully applied for a traveler's visa in January 1947, after she and her fiancé Isaac decided to marry. She journeyed from Amsterdam to Ottawa and immediately moved into her future mother-in-law's house. There she found that the preparations for her wedding and for her move to Montreal, where Isaac now worked, were well underway.[33]

In these cases, the war brides offered little input in their own weddings, knew few people in attendance, and likely missed their parents, family members, and friends.[34] Their mothers-in-law arranged the wedding ceremonies and celebrations. As Sala K. remembered, Sidney's controlling mother wanted to schedule her son and daughter-in-law's wedding to take place shortly after Sala's arrival. Finding a banquet hall free, she planned everything, even obtaining Sala's wedding dress. "My mother-in-law, that's how she was, she put me in that dress the next week and took me to the wedding. It didn't fit me, believe me, I would have never worn it. And it was very sad."[35] Alice similarly attended her own wedding at Chesty's family's synagogue, the Orthodox Adath Jeshurun; she knew none of the guests and the East End synagogue was unlike the one in which she had grown up.[36]

The absence of parents, siblings, children, and friends—especially when juxtaposed against the spouse's extensive circles and networks—was painful. In their reflections on their early years in North America and Britain, Jewish war brides emphasized that they felt most alone when they experienced life-cycle events while surrounded by their spouses' families. This likely intensified the already devastating phenomenon that Holocaust testimony scholar Lawrence Langer has called the "disintegrated self": the tendency of survivors to coexist alongside family members and loved ones who did not survive, experiencing life-cycle events, as well as ordinary daily activities, in the presence of their murdered family members.[37] Many Jewish war brides described this strange coexistence as they settled into their spouses' families' homes and began to navigate their new lives. Leesha's longing for her parents was most acute during life-cycle events, such as her wedding to Isaac and the birth of her children; it was then that she most keenly missed her mother's "consoling and helpful hand."[38] Living with Norman's sisters in London as she tried to create a new life for herself, Gena ached for the family the Nazis had murdered. "It was difficult to push away the memories of my sisters and brothers who had died," she remembered.[39]

As young adults who had come of age immediately before, during, or right after the war, many of these war brides had missed opportunities to observe child-rearing practices and adult relationships, and they had been deprived of the family members with whom they could experience pregnancy, childbirth, and parenting.[40] Lala became pregnant while living in the Fishmans' home, and she remembered feeling as if she lacked any kind of parental or spousal guidance. "I had no one to go to for advice," she lamented. "I hardly knew what to do. . . . I had to learn the rudiments of parenting 'under fire.'"[41] With her mother still in France and with little possibility that they would be reunited in the United States, Bella worried about her pregnancy and mothering in the absence of her own mother.[42] She and other Jewish war brides also wondered how they could cope with pregnancy and parenting so soon after experiencing trauma. "I wasn't very happy about this," Gena remembered about her first pregnancy. "I felt I needed more time to adjust to my new way of life before being ready to face the challenge of motherhood. I was frightened and emotionally very unprepared."[43] While bearing children served as proof that they had survived, demonstrated their ability to renew their decimated population, and affirmed agency over their bodies, it also intensified their sense of isolation.

Several women also found that medical difficulties stemming from their years living under Nazi occupation complicated their pregnancies and early child-rearing years, making their sense of unbelonging more acute. Still "thin and undernourished," Gena had an uneasy relationship with her own body during and immediately after her pregnancy. She could not fully understand how she had become pregnant and was unsure how it could be "possible after so many years of malnutrition and menstrual difficulties."[44] She was miserable. As her physician and husband showered her with words of encouragement, she felt "terribly sick."[45] She may have felt atypical, but several military spouses also faced medical complications that became exaggerated when pregnant. Judith S. was ill before and after giving birth to her son. "I had to be in bed for a long time," she remembered. "I wasn't allowed to get pregnant [again]."[46] "Being pregnant," another woman succinctly explained, "it was a lot."[47] And yet the apparent "ease" with which some became pregnant exacerbated the pain others experienced when dealing with infertility. Clara desperately wanted to expand her family after she had settled with Daniel and his parents, especially after her sister had given birth to her first child. But her physicians diagnosed her as infertile and explained that her years in hiding had resulted in her medical condition. According to her doctors, "The Holocaust did this to me."[48] Clara was not alone. As Peggy Kleinplatz and Paul Weindling have shown, survivors faced real difficulty conceiving or bringing to term their desired number of children. Infertility—or being unable to have as many children as one wanted—made it tough to acculturate to one's new home and muddied triumphant notions of the "reproduction frenzy" of the postwar period.[49]

In addition to infertility and difficult pregnancies, other medical afflictions plagued the spouses' early years. Like other survivors more generally, they suffered from tuberculosis, gastrointestinal diseases, and anxiety and depression. In addition to her difficult pregnancy, Gena endured stomach problems, depressive episodes, and "poor lungs." Thin and undernourished, for years she was unable to eat the foods eaten by her husband's family and instead followed a strict diet of bland foods until her stomach could handle additional fats and sugars. She had trouble sleeping and suffered from night terrors.[50] Lala similarly wrestled with nightmares and painful feelings of loneliness. During the day, she tried to juggle the many demands on her time, but she felt "so alone." At night, she would be "jolted awake by vivid nightmares about the war." She and the other war brides lacked the language, terminology, and medical support to fully understand the challenges that plagued them.[51]

Some spouses emigrated from Europe or North Africa with cases of latent TB. In these situations, the infection went undetected unless symptoms developed. Other spouses were diagnosed with TB or similar diseases within a few years of their immigration, likely due to weak immune systems and/ or stress.[52] Less than a year after her arrival in Columbus, Ohio, Judith S. showed symptoms of jaundice and then TB, "a souvenir from Auschwitz."[53] Gena's tentative health deteriorated more quickly. Almost immediately after settling in London, she collapsed from "poor lungs" and required immediate care. Her in-laws sent her to a sanitarium; for two years after her release, she visited doctors at a Middlesex hospital every six weeks.[54]

Class and residence shaped these women's treatment regimens. In the United States and married to a dentist with an established practice, Judith had access to streptomycin, the recently discovered antibiotic that was most effective at treating TB and still difficult to obtain. Once she was released from bedrest, she could slowly return to her new daily routines. In London, antibiotics were more difficult to procure, and Gena's treatment regimen was more drawn out, lasting several years. Nevertheless, in both cases, the women had to quarantine to protect their spouses, in-laws, and children. Physically isolated, they were unable to care for their children, assist in the housekeeping, or acclimate to their new homes and surroundings. But unlike many other recently arrived survivors who not only had to seek medical care in languages they did not speak but also lacked access to certain forms of medical assistance, Gena and Judith had spouses and in-laws who knew how to navigate their health systems.[55]

Many of the spouses gave voice to some of their distress, but family members, physicians, and neighbors were often indifferent to their complaints. Sala K.'s doctor, husband, and mother-in-law minimized her anxieties and encouraged her to devote her time and energies to her household. She frequently left the apartment and cried in a nearby park, something her husband "knew [about] but not really."[56] Gena's doctor, husband, and parents-in-law likewise dismissed her fears, instructing her to "cheer up, be happy" and reminding her that she would be a "better" wife and mother if she devoted herself to her household.[57] The dismissal of depressive episodes was consistent with experiences of other survivors in North America and Britain. As Beth Cohen, Adara Goldberg, and Rebecca Clifford have shown, victims of Nazism often discussed their ailments, but medical providers, family members, and neighbors frequently did not take these pains and agonies seriously or associate them with the immigrants' traumatic pasts. Most mental health professionals "seemed very nearly oblivious to the aftereffects of the Holocaust for their clients," and if they discussed psychic distress, postwar psychiatrists largely envisioned psychological trauma as something temporary.[58] Instead, they imagined psychic distress as caused by physical injuries in the brain or their genetic makeup. When a Polish-born Jewish survivor in Toronto climbed out of a window at the city's National Employment Service and leaped onto a narrow metal pole, for example, professionals and newspaper accounts across Canada depicted her as animalistic and "a definite mental case." They made little linkage to the anguish caused by her experiences in the camps.[59]

Certainly, some social workers and chaplains recognized the depth of survivors' psychological needs. As early as May 1945, Chaplain Abraham Klausner identified mental anguish among Holocaust survivors as a real concern: "Just as they are undernourished and will carry the effects of their undernourishment for the rest of their lives, as they will their serial numbers which were tattooed on their left arm, will not these conditions under which they lived and which have caused permanent physical changes also leave permanent emotional changes?"[60] Polish-born psychiatrist Paul Friedman shared similar observations when, three years later, he published an article in the American Jewish magazine *Commentary* on the mental health needs of the DPs he had met in Europe. Aptly titled, "The Road Back for the DPs: Healing the Scars of Nazism," the article recognized a "pressing need for psychological assistance." According to Friedman, early rehabilitation programs focused only on material aid; now aid workers needed to consider the psychiatric care of former Nazi victims. Yet Friedman worried that few DPs would receive the assistance they so desperately required. Health care workers, he asserted, denied survivors psychiatric care because of their own guilty feelings. They had been safe while European Jews faced an attempted genocide.[61]

Instead of focusing on their traumas, the Jewish war brides' health practitioners and contemporaries imagined the survivors as particularly resilient and/or distanced them from their European or North African pasts. This was consistent with the conflicting messages survivors tended to receive more generally, namely that they were too dissimilar from "authentic" Nazi victims to themselves be victims; that they had done something immoral to survive; and that their survival suggested proof of physical and psychological superiority.[62] Such understandings likely were influenced by the photographs that had emerged from the liberated camps of the skeletal, diseased, and malnourished Nazi victims. While the earliest images of the Nazi camps were not widely shared in the United States, Canada, or Britain, the discovery of Ohrdruf, an annex of the Buchenwald camp, in 1945 led to the slow dissemination of liberation photography. After visiting Ohrdruf, Dwight Eisenhower, the supreme commander of Allied forces in Europe, encouraged war correspondents and photographers to go to former Nazi sites to document the Nazi atrocities. The publication of these images was supplemented by those pictures captured by the few military personnel who had access to cameras and led to a shared understanding of a Nazi victim.[63] Family members and neighbors differentiated Jewish war brides from other Nazi victims. A reconciliation of the two would be difficult. How could one's spouse, one's sibling-in-law, or one's child-in-law be a skeletal traumatized figure?

Newspaper, radio, and television coverage portrayed Jewish war brides as "surprisingly" like other wives and mothers. One *Chicago Tribune* article described Ruth A. as "typical" among her neighbors. Like other local housewives, she was attractive, neat, friendly, child-centered, and outgoing. "You might not notice anything that would set her apart," asserted journalist Jean Komaiko. Ruth was "warm, friendly, and smiling"; however, she shockingly had "known some of the worst horrors that our cruel century has produced."[64] The article's accompanying photograph reinforced the image of Ruth as a 1950s housewife. Deeply engaged in her handiwork, she sat erect in a wingback chair near a lamp and filled ashtray while her husband, flanked by their children, remained slightly aloof, focused on reading his newspaper in the background. A photograph of Ruth and her children was reflected in the mirror above the couch.[65] Ruth's past traumas remained deeply hidden and, ostensibly, would not interfere with her mothering. Newspaper depictions of Leesha similarly insisted that it was "hard to believe" that the "good-natured, chubby little girl" had survived years of hiding, let alone participated in the resistance.[66] According to reporters, the "Holland Heroine" now was occupied with the domestic tasks of being a wife and, hopefully, one day a mother, roles in which her "immediate zest for action and service" would serve her well.[67] Here, too, photographs of Leesha and Isaac positioned the bride as diminutive and unthreatening.[68] Her portraits—much like those of Ruth— acknowledged her past but insisted that her traumas remained unseen and dormant. Marriage, they implied, could allow for such a transformation.

American television and radio broadcasts similarly submerged the Jewish spouses' traumatic pasts and showcased their current roles as spouses, parents, and new immigrants.[69] Just as the host of *This Is Your Life* fawned over glamorous Hanna, saying she looked younger than her years, the organizers of "I'm an American Day" featured Freide, a newly arrived war bride (and Clara's sister), as someone who had quickly shed her traumatic European past. "I'm an American Day" celebrated the disparate contributions of immigrants to American culture and life,[70] and within a few months of her immigration, Freide sang the "Star-Spangled Banner" on the radio broadcast. Over the next several years, she appeared as one of the entertainers, singing an eclectic array of American patriotic jingles, "Jewish songs," lieder, and operatic pieces.[71] Likewise, on Thanksgiving Day 1947, Gregor sang on the *We the People* radio program.[72] Gregor, Hanna, and Freide allegedly had integrated into the American fabric of everyday life.

Feeling as if societal expectations demanded their silences, most Jewish spouses avoided talking about their wartime experiences with their family and neighbors. Sala B., who insisted that she "never talked about the war," identified three different reasons for her silence: the disinterest of her neighbors, her wish to avoid revisiting past traumas, and her strong desire to prevent her children from experiencing pain.[73] Anna also asserted that she engaged in similar self-censorship to protect her child from her mother's memories and because her neighbors "didn't believe one word" of her stories about the camps. "I left it at that," she recalled. "I never really spoke about it again."[74] Thousands of miles away, Sala K., also decided that she was "never, never going to talk about camps." She imagined that her obligations as a parent demanded her silence; she "wasn't going to be a good mother" if she spoke about the Nazi horrors. "The only way I knew how to raise them normal," she argued, "was not to talk about it."[75] Like many survivors, the Jewish war brides struggled—into the 1950s and 1960s—over the degree to which they should share stories of the past. While work on multigenerational trauma suggests that these women likely—and unintentionally—transmitted their burdens to their children in some way, Jewish war brides insisted that they intended to suppress their traumatic pasts.[76]

The impulse toward self-censorship also was consistent with the behavior of veterans, the very people the war brides had married, and it is likely that the wartime traumas of the military personnel they married compounded and/or complicated the ways Jewish war brides engaged with their own pasts. While many psychiatrists affirmed the existence of nervous strains in soldiers because of prolonged stress, few medical officials then discussed the long-term consequences of trauma on veterans.[77] The Jewish war brides—like war brides more generally—lived in homes with men (and women) who struggled with their own wartime demons, yet likewise remained silent about those experiences, sometimes even ignoring their time in combat.[78] Sala B., for example, unintentionally juxtaposed her past with Abe's. Ignoring that her husband had witnessed the horrors of combat and liberation, she explained to her interviewer that her attraction to Abe lay in his "cheery" Canadian persona. She wanted to marry an American or a Canadian, not "someone from the caf-zet [camp]."[79] One daughter of a civilian-military couple similarly remembered that her mother wanted to be "separated from the camps," and her father, an attractive young GI, offered that form of avoidance.[80] Ignoring the wartime experiences of their military spouses allowed the Jewish war brides one path toward recovery and rebuilding.

· ·

Several other variables emerged as central to the Jewish war brides' understanding of their own healing. They uniformly characterized acquiring their own living spaces as fundamental to their recuperation and renewal. After Sala K. had given birth to their two children, she and Sidney moved from the Kirschners' third-floor walk-up in Harlem to an apartment in Queens. The young family had spent five years cohabitating with Sidney's mother and it "was time for us to move."[81] She quietly remembered the luxury of living only with her husband and children. "Nothing excited me as much as getting my own bathroom," she recalled. "I had my own bathroom for the first time in my life. . . . That was my kingdom. It was like a palace."[82] For Anna, it did not matter that Cardiff was "bleak, rainy, windy, and grey," the residence she and her husband acquired for their family allowed her a sense of independence and stability. After years of incarceration, this was the "first home, mine, really after the war."[83] Anna and others had gone from prewar homes to wartime incarceration or hiding, to postwar shared apartments and DP camps, to war bride processing centers, and then to the homes of their in-laws. Obtaining homes of their own offered them a sense of agency after years of powerlessness.[84]

Many of these families took advantage of the passage of the GI Bill and its Canadian equivalent, the Veteran's Rehabilitation Act, which allowed veterans to purchase homes and/or attend university more easily.[85] Because of the even more extensive devastation of the British housing market, however,

Jewish military couples in the United Kingdom found that it took longer to obtain their own homes. When they learned an apartment was available in London, Gena and Norman desperately lobbied the landlord to rent it to them. Now that Gena had children of her own, she strongly wanted to move away from her in-laws' home and settle into her own space. Once she had a "home of her own," she began to sleep better and gain weight.[86]

Even though it also intensified their sense of loneliness, Jewish war brides emphasized the role parenting played in their rebuilding. For one thing, having children led several of the Jewish war brides to socialize and acculturate. Some found comfort in speaking (and sometimes reading) English when their children attended school or when they met other young families in their predominantly English-speaking neighborhoods. This, they argued, was even more significant than mimicking the English they heard spoken by their husband's family or on the radio. Ann Kirschner remembered that her mother "acquired English as her children did,"[87] and, though Bella had started to learn English while living with Ray's mother and sisters, it was her own growing family that pushed her to gain comfort with the language.[88]

Children served another acculturation purpose. Walking with a baby carriage encouraged new parents to meet other young mothers in neighborhood parks, on the street, and in local stores. Many women also met other new parents when they took advantage of the different kinds of programming offered to spouses of military personnel and to new immigrants.

War bride clubs had existed in Canada and the United States since the end of the First World War. They offered networking activities for the newly arrived British spouses—and later Australian and New Zealand—women to meet other "brides" who had immigrated during the previous decades.[89] As those clubs grew and were joined by new associations in cities and towns that had not previously hosted war bride clubs, their leadership reached out to white military spouses who emigrated from outside of Britain and Commonwealth countries. Several of these organizations collaborated with the Maple Leaf Association, the American Red Cross, and local veterans' societies to organize welcome teas, childcare classes, and cooking workshops. In New York City, in 1945, the Manhattan Cosmopolitan Associates club, founded by and for British brides, expanded its membership to include all foreign-born military spouses. As the club's founder explained, "There were other women who had married GIs but weren't British. They had the same problems we did, but only worse because they didn't speak the language." Because those women "really were isolated," the New York club expanded its programming to include a wider range of efforts to acculturate the newcomers into

American customs and languages. These offerings slowly attracted some of the war brides who lacked a deep familiarity with both English and American customs.[90]

The ability of these newly arrived war brides to take part in these distinct programs helped further their integration but also frequently emphasized their sense of in-betweenness. They could never fully fit into either the predominantly Christian white war bride communities or the circles of Jewish Holocaust survivors. Across the United States and Canada, Jewish women participated in disparate programs intended for war brides, most frequently taking advantage of those offerings that targeted their specific demographic, class, and background. These programs occupied a central role in their managing their isolation and acculturation. In Brooklyn, Lala was one of many new mothers originating from somewhere other than Britain who attended a pregnancy and childcare course organized by the Red Cross and a local war brides' group in which they learned how to raise their children in an American landscape.[91] About eighty miles away, Bella attended several teas sponsored by a Philadelphia group that had been formed by French-speaking war brides. For Bella, who now lived in a household where no one spoke French, this group was attractive because it allowed her to converse in the language of her childhood friendships, encouraged mothers to bring their children, and was located in a nearby neighborhood.[92] Charlotte R. eagerly socialized with the mostly English-speaking middle-class members of the "GI bride" group in her New Jersey town. Having escaped to England at the beginning of the war, Charlotte likely was comfortable participating in English-language programs, which included childcare workshops, children's playdates, a film series, teas, and an annual Mrs. GI contest, for which she won an honorable mention. And, because she lived in a Jewish neighborhood, it is probable that some of her fellow club participants also were Jewish, though no specifically Jewish content was offered at her club.[93]

Ruth B. patronized social gatherings sponsored by a Montreal war bride club that attracted British-born women, but, unlike Charlotte R., she also took part in local programming that focused specifically on Jewish war brides. After prompting from Jewish chaplains associated with the Maple Leaf Association, a few synagogue sisterhoods in Montreal and Toronto developed programming to help the brides acclimate. They reached out to the newly arrived brides, invited them to join the sisterhood, and offered social networking opportunities and English tutorials.[94] It is unclear whether the Canadian rabbis had been aware of the ambivalence several Jewish women's groups had expressed about their newly arrived coreligionists, but Montreal and Toronto saw the creation of short-lived Jewish war bride clubs.[95]

Such targeted opportunities for support were exceptional. Most of the North American Jewish spouses participated in the general war bride activities described above and in English classes, citizenship workshops, and childcare programs that local and national Jewish organizations offered for survivors.[96] In the United States, those courses were mostly—but not exclusively—run by local chapters of the National Council of Jewish Women (NCJW); in Winnipeg, Toronto, and Montreal, the Jewish Immigrant Aid Society (JIAS), often with provincial school boards, ran twice-weekly language and citizenship classes. Both the NCJW and JIAS classes envisioned that teaching immigrants American and Canadian languages and customs would produce well-rounded new citizens. The course goals focused first on teaching elementary English skills, as well as rudimentary American or Canadian history, citizenship, and politics.[97] Both Arlene J. and Sala B. recalled the important role these courses played in their acculturation. For over half a century, Arlene visibly displayed the photograph of her "Adult Student Club," an English and Americanization class run by the local chapter of the National Council of Jewish women at the Yonkers Jewish Community Center. The instructor, Frances C., was the president of the Yonkers branch of the NCJW, a field officer of the Girl Scouts, and an active member of her parent teacher association and synagogue.[98] Here, too, understandings of class and culture shaped their experiences. Arlene imagined that she and her husband Joe befriended Frances and her husband in part because Joe, a refugee GI, already was comfortable speaking English and, in part, because, despite their current poverty, she had grown up in a cultured, bourgeois home. A graduate of the gymnasium, Arlene spoke French, German, Hungarian, Latin, Czech, Slovak, and some Russian. Within a few years, her English became strong enough that she could translate prayers into English and become recording secretary of the "Adult Student Club."[99] Sala left no record of her relationship with her instructor, but she remembered the English and citizenship classes that she patronized after her arrival and continued to take advantage of adult education opportunities long after she had learned English. Both women also received language and citizenship instruction by taking part in informal and formal community-sponsored events at local libraries, synagogues, and clubs. Sala patronized the offerings at Montreal's Jewish Public Library and the Arbeiter Ring; Arlene joined the Yonkers branch of the NCJW, the parents' association of her son's Jewish day school, and the sisterhood of the Orthodox synagogue she and Joe attended.[100]

Americanization class, Yonkers, NY, undated.
From the author's private collection.

In addition to these support activities, some Jewish war brides took advantage of clubs created by Jewish newcomers. *Landsmanschaftn* (mutual benefit or aid societies) and "survivors clubs" provided emotional support and connections, offered practical advice, and hosted social activities of all kinds. Bella and Ray participated in such an organization, even though most of the survivors originated from places other than France. As Bella explained, the mainstream Jewish institutions near their home were expensive; she already participated in the French (Christian) war bride group; it was far more affordable to take advantage of the programs that catered specifically to Jewish immigrants; and Ray already was comfortable in a Yiddish-speaking milieu.[101]

Other women, though, were unable to take advantage of survivor clubs and *landsmanschaftn* opportunities because their husbands' families sought to shed any vestige of an immigrant past. While Sala K. initially strove to meet new immigrants, she found it difficult to maintain those ties because her husband and his family socialized with a different network. "I didn't have that much contact with the people, with my own people." she recalled.[102] As her daughter remembered, "My father must have put his foot down." Once Sidney, Sala, and their children moved to Rockaway, to be closer to his brothers, "there was no contact with the immigrant, survivor community there."[103] In

Hendon, Gena found it was far "simpler" for her to associate with Norman's neighbors and colleagues. She only would participate in survivor networks and circles later in her life.[104]

Most Jewish war brides likewise were excluded from postwar efforts that focused on survivors' resettlement and employment. The most robust of these programs took place in the United States, which witnessed the arrival of approximately 140,000 Holocaust survivors between 1945 and 1953, but Canadian Jewish organizations also oversaw the resettlement and relief of about 35,000 survivors during this time. In cities across North America, Jewish communal leaders agreed to accept a certain number of survivors and assume responsibility for their resettlement and adjustment.[105] The war brides could not join these programs. They were nonquota immigrants who lived with their spouses and families, and Jewish agencies assumed that they therefore did not require this kind of relief.[106] Jewish communal leaders imagined that the war brides might supplement the family income, but they would not be responsible for it. This was generally true. Only a small number of Jewish war brides described working for a salary. Those who did assisted family or friends in small businesses, worked as seamstresses or domestic help, and, in some exceptional cases, in later years, sought educational opportunities and became employed in a wider range of professions. They did not participate in work-matching programs or in the English classes explicitly tied to gaining employment.

As spouses began learning English, having children, and acquiring their own homes, they also began to arrange for their family members' immigration and, if needed, their own naturalization. Soon after Gena's children were born, she and Norman successfully brought her mother to London; there now were policies in place that allowed Norman to sponsor his mother-in-law, and Gena wanted her mother to help her raise her children.[107] Likewise, after Freide and Clara had respectively settled in New York and Philadelphia with their husbands and children, the men served as sponsors of Freide and Clara's mother, Rosa.[108] The mothers each came to their daughters' new homes following the immigration policies of those countries. Gena's mother entered Britain under the "Distressed Relatives scheme." Created in October 1945, this immigration plan was intended for survivors of concentration camps who had relatives in Britain who could support them. British governmental policy made it difficult for Jewish survivors to come to the United Kingdom because it subjected them to alien restriction legislation; the "Distressed Relatives scheme" allowed survivors to bypass many of the existing restrictions.[109] Because Norman and his father could serve as Gena's mother's sponsor and because she was a survivor of the camps, she could immigrate to England and reunite with her daughter.[110]

Canada implemented a similar immigration policy in 1946 that allowed for the sponsorship of first-degree relatives, although, unlike the UK program, it did not favor survivors of the camps. Sponsoring Canadian relatives had to prove their ability to pay for all transportation and care. They also had to guarantee that the immigrant would not be a public charge.[111] As soon as her immigration papers to Canada were finalized, Ruth B. began to encourage her husband Nathan B. to complete the necessary paperwork to arrange for her parents' sponsorship. Just as she was about to board the war bride ship in Southampton that would take her to Halifax, she wrote a letter to her husband, asking him to bring her parents to Canada as soon as possible. "Darling," she wrote, "I know you will do your very best for them, but please don't delay it any longer than absolutely necessary."[112]

In the United States, the Truman Directive of December 1945 authorized preferential treatment for the admission of DPs within existing immigration law, but it, too, remained restrictive toward European Jews.[113] Immigrants continued to need sponsors (individuals or welfare agencies) willing to provide affidavits promising that the newcomers would not become public charges. Sponsors had to guarantee suitable employment and safe and sanitary housing for the eligible DP and those accompanying him or her. They also had to receive the DP at the port of entry and pay for his or her travel.[114] If they had the wherewithal to sponsor members of their spouses' families, many American veterans did so. Soon after their children were born, the husbands of Judith I., Judith S., and Sala K. all began to arrange for their spouses' surviving family members to move to the United States.[115] While Judith I.'s mother and Sala K.'s sisters immigrated within a half-decade of the war brides' arrivals, it would be several more years before Judith S. would be reunited with her mother. Her husband, Sam, was killed in a car accident not long after the couple arrived in Columbus, Ohio, before he could finalize the paperwork. Judith S.'s mother only came to the United States once Judith had received her citizenship papers and could serve as her mother's sponsor.[116]

For some, like Judith S., a reunion was impossible or a long way off. It could be made infeasible by the costs of sponsoring someone to come to the United States, Canada, or Britain; the political context of the time; and the eagerness of the relatives to migrate and unite. When they settled in Philadelphia with Ray's family, Bella and her husband lacked the funds to sponsor her siblings and mother to come to the United States. Bella's brother and his wife eventually immigrated to the United States because his wife's family in Cleveland served as their sponsors; Bella's mother remained in France.[117] Helen L. similarly found herself separated from her mother for many years after the war; her husband, Al, had sufficient funds to help sponsor her mother, but the older woman had escaped to Shanghai before the war broke out and the postwar political situation meant that the American consul was unable to process and facilitate the family's immigration requests.[118]

After her husband's tragic death, Judith S. was even more determined to obtain her citizenship. She was not alone. Many of the British and American Jewish war brides became citizens as quickly as possible. Governmental officials in Britain, Canada, and the United States had expected the new spouses to quickly petition for naturalization. While it is certainly true that "immigration law is about who gets in, while naturalization law is about who stays in," naturalization policy had long been intertwined with that of immigration law.[119] Officials envisioned that many of those who immigrated would—one day—desire permanent residence. This was particularly the case with the war brides, who were imagined as candidates for citizenship as soon as military personnel petitioned for permission to marry them. Most spouses received their citizenship in one of two ways: through marriage or an expedited process established for spouses of current citizens. The timing of their immigration and their country of arrival dictated what their naturalization process looked like and whether it was the same for men and women.

US nationality laws during this period did not permit an individual to gain citizenship through marriage. That had not been the case earlier in the twentieth century. Until 1922, a woman's citizenship status had been derivative. As a child, she became a citizen through her father, and as a married woman, she became a citizen through her husband. However, after the passage of the Cable Act in 1922, marriages to US citizens no longer resulted in alien women becoming US citizens. Nor did they result in US citizens losing their citizenship if they married alien men.[120] Instead, during the 1940s, alien spouses of US citizens could become citizens within three years. They did not need to file a declaration of intention but could initiate naturalization proceedings with a petition alone.[121] Within days of arriving in Chicago, Ruth A. identified the steps required for naturalization. "If I told you that I applied for my citizenship my second day in Chicago you'd have an idea," she explained to her interviewer to describe how important it was that she become a citizen.[122]

Until 1948, in Britain a clear distinction existed between naturalization laws intended for women and those for men. Alien women who married British citizens automatically became British citizens; upon marriage, they lost the citizenship of their countries of origin or, if they were stateless, their status as stateless individuals. According to the 1914 British Nationality and Status of Aliens Act, "The wife of a British subject shall be deemed to be a British subject, and the wife of an alien shall be deemed to be an alien."[123] It was in this way that Gena became a British subject upon her marriage to Norman in 1945. Alien men who married British women during this period did not gain British naturalization rights; they retained their alien status while their wives lost their status as British subjects. With Parliament's passage of the British Nationality Act in 1948, alien women married to British men no longer automatically became British subjects; nor did British women who married alien men lose their British citizenship. Alien spouses had to register to become citizens, although that process was expedited in comparison to the naturalization petitions of aliens who were not married to citizens. This was why, unlike Gena, who had become a citizen upon marriage to Norman, Anna had to wait a full year to petition to become a British subject. She married after the passage of the new citizenship law.[124] She applied for her "nationality" after twelve months of residence in Cardiff and experienced the process as simple and pedestrian. "We got it by return post," she recalled. "It was no problem really."[125]

Until 1947, alien women who married Canadian men automatically became Canadian citizens and British subjects; alien men who married Canadian women retained their alien status. When Ruth B. married Nathan B. in 1946, she immediately changed in status from being "stateless" to becoming a British subject. Beginning in January 1947, however, a wife no longer gained or lost naturalization or British subject status through marriage. Instead, women and men married to Canadian citizens became naturalized Canadians by following the same process, albeit an expedited one.[126] Still, Canadian war brides who married before 1945 would find that they were not automatically naturalized, despite the promise that upon marriage they would become "Canadians all." Immigration officials had stamped on their war bride travel certificates, "Landed Immigrants." This meant that unless the war brides completed the paperwork to become full citizens, they never possessed legal Canadian nationality.[127]

Whatever path toward naturalization they pursued, several spouses articulated the important place it played in their lives. When asked why she applied so quickly for American citizenship after her immigration, Ruth A. insisted that she "loved Americans" and wanted to be fully included in US society; Anna likewise remembered that becoming a British subject "was like being crowned or something."[128] Judith S. similarly recalled explaining to her confused husband why it was so crucial that she "couldn't wait" to become a citizen. She allegedly retorted, "Honey . . . you don't understand what an American passport would have meant to me in Europe."[129] Many of the Jewish war brides had been stripped of their citizenship; some had never reached the age of citizenry's benefits or obligations. An accelerated process toward naturalization made them feel accepted by government and society, and it offered them the possibility of an "escape route" if their new homes turned against them.[130]

Worry about the security of their new home was one way postwar trauma remained present in the narratives and experiences of the early years. War brides remembered an ambivalence and vulnerability that intensified as they settled with their spouses' families, surrounded by unfamiliar cultures and languages. Longing for their murdered family members, they wondered how to create viable relationships with their spouses and children without strong family networks or the lived experiences of healthy adolescences or early adulthood. They battled with night terrors, gastronomical distress, depression, and a wide range of diseases that had lingered from their years in Hitler's Europe. They told stories of highs and lows as they navigated among war bride clubs, DP groups, survivor associations, and veterans' clubs; *landsmanschaftn*, Western European immigrant circles, Ashkenazic synagogues, and Sephardic synagogues; Red Cross or Maple Leaf clubs, Jewish synagogue sisterhoods, Jewish women's groups, and local parent associations. In each space, they encountered individuals with whom they simultaneously did—and did not—fit. In remembering those years, they emphasized their traumas, but they also offered narratives of recovery and rebuilding, describing marriages, children, and communities who helped them "survive" their pasts.[131]

. . . .

When I first met Lala in 2009, she had published a memoir, been interviewed several times, and was heavily involved in creating a local Holocaust museum and education center. Preparing to sell her home and donate some of her photographs and memorabilia, she opened her front door before I had even stepped out of my car, eager to show me the boxes of materials she had readied for my arrival. She was open and forthcoming, and I found it difficult to reconcile her smooth recounting of her war years with the fact that she had spent her first decades in the United States revealing little about her past. Like other Jewish war brides—and survivors more generally—Lala had remained silent about her past for much of her adulthood. Indeed, once they settled into their new homes, Jewish war brides tended to be reticent about their wartime experiences, even if they initially had shared them with reporters or neighbors.[132] According to Lala, she had stayed quiet for a reason: postwar years were occupied with marriage, parenting, recovery, and acculturation, all efforts that rested on the suppression of wartime traumas.

Like many of their fellow survivors, several Jewish war brides waited decades to cultivate stories of their past and share them with family, friends, and, in some cases, the public. Influenced by the growing interest in—and collection of—individual survivor experiences, the widening circulation of Holocaust narratives, and their own acute awareness of their generation's mortality, they transitioned from silence, to quietly divulging their painful pasts to their children and grandchildren, to becoming involved in Holocaust education efforts. Some, like Lala, published memoirs and gave interviews; others participated in projects that lay outside of the traditional realm of memorialization: curating music, authoring children's books, or producing plays.[133] "I thought, if my son, the future generation, is interested in what happened," one war bride explained in the 1980s, "then all the other generations [will] want to know and must know."[134]

Drawn to serving as "public witnesses," these Jewish war brides developed narratives that followed the templates of survivor interviews more generally. They focused on their lives before and during the war. They revealed stories of wartime horrors and depravations and talked about their current relationships, when relevant, to the Holocaust and contemporary Jewish life and community.[135] When I spoke with Lala, she began our interview by repeating the narrative that she had shared with others. She jumped immediately into her childhood, moved quickly to her experiences during the war, and then pivoted to her work in Holocaust education.

These public accounts, then, while crucial, often overlooked the Jewish war brides' uniqueness. They tended not to disclose experiences of courtship, marriage, and immigration. They obfuscated the multiple communities in which war brides lived and moved, in which they felt included and excluded: military circles, Christian war brides, displaced persons, Jewish survivors, European and North African civilians, their own biological relatives, and the families of the military personnel they married. And they minimized the unique strategies Jewish war brides employed when they engaged with the very real "problem of survival" in the aftermath of trauma.[136]

CONCLUSION

Ever since I was eight years old and first learned about my paternal grandmother's story, I have been interested in the history of the Holocaust. For years, I imagined that the survival, marriage, and immigration experiences of my grandmother Arlene (born Aurelia) were unique. But as I read memoirs by survivors of the Holocaust, I noticed an interesting pattern. Several of the books written by women concluded with a description of the authors' encounters with the American, British, or Canadian military personnel they later married; in contrast, the accounts written by male survivors infrequently mentioned such marriages.[1] Was it unusual, I wondered, for Jewish survivors to have married Allied soldiers or officers? What began as a curiosity evolved into the understanding that my grandmother's story was more common than I had long imagined. Jewish war brides, I came to realize, were worthy of attention.

Unlike Gena or Lala, who published memoirs, or Bella and Sala B., who consented to interviews, Arlene refused to talk about her war years or her experiences at liberation.[2] Joe, the man I knew as my grandfather, respected his wife's silence. He knew about some of Arlene's experiences but refused to share them. When I pushed him to reveal my grandmother's secrets, he employed one of the many strategies that diverted my attention. He would place a few chocolate chip cookies on a napkin and slide them my way, pour me a large glass of otherwise forbidden bright red Hawaiian punch, or turn on the television and allow me and my sister to watch hours of TV unsupervised.

When my brother Jason was born and named after Ignatz Judkowicz, my sister and I gained a greater understanding of my grandparents' silence. Ignatz, we were told, had been my father's biological father—my grandmother's first husband. He, Aurelia (Arlene), and my father had spent some of the war years hiding in the Tatras mountains. They were freed by partisans in Banská Bystrica on March 26, 1945, and Ignatz died from typhoid five days later in the Slovakian town of Brezno.[3] Several months later, Joe, an American GI stationed in Austria, made his way to his childhood home of Humenné, Czechoslovakia, where he was reunited with his older sister Anna and her eldest son Gershon, both of whom who had survived Auschwitz. He also met my father and grandmother, the son and widow of his younger brother Ignatz.

Just as they remained silent about my grandmother's war years, Joe and Arlene never spoke in detail about their courtship or wedding. They mostly relayed that after he arrived in Humenné, Joe had searched for ways to bring Anna, my father, and grandmother to the United States.[4] When no other viable plan emerged, he proposed marriage to my grandmother and enticed Martin, a distant cousin and a member of the American armed forces serving in Europe, to do the same with Anna.

Over the years, my siblings and I mimicked our grandparents' downplaying of their complicated and somewhat unusual courtship narrative. After all, both Joe and Arlene suffered mind-boggling losses during the war, a trauma that clearly remained with my grandmother, who was known to weep frequently over the murder of her sisters, parents, and first husband. My grandmother remembered her courtship and marriage to Ignatz with tremendous nostalgia, and Joe and Ignatz, separated by only two years, had been close as children. That Joe and Arlene would marry—and then remain married until Joe's death in 1984—presented a family history that was difficult to unpack psychologically.

Moreover, Judaism has been understood to prohibit such marriages. When a brother dies, Jewish law mandates that the surviving brother marry the widow *if there are no children from the original marriage*; some have interpreted that to mean an injunction against marrying one's deceased brother's widow if there was a child.[5] Joe, Ignatz, and my grandmother had been raised in religiously observant Jewish homes, and my grandmother remained Sabbath- and holiday-observant until her death. Transgressing what she thought was Jewish law would not have been a minor matter for her. Indeed, once I learned of my complicated family tree, my grandmother quickly reassured me—even though I was eight years old and would not have been familiar then with Jewish law—that she and Joe had received rabbinic dispensation for their marriage from the rabbi at Prague's Alt-Neue-Schule.

Even as I entered adulthood and began to study history with increasing rigor, my grandmother—the only living member of that generation of the

Judkowicz family—still refused to discuss certain portions of her past with me. A dutiful granddaughter and respectful historian, I limited my interviews to the periods of her life about which she consented to speak: her childhood, adolescence, and early adulthood in Czechoslovakia, as well as her life as an established mother and wife in New York.[6] Much of what I learned about my grandparents' lives during and immediately after the war, I pieced together from archival research.[7]

. . . .

While *Between Two Worlds* rests on other personal narratives with deep evidentiary foundations, my grandparents' experiences were consistent with many of the book's conclusions. Like so many of the Jews studied here, when Ignatz, my grandmother, and my father emerged from hiding, they experienced "liberation" as anything but certain or joyous. After they were freed by the partisans, the lines of fighting continued to move. Roadways had been destroyed, and it was difficult to traverse from place to place. Devastatingly ill, Ignatz died en route to Humenné. After his death and the cessation of the war in Europe, my grandmother came to realize that of her large family, only she, her two-year-old son, Anna, and Anna's seventeen-year-old son had survived. The Nazis and their collaborators had killed my grandmother's parents, her siblings, and their families; Anna's husband and younger son, mother, and other siblings and their families all had been murdered.

In fact, the Slovakians and Nazis had murdered about 90 percent of Humenné's Jewish population, and only six Jewish children from that town were known to have survived the war.[8] My father was one of them. Most neighbors, therefore, were surprised by my grandmother's and father's return. Several had seized and looted their home and, while the possessions that my grandmother had put into safekeeping were returned to her by Ignatz's friend and coworker, she and my father lacked money or resources. My grandmother likely bartered what she could and probably depended on local partisans, on Gershon, and, eventually, on Joe, for support.

As Anna and Aurelia and their sons struggled with their daily existence in postwar Humenné, Joe was overwhelmed by the scale of destruction he had witnessed as he made his way into and through Italy, Germany, Austria, and Czechoslovakia. Like some of the refugee soldiers studied here, he had left Czechoslovakia in the 1930s, going first to Belgium, then to Palestine, and, finally, to Yonkers, New York, where his older brother Harry then lived. During the late 1930s and early 1940s, Harry and Joe had tried to bring their mother, their siblings, and their siblings' families to the United States. They were unsuccessful in their efforts, and when Joe enlisted in 1942, he innocently hoped that he would be assigned to serve in Europe, where he might be able to assist his loved ones.[9]

Soon after he was naturalized in Oklahoma in 1943, Joe was sent to Italy, and when the war in Europe concluded, he felt compelled to become involved in relief. Like Karl, who would also meet and marry his future wife in Czechoslovakia, Joe extended his service to remain in Europe to search for his family and went to his childhood home as soon, and as often, as he could. He never discussed the wreckage he saw during the war and its aftermath, only telling his granddaughters that it had been heartbreaking to witness such barbaric loss.

Like the couples featured in *Between Two Worlds*, Joe and Aurelia's encounter and courtship narratives invoked themes of agency, strategy, religious authority, and familial rebuilding, as well as loss, exclusion, and restrictions. Joe had been terrified about what he might find in his childhood home; when he arrived there, he was simultaneously shattered by the enormity of his loss and comforted to find Anna, her son, my grandmother, and my father still alive. Joe had a clear vision of how the Judkowicz family needed to slowly rebuild. A smoker, he traded cigarettes he had brought for the fuel, clothing, fresh fruits, and vegetables crucial to his family's recovery.

Joe and Aurelia agreed that the one remaining child, my father, needed to be brought to the United States, where he could be reunited with Joe and Harry, and raised in "freedom." Representatives of Jewish aid organizations in Vienna and New York warned that it would take significant time for a single woman and her child to gain entry to the United States. They recommended that my father immigrate to New York as an orphan. My grandmother refused; she would not permit her son to leave Europe without her.

When exactly my grandparents decided to wed, I do not know. But it is clear that they understood that marriage and immigration were inexorably linked. Just as Morris had advised Lala that if she wished to emigrate, she should "go like a war bride," my grandparents came to understand that the simplest way to bring my grandmother and father, as well as Anna, to the United States would be for them to travel as dependents of US military personnel. As an unmarried American GI, Joe could marry my grandmother and arrange for her and my father's joint immigration to the United States and then for his adoption of my father; Martin, whom Anna had never previously met, could arrange for Anna to come to the United States.

Like so many women and men studied here, my grandparents also found that the legal act of solemnizing a marriage was complicated. Putting the psychological barriers aside—which is no small feat—my grandparents had to undergo the laborious petition process, marry, apply for my grandmother's travel papers, and contend with Judaism's supposed prohibition of such a marriage. Joe and Arlene continued to rely on family in Europe and in the United States, fellow soldiers, rabbinic authorities in Prague, and JDC and ARC representatives in Vienna and New York for assistance. It appears that Joe faced no difficulty getting his military commander to grant him permission to marry my grandmother. Marriage policies had been shaped by interpretations of victimhood, respectability, and reward, and his commander likely believed that Joe deserved remuneration for service, courage, and bravery, and that my grandmother would serve as an appropriate wife. Perhaps, too, he was sympathetic to the story of my father's survival and Joe's desire to bring him out of Czechoslovakia; maybe he also shared the concern about Czechoslovakia's stability as a sovereign state and its vulnerability to Soviet invasion. No matter what prompted him to approve Joe's petition, my grandfather received word that he could marry my grandmother and began to process her paperwork to bring her to the United States.

The military records do not tell us whether Joe attempted to speak with his chaplain. Instead, Joe and Aurelia, like Judith S. and Sam, went to the rabbinic authorities in Prague, who already had expressed and acted on their sympathy to Jews affected by the war. On June 14, 1946, several months after the implementation of the War Brides Act, Joe and Aurelia received their much-desired rabbinic exemption and exchanged their wedding vows at the Alt-Neue-Schule.

Almost immediately after their wedding, the couple separated again. Joe returned to Austria, where he was based and would remain for another year. My grandmother returned to Humenné, likely to retrieve my father from Anna's care. In Humenné, Aurelia, my father, and Anna continued to live among the few Jewish survivors who had returned to the region, but when the women began their journeys as war brides, immigration regulations and processes would treat them differently from the Jewish migrants with whom they shared languages, cultures, and histories. Once she received word of their departure date, Aurelia and my father traveled to Hanau, Germany, and Le Havre, France, where they settled in one of the cigarette camps with other war brides and their dependents. There, they had their paperwork processed and luggage checked and underwent medical inspections.

In Europe, my grandmother and father came in and out of contact with European Christian civilians, European and North African war brides, Allied military personnel, Slovakian partisans, and Jewish DPs, refugees, and émigrés. In Hanau and Le Havre, my grandmother and father lived, traveled, and were screened with mostly Christian women who also had married American military personnel. Aurelia could communicate with a few of them. She spoke French and German, along with Hungarian, Slovakian, Czech, and to a lesser degree, Russian. She did not speak English. She probably understood some of her surroundings in Germany and France, but it is possible that she often felt as if she did not fully belong with the mostly French-speaking Christian war brides she encountered. There were a few German-born non-Jewish war brides in Hanau, but given her recent traumas and personality, it is hard to imagine that she would have socialized with them. My father likely gave her an excuse to keep to herself.[10]

My grandmother—like many of the other German, Polish, and French war brides—probably experienced greater difficulty comprehending her surroundings when the ship, the *Henry Gibbins*, docked in Southampton. The troop transport ship, which had been outfitted after the war to accommodate brides and their children, began its journey in France and stopped in Southampton to collect its largest group of migrants before continuing on its long voyage to the United States. I wonder what it was like when the *Gibbins*'s bride population was more than quadrupled by the English-speaking war brides from Tidworth. The enormous *Gibbins* carried 390 brides and dependents, as well as demobilized military personnel and European refugees. It included two formal staircases, a dining room, and three decks of cabins. My grandmother and father would have roomed with a group of women who also were traveling with their young children. I never discovered whether my grandmother befriended any of them, the other war brides, or the Jewish refugees with whom she traveled. Nor did I ever learn whether my father contracted the diarrhea that had spread among several of the children on the ship, killing one infant. I can only imagine how terrifying it must have been for my grandmother to witness another infectious disease impacting a population in close quarters so soon after Ignatz's death.

Like so many brides and dependents, my grandmother arrived at Ellis Island to be greeted by her husband's family: Harry, his wife Sophie, and several of Sophie's relatives. Joe would not return to the United States for nearly another year, and Arlene and my father lived with Harry and Sophie until Joe's demobilization. Once Joe returned to the United States, Harry purchased a three-story brownstone in Yonkers where his extended family could live. Joe, my grandmother, and my father moved into the third-floor apartment; Harry and Sophie lived on the middle floor; and Anna later settled on the first floor with her new husband. They remained in that apartment building until after my grandfather's death.

As I researched and wrote about the war brides' arrivals to their new home, I kept thinking about those first few months in Yonkers: the nearly suffocating presence of Harry and his wife, my grandmother's feelings of foreignness, her desperate longing for her murdered family members, and the unprecedented physical and emotional marks left by the Holocaust. With whom—if anyone—did my grandmother spend time when she first arrived? She could communicate with Harry, but he was at work all day long. In what language did she speak with Sophie, who also would have been in the apartment alongside my grandmother and father? My grandmother spoke no English, and Sophie was American-born. So too were Sophie's family with whom she and Harry socialized and worked. Other questions also linger. Did any of the diseases from their time in hiding or on the ship affect them upon their arrival? Did my grandmother welcome or resent Sophie and Harry's offers to help care for my father? Did Joe's return to the United States offer my grandmother solace or serve as a reminder of what—and whom—she had lost?

My grandmother shared other commonalties with other Jewish war brides who settled in the United States. She quickly acquired certain characteristics of acculturation. As a spouse of a GI and as a beneficiary of a family that had been in the United States for a significant period, she had access to unique educational opportunities and support systems to speed her assimilation. She enrolled in English and Americanization classes offered by the National Council of Jewish Women, attended synagogue with Harry and Sophie, and eventually sent my father to a nearby Jewish school. Soon after Joe's demobilization, she completed her paperwork to become naturalized, and she and my father ultimately became US citizens. She, Joe, and my father moved into their own apartment with relative speed, albeit an apartment in the same building as her husband's surviving siblings and their spouses. At home with Joe and Harry, she spoke Czech and Slovak. With my father, she spoke English to perfect her language skills. For much of her life, she participated in four communities: that of Jewish Slovakian refugees and immigrants, the modern Orthodox Jewish community of Yonkers (many of whose members were Czech or Slovak), Sophie's American-born family and

Arlene, Joe, and Gary Judd, undated.
From the author's private collection.

their business partners and friends, and my grandfather's few non-Jewish army buddies and their wives. There is no record of my grandmother or Anna joining local war bride clubs.

Finally, like that of the couples at the heart of *Between Two Worlds*, my grandparents' history underscores the messiness of memory. This is evident not only in their silences but also in the ways my grandmother reimagined and retold her past. The only detail she ever shared about her time on the ship was that Joe somehow managed to send oranges for my father, who was a picky eater.[11] Despite the fanciful nature of such a task, we never questioned her or the veracity of this tale. The historical record, however, elucidates that my father's oranges had nothing to do with his adoptive father. Rather, after the outbreak of the gastrointestinal disease on board the *Gibbins*, the medical staff ordered that citrus be distributed among the vulnerable children. We tell ourselves—and others—stories to make sense of our pasts and to give us ways to reconcile with them. By reimagining this innocuous story, my grandmother elevated and shifted Joe's role in their immigration narrative and deflected the fear that must have plagued her during the outbreak.

. . . .

It is a truism that marriage is complicated, and the marriages between the Jewish war brides and their spouses were no exception. Nor was that of my grandparents. I often am asked whether the couples I study were "successful," by which the questioner often means whether the couples remained married. I find the query fascinating, often telling me much about the questioner. Not only was divorce uncommon, but these Jewish war brides infrequently had family or previous homes to return to. Most couples remained married, at least through the 1940s and early 1950s. Some like Freide and Ruby, separated later, finding that their relationships were no longer viable as they—and their children—aged.[12] My grandparents remained married for almost forty years, until my grandfather's death. They were tremendously fond of one another: my grandfather never took for granted my grandmother's and father's survival, and my grandmother was steadfast in her appreciation for Joe and for the life in the United States that he made possible by marrying her. Both framed the war bride story as one that "saved" the lineage of the Judkowicz family. In their home, recovery and reconstruction focused on a deep affiliation with Jewish religious and cultural life, a hoped-for return to their middle-class origins, and the foods and languages of their childhood homes. It also rested on an agreed-upon silence concerning their traumatic pasts.

It was partly that tacitly agreed-upon silence that kept me quiet about my grandparents' story. But, like many of scholars of the Second World War and like the Jewish spouses themselves, I was complicit in the little attention paid to the Jewish war bride experience, focusing instead on larger narratives of the Holocaust. In researching and writing this book—as well as in unearthing information about my own family's past—I wanted to add a new dimension to how survivors and their families approached the thorny, complicated act of surviving in the aftermath of war. I hope *Between Two Worlds: Jewish War Brides after the Holocaust* has done justice to the women and men whose stories it tells while also highlighting the very messy, human nature of history.

ACKNOWLEDGMENTS

I could not have written *Between Two Worlds* without the stories, input, cups of tea, and advice from the Holocaust survivors, World War II veterans, ARC staff, and family members who opened their homes to me. I deeply regret that I could not publish this book in time to share it with Lala Fishman, Halina Horvitz, Judith Isaacson, Flory and Harry Jagoda, Arlene and Joe Judd, Manny Luttinger, Irene Orlaska, Bella and Ray Ostroff, Lily Schachter, Lydia Servetnick, Judith Summer, Alfred Tibor, Gena Turgel, or Gerda Weissmann Klein. Conversations with them and with Ann Kirschner, Susan Erlebacher, Dave Kasik, Elisabeth Petuchowski, Val Prestage, and Gershon Ron made this book better, and I am grateful for their time and insights.

I wrote *Between Two Worlds* as a faculty member at The Ohio State University. There, the Department of History, the Melton Center for Jewish Studies, the Center for Slavic and East European Studies, the College of Arts and Sciences, and the OSU Global Arts and Humanities Discovery Theme provided crucial support. Discussions with OSU colleagues (and friends) Bruno Cabanes, Clay Howard, Hasan Jeffries, Scott Levi, Pete Mansoor, Geoffrey Parker, Paul Reitter, Stephanie Smith, David Stebenne, and Dave Steigerwald improved this book. Zoom calls and text messages with Tina Sessa, Mytheli Sreenivas, and Ying Zhang kept me focused and supported. My undergraduate students made me want to write a book that they would want to read, and my graduate students weighed in and pushed me to think in new directions. I am particularly indebted to Darcy Benson, Nikki Freeman, Sara Halpern, Lauren Henry, and Renae Sullivan for their critical insights. Wendy Soltz assisted with early periodical research, and Carrie Esker swept in at just the right moment to assist with my bibliography.

Several institutions offered their support, and archivists, librarians, and scholars throughout the world aided me with their knowledge and expertise. My thanks to the American Council for Learned Societies, the Hadassah Brandeis Institute Research Award, the Hartmann Institute, and the American Jewish Archives. Presentations at Brandeis University, Miami University, the Jewish Theological Seminary, Salem State, the University of British Columbia (Vancouver), University of Edinburgh, University of Washington, University of Wisconsin (Milwaukee), Wellesley College, the US Holocaust Memorial Museum, the Milwaukee Jewish Museum, the Leo Baeck Institute, and the Museum of Jewish Heritage sharpened my thinking. I am grateful to Rhona and Ben Carniol, Ruth and Charles Dixter, Sara and David Dixter, Amy and Eric Fingerhut, Shelley Harten, Daniel Kapp, Joan and Jack McAvoy, Katie and Jon McAvoy, Dina Shiner, and Naomi and Burt Siegel for housing and feeding me.

An impressive number of scholars commented on conference papers and chapter drafts. These included Eliyana Adler, Alina Bothe, Katerina Capkova, Beth Cohen, David Feldman, Michael Flamm, Sylvia Fried, Judy Gerson, Ethan Katz, Patricia Kollander, Richard Menkis, Deborah Dash Moore, Jessica Rheinisch, Christine Schmidt, Eugene Sheppard, Ronit Stahl, Andrea Strutz, and Veerle Verden Daelen. I am particularly grateful to Pam Nadell, who first pushed me to think about writing a larger book for a crossover audience, and to her, Hasia Diner, Atina Grossmann, Marion Kaplan, Frances Malino, and Marsha Rozenblit for being remarkable mentors. My thanks, too, to Lila Corwin Berman, Christine Hayes, Laura Leibman, Ari Kelman, Jeffrey Shoulson, and Warren Hoffman who worked closely with me at the AJS.

This book benefited greatly from suggestions offered by UNC Press's two anonymous readers and from Debbie Gershenowitz's stewardship. She, JessieAnne D'Amico, Erin Granville, Alex Martin, and Lindsay Starr helped bring it to press. Amaryah Orenstein read every word, multiple times, and expressed unwavering belief in this project when my confidence waned. She is a brilliant warrior, reader, agent, and friend.

Between Two Worlds "survived" a freak tornado and disparate medical challenges for me and my family. Our village provided support, meals, groceries, and rides, and they continued to help during COVID and writing. Thank you to Ruth Adler, Andrea Berg, Ari Berger, David Bernstein, Naomi Brenner, Nick Breyfogle, Sara Butler, Daniel Frank, Rebecca Gurk, Jillian Gustin, Donna and Gordon Hecker, Elyse and Ron Less, Sharon Mars, Or Mars, Abby Maier, Dodie McDow, Jay and Bat-Ami Moses, Allison Norris, Amy and Marc Rotenberg, Leah Strigler, Lewis Warshauer, Isaac and Rayna

Weiner, Linda and Howard Zack, and Tali and Benny Zelkowicz. I am in-debted to physicians E. Batchos, M. Bechtel, S. Bowman-Burpee, R. Conroy, K. Epstein, B. Fahey, R. Rosenthal, W. Shiels (z'l), and M. Weber. They may never read this book, but their care allowed me to write it.

There are others who deserve recognition. Kristin Dykema Barbieri, Joel Berkowitz, Alice Conklin, Meg Malone, Maud Mandel, Margaret Newell, Kierra Crago Schneider, and Jodi R. R. Smith have supported me for decades. Since June 2020, monthly calls with my Shafer '90 sisters (particularly Holly Benton, Chris Bicknell, Suzy Brandzel, Amy Hespenheide, Lyn Harris, Erika Jenssen, Melissa Meredith, Laura Mills-Chen, Amy Putnam, and Kate Rut-ter) have uplifted my spirits. Birgitte Soland has been my champion ever since I arrived in Columbus with an energetic toddler and an exhausted husband. I wrote early drafts of *Between Two Worlds* at Theodora Dragostinova's table; she is a remarkable thought-partner, writing coach, and friend. Now that she has moved to Durham, fewer people mistake me for Jennifer Siegel, but she continues to have a transformative impact on my life. For over twenty years, Andrea Lourie and I have devoted Sunday mornings to walking, thinking, and being there for one another, while I have spent countless *shabbatot, cha-gim,* and weekdays with Natalie Cohen. I am fiercely cared for—sometimes even coddled by—Natalie and Dan Cohen and my other Columbus fami-lies-by-choice, Tobi and Ken Gold, Adam Davis and Alexandra Schimmer, and Steph and Andy Wapner. I could not love them more. I marvel at the relationships I have developed with their children and with Kendall Hecker. I am moved, too, by the love I have cultivated for the four-legged-creatures that have been a major part of our household: Porkchop, George, Stella, and Stanley.

No acknowledgment would be complete without recognizing the love and assistance of my family. Jeff, Jenn, Jason, Amy, Tova, Joseph, Samson, Sigal, and Mila and Mike, Dorothy, Jay, Gloria, Shai, Levi, and Yael provide me with tremendous support and friendship. Ted and Carol welcomed me into the fold of the Steinman family and have kept me nourished with good wine, fabulous clothing, and lots of love. I love that Jason and his family have grown up in such proximity to mine. Jenn helps me navigate the world. She is there when I need her, which is often; I hope I do the same for her. Rosalind and Gary Judd remain my models for how I want to parent, partner, and serve. My epilogue could not have been easy for my father to read, and yet he encouraged me to write it.

I am humbled by my sons who have grown up with this book project. Jesse and Gavi are compassionate, warm-hearted, empathetic men. May they one day know the glory of what it is like to love someone as intensely, as unconditionally, and as fiercely as I love them both.

This book is dedicated to Kenny, my kind, brilliant, funny husband whose genuine goodness continues to delight and inspire me. Together, we have tried to build a home centered on warmth, laughter, intellectual curiosity, and a desire to make this world a better place. For him, for our sons, and for all of my tremendous privilege, I am breathtakingly grateful.

NOTES

ABBREVIATIONS

ACFBP Papers of the American Committee for the Foreign-Born, Labadie
Collection, box 23, case file: Bilotta, James, University of Michigan
Library (Special Collections Library), Ann Arbor, Michigan

ACLUP American Civil Liberties Union Papers 1912–1990, MS Years of
Expansion, Knauff, Ellen (Deportation) 1948–1953, series 4, box 1483,
folder 96, Mudd Library, Princeton University, Princeton, New Jersey,
Gale Primary Sources, https://www.gale.com/intl/primary-sources

ADM Admiralty Record Cases ADM 116, National Archives,
Kew, Richmond, United Kingdom

AJA American Jewish Archives, Cincinnati, Ohio

AJHS American Jewish Historical Archives, New York City

AJHSB American Jewish Historical Society, Boston

BHL Bentley Historical Library, Ann Arbor, Michigan

CAHJP Central Archives for the History of the Jewish People, Jerusalem

CJA Alex Dworkin Canadian Jewish Archives, Montreal

CJC001 Canadian Jewish Congress Organizational Records, Alex
Dworkin Canadian Jewish Archives, Montreal

FBIC Central Records Center 100-BS-12931, National
Archives, College Park, Maryland

FBIT Transfer Call 421, 100-HQ 328147, section 1, National
Archives, College Park, Maryland

HC Deb House of Commons Debates, London

ITS International Tracing Service Collection, Weiner Library, London

IWM Imperial War Museum, London

JCRA Jewish Committee for Relief Abroad, Papers,
WL 1232, Wiener Library, London

JDCJ Joint Distribution Committee Archives, Jerusalem

JPL   Jewish Public Library, Montreal

JWB   Records of the JWB Chaplaincy I-249, series VI, American
Jewish Historical Archives, New York City

LBI   Leo Baeck Institute, New York City

LMA   London Metropolitan Archive, City of London

NACP   National Archives College Park, College Park, Maryland

NAK   The National Archives, Kew, Richmond, United Kingdom

NJWB   National Jewish Welfare Board I-337, subgroup III, series B,
American Jewish Historical Society, New York City

NYPL   New York Public Library, New York City

RG24-C-1-a   Directorate of Repatriation, Library and Archives of Canada, Ottawa

UPT   University of Pennsylvania Archives and Records Center, Philadelphia

USHMM   United States Holocaust Memorial and Museum, Washington, DC

USNA   United Service for New Americans Inc., New York City

WHB   William Haber Collection, Collection, 85198, Bentley
Historical Library, Ann Arbor, Michigan

WJC   World Jewish Congress Records MS-361, Series D,
American Jewish Archives, Cincinnati, Ohio

WL   Wiener Library, London

WRJ   Women of Reform Judaism MS-73, American
Jewish Archives, Cincinnati, Ohio

YVA   Yad Vashem Archives, Jerusalem

INTRODUCTION

1. *This Is Your Life* began as a radio show in the late 1940s to help returning World War II veterans, especially paraplegics, and, as such, first profiled returning heroes. By 1952, the radio show had become a popular television show. "About," *This Is Your Life*, http://www.thisisyourlife.com/, accessed February 15, 2023.

2. "This Is Your Life, Hanna Kohner," 0:02–25:18. For narrative purposes, after first mention, I refer to individuals by their first name.

3. Shandler, *While America Watches*; Shandler, "This Is Your Life." Of the three Holocaust survivors featured by *This Is Your Life*, two immigrated to the United States as war brides. The second military spouse honored also was a survivor of the Holocaust and a man. In February 1954, the show feted Cantor Gregor "Greg" Shelkan, who had been born in Latvia and survived the Riga ghetto and four different Nazi camps. Gregor immigrated to the United States as a war bride. Shelkan, interview 15025; "Cantor Gregor Shelkan," *This Is Your Life*, http://www.thisisyourlife.com/search/160709TL98334900_5348.html, accessed February 14, 2023.

4. Kohner, Kohner, and Kohner, *Hanna and Walter*. Hanna's brother reunited with her on *This Is Your Life*. On Gottfried Bloch, see Bloch, interview 107.

5. On émigré soldiers more generally, see Kollander, "Reflections on the Experience of German Émigré Soldiers"; and Reinisch, *The Perils of Peace*, esp. chap. 3.

6. See, e.g., Sabloff, "How Pre-modern State Rulers Used Marriage."

7. The territories and lands of nineteenth-century Canada tended to follow the laws of England when it came to matrimony, including the marriages of Canadians living or serving abroad. Raney, *Marriage and Divorce Laws of Canada*.

8. During the nineteenth century, only single men were permitted to enlist in the British Army, and British officers were encouraged to deny permission to those individuals who requested the right to marry. "Army, February 27, 1907," *Parliamentary Debates*, 85–86; Hurl-Eamon, *Marriage and the British Army*; Lomas, "'Delicate Duties.'"

9. Zeiger, *Entangling Alliances*, 3.

10. Until 1938, the marriage allowance for soldiers on the Married Quarters Roll of their units varied, according to the man's rate of pay and length of service. Brereton, *The British Soldier*, 159.

11. Between 1917 and 1919, dependents of Canadian soldiers received a special rate on a secure ship for their passage to Canada. After 1919, they received free third-class passage. While there is no official number of war brides who married Canadian soldiers during the First World War, scholars estimate that approximately 54,000 individuals accompanied the troops who were returning to Canada after their demobilization. Repatriation Committee, *Information for Wives of Soldiers*.

12. Branstetter, "Family Law," 7; Zeiger, *Entangling Alliances*, 13–37.

13. Scholars have not yet considered ethnicity and religion when studying the war brides of World War I.

14. Canadian soldiers began to petition for approval of their marriages almost immediately after Canada entered World War II in September 1939. The first such marriage took place on January 28, 1940. Jarratt, *War Brides*, 15.

15. Girard, "If Two Ride a Horse"; Wolgin and Bloemraad, "'Our Gratitude,'" 53–54.

16. These early laws gave no consideration to the war or reconstruction in the Pacific. Eventually, the war bride legislation created a new discourse that would "gradually substitute a discourse of family for the previous one of race." Wolgin and Bloemraad, "'Our Gratitude,'" 29. Also see Friedman, *Citizenship in Cold War America*, chap. 2; and Zeiger, *Entangling Alliances*.

17. HC Deb, December 7, 1951, vol. 494, cols. 2755–65, Historic Hansard Commons, https://api.parliament.uk/historic-hansard/commons/1951/dec/07/british-soldiers -german-wives. Also see Knowles, *Winning the Peace*.

18. Wolgin and Bloemraad, "'Our Gratitude,'" 27–60, esp. 55.

19. Nakano Glenn, *Issei, Nisei, War Bride*; Lee, *At America's Gates*.

20. Philip Wolgin and Irene Bloemraad argue that Canadian war bride debates focused much more on *when* the women might enter Canada and not *whether* they ought to enter. Wolgin and Bloemraad, "'Our Gratitude,'" 55.

21. The scholarship is extensive. Some of the work on which I rely includes Berkowitz, *The Crime of My Very Existence*; Crago Schneider, "Jewish 'Shtetls' in Postwar Germany"; Grossmann, *Jews, Germans, and Allies*; Lavsky, *New Beginnings*; and Patt, *Finding Home*.

22. On British war brides, see Friedman, *From the Battlefront*; Goodman, "'Only the Best British Brides'"; Jarratt, *War Brides*; Rose, *Which People's War?*; Virden, *Good-bye Piccadilly*; Winfield and Wilson Hasty, *Sentimental Journey*. On the war brides in the Pacific, see Nakano

Glenn, *Issei, Nisei, War Bride*. On German and Austrian brides, see Bauer, "Austria's Prestige"; Bauer, "Frauen, Männer, Beziehungen"; and Höhn, *GIs and Fräuleins*. Two studies that concern multiple places of origin are Wolgin and Bloemraad, "'Our Gratitude'"; and Zeiger, *Entangling Alliances*. War bride memoirs and memoir collections include Ward Crawford, Hayashi, and Suenaga, *Japanese War Brides in America*; Hennessy, *The Bride and the Beetle*; Kaiser, *French War Brides*; and Kneeland, *Paulette*.

23. National Federation of Temple Sisterhoods, Transcript of Conference, February 26, 1945, WRJ, box 21, folder 2, AJA.

24. On the term "survivor," see Bothe and Nesselrodt, "Survivor"; Michman, *Holocaust Historiography*, 329; and Orgad, "The Survivor in Contemporary Culture." I appreciate the time that Dr. Bothe spent with me on email and Skype.

25. Bothe and Nesselrodt, "Survivor," 64.

26. General Assembly, "Resolutions Adopted on the Reports of the Third Committee," December 15, 1946, UN Refugee Agency, https://www.unhcr.org/en-us/excom/bgares/3ae69ef14/refugees-displaced-persons.html.

27. Orgad, "The Survivor in Contemporary Culture," 134.

28. Bothe and Nesselrodt, "Survivor," 61; Arendt, *Eichmann in Jerusalem*, 223.

29. Other shifts took place as well. The many different national restitution and reparation processes used their own specific definitions of survival and victimhood, while the push to record and share Holocaust testimony focused attention on individual survivor experiences. Bothe and Nesselrodt, "Survivor."

30. Flory Jagoda, interview by author, February 3, 2009, Alexandria, VA (hereafter Flory Jagoda, interview by author).

31. I lack the research languages to study the spouses of Soviet soldiers, and I do not examine them or the marriages in the Pacific. I also worried that expanding my study in this way would push the project in unwanted directions.

32. This book only studies those fiancées who eventually married their partners.

33. Zeiger, *Entangling Alliances*, 3.

34. Most war brides were women. I try to introduce the stories of male war brides, but I found far less material on them.

35. Shaye Cohen, *The Beginnings of Jewishness*.

36. "Drippy Chicago Is Homelike to British Brides," *Chicago Tribune*, February 6, 1946, 8; Jean Komaiko, "A War Bride Looks at America: Polish Born Wife of Ex-GI Sees Nothing But the Good in Her Adopted Country," *Chicago Tribune*, June 5, 1955, 35. I identified couples by researching wedding announcements, chaplains' reports, newspaper articles, obituaries, ship logs, war bride club newsletters, and memoirs. I also identified some by placing classified advertisements in different Jewish newspapers.

37. Gerda Weissmann Klein's 1957 *All but My Life* was the first Holocaust memoir published by a Jewish war bride. Also see Fox, *My Heart in a Suitcase*; Isaacman, *Clara's Story*; Isaacson, *Seed of Sarah*; Fishman and Weingartner, *Lala's Story*; Rose, *The Tulips Are Red*; and Turgel, *I Light a Candle*. These publications were in English. On the use of English in Holocaust memory-making, see Matthäus, "Displacing Memory."

38. For an erudite discussion of the worthiness of testimonies in crafting historical studies of the Holocaust, see Browning, *Collected Memories*; Greenspan, "The Awakening of Memory"; Hartman, *Holocaust Remembrance*; and Langer, *Holocaust Testimonies*.

39. Dean, *The Moral Witness*, 20; Popkin, "From Displaced Persons to 'Secular Saints.'"

40. Gardner, *The Qualities of a Citizen*, 224.

CHAPTER ONE

1. They also were prohibited from marrying non-Jews. See Tomasevich, *War and Revolution in Yugoslavia*; Zakić, *Ethnic Germans and National Socialism*; Goldstein and Goldstein, *The Holocaust in Croatia*; and Flory Jagoda, interview by author. For more on Jagoda, see Jagoda, interview by Ringleheim; and Jagoda, interview by Bass.

2. Flory Jagoda, interview by author.

3. The interment of Jews on the island of Korčula predated Mussolini's November 1942 order for the imprisonment of Jews in Italian-occupied Croatia. There were two internment camps on the island: one in the village of Korčula and one in the village of Vela Luka (Valle Grande). See Hoppe, "Curzola Island"; and Tomasevich, *War and Revolution in Yugoslavia*, 600–602.

4. Flory Jagoda, interview by author.

5. Bonder, interview 40845, segment 132.

6. Engelking and Leociak, *The Warsaw Ghetto*; Prais, *Displaced Persons at Home*.

7. Bonder, interview 40845, segment 132.

8. She knew that one of her sisters had emigrated to Palestine.

9. Bonder, interview 40845, segments 131–33.

10. I am influenced by the recent scholarship, which has offered more nuanced interpretations of this period. It has challenged the chronology of the Holocaust's end, paid attention to regional distinctions, and looked closely at Jews in Axis-controlled territories outside of Europe. See, e.g., Adler, *Jews and Gender in Liberation France*; Bardgett and Cesarani, *Belsen 1945*; Hitchcock, *The Bitter Road to Freedom*; and Stone, *The Liberation of the Camps*. For a global microhistory outside of Europe, see Sara Halpern's recent dissertation, "Saving the Unwanted." Recent, more traditional histories of liberation can be found in Blank, *Bitter Ends*; Celinscak, *Distance from the Belsen Heap*; and McManus, *Hell before Their Very Eyes*.

11. In 1943 the Jews of Tunisia were liberated, anti-Jewish laws in Algeria were cancelled, and French citizenship for Algerian Jews was reinstated.

12. Several of the liberated camps had fewer prisoners in number because the Nazis already had tried to murder or move those populations; this was particularly true of the camps liberated by the Soviets.

13. Isaacman, interview 24614.

14. Robert S. Marcus, memo, May 12, 1945, WJC, box 64, folder 3, AJA. Paris Papamichos Chronakis has made clear that while many victims and perpetrators used the category of "Greek" to describe groups of individuals, that usage overlooked the national and ethnic diversity among them. Papamichos Chronakis, "We Lived as Greeks."

15. Turgel, interview 39187, segments 160–62; Bonder, interview 40845, segments 132–34.

16. Flory Jagoda, interview by author. When the Allies first invaded Italy in July 1943, they moved slowly from Sicily to Reggio (British Eighth Army) and Salerno (US Fifth Army). Italian authorities declared an armistice with the Allied Forces in September 1943 but the fighting against the Germans continued for nearly two years. Overy, *The Bombers and Bombed*, 318–60.

17. The neighbors had not known that Jews were hiding on Stadion Street.

18. Isaacman, interview 24614, segments 43–44. On the bombings, see Overy, *The Bombers and Bombed*, 424–25; Veranneman de Watervliet, *Belgium in the Second World War*. On the physical damages of the war, see Lowe, *Savage Continent*, 3–11.

19. Allan Allport has argued that the last days of the war were particularly horrific because many Wehrmacht troops continued fighting even after delegates from the de facto Nazi capital in Flensburg surrendered. Allport, *Demobbed*, 6.

20. SHAEF was dissolved on July 14, 1945. Over the course of the spring and summer, the control over these camps shifted from the military command to the UN Relief and Rehabilitation Association (UNRRA). Armstrong-Reid and Murray, *Armies of Peace*; Dinnerstein, "The US Army and the Jews"; Reinisch, "Internationalism in Relief"; Shepard, *The Long Road Home*; Salvatici, "'Help the People.'"

21. A corollary to the Yalta agreement stipulated that all Soviet prisoners of war (POWs) and civilians be repatriated to the USSR.

22. There, they lived among members of their assumed-shared nationality. Polish Jewish DPs might be living alongside Polish non-Jews; Hungarian-born Jewish DPs alongside displaced Hungarian non-Jews.

23. In addition to some of the works cited above, see Holian, "The Ambivalent Exception."

24. Margarete Myers Feinstein argues that the housing crisis in Germany brought these disparate groups into intimate contact with one another. Myers Feinstein, "All under One Roof."

25. In the immediate postwar period, Allied Forces asserted a moral order for housing priorities: victors, victims, refugees, and politically untainted Germans, at the bottom. See, e.g., Cunningham-Sabot and Fol, "Shrinking Cities"; Myers Feinstein, "All under One Roof"; Heynen, "Belgium and the Netherlands"; Nasiali, "Citizens, Squatters, and Asocials."

26. Shepard, "'Becoming Planning Minded.'" As Paul Weindling has shown, frontline Allied troops expected an epidemic. British troops wore uniforms that included DDT, established delousing stations, and were supplied with DDT powder. Weindling, *Epidemics and Genocide*, 373–81.

27. American Jewish Joint Distribution Committee, "Workbook"; Glyn Hughes, "Belsen Concentration Camp: Appendix B," April 15–18, 1945, Collections of the Office of the Chief Rabbi, ACC 2805/05/05/01, LMA. On medical concerns in Bergen-Belsen, see Celinscak, *Distance from the Belsen Heap*, 162–68; Lavsky, *New Beginnings*, 44–45; Shepard, "The Medical Relief Effort at Belsen"; and Weindling, "Belsenitis."

28. In Belsen, both typhus and typhoid existed, and it is possible that Gena's mother suffered from typhoid. Ironically, typhus had been the pretext the Germans gave for ghettoization.

29. The Red Army declared the ghetto-camp of Theresienstadt (Terezin) a quarantine zone on May 14, 1945. They had liberated the ghetto-camp on May 9, 1945. Stone, *The Liberation of the Camps*, 57–61.

30. Bonder, interview 40845, segments 131–35.

31. Bonder, interview 40845, segments 131–35 and 141; Bonder, interview 54741, segment 97.

32. As scholars have demonstrated, rape became a part of the "social history of the Soviet zone." Grossmann, "A Question of Silence," 53. Also see Baldwin, "Sexual Violence and the

Holocaust," 121; Dror and Linn, "The Shame Is Always There," 277–78; Levenkron, "'Death and the Maidens,'" 18–19; Sander and Johr, *Befreier und Befreite*; Jeges, "Gendering the Cultural Memory of the Holocaust," 250.

33. Sala Bonder, interview 40845, segments 135 and 141.

34. Grossmann, "A Question of Silence," 53.

35. The works of Mary Lou Roberts, Peter Schrijvers, and Paul Jackson are particularly significant here. While Roberts and Schrikjvers set out to study occupation practices in continental Europe, Jackson's book examines the struggle of queer servicemen in the Canadian military. Roberts, *What Soldiers Do*, 76–77; Schrijvers, *Liberators*, 229–30; Jackson, *One of the Boys*, 84, 90, and 237–38. Also see Herzog, "European Sexualities"; and Pratt, "Medicine and Obedience," 81–82.

36. Flory Jagoda, interview by author.

37. Daniel Isaacman, letter, March 26, 1945, 50/173, box 2, folder 3, UPT. Daniel's Zionist movement called for the redemption of the Jewish people in the land of Israel (*Eretz Yisrael*) through the revival of the Hebrew language and manual labor.

38. Robert S. Marcus to Stephen S. Wise, letter, April 17, 1945, WJC, box 64, folder 3, AJA. Also see Robert S. Marcus, memo, May 12, 1945, WJC, box 64, folder 3, AJA.

39. Herbert S. Eskin, Chaplain Report (June), July 10, 1945, NJWB, box 55, file Eskin, AJHS; Myer Hendelman to Bert Klausner, letter, January 24, 1945, CJC001, DA 18, box 5, folder 15, CJA; Ernst M. Lorge to Judah Nadich, letter, May 1, 1945, WJC, box 65, folder 1; Abraham Klausner to Central Office, US Army, letter, July 22, 1945, P68, I, CAHJP. Founded in 1917, the National Jewish Welfare Board (NJWB) provided support for soldiers; it oversaw the Jewish chaplaincy and on-leave morale and recreational needs of the Armed Forces. See Cooperman, *Making Judaism Safe for America*; and Slomovitz, *The Fighting Rabbis*.

40. In her work, Rebecca Clifford similarly notes that with the end of the war, survivors shifted their orientation from the present to the future. Clifford, *Survivors*, 17.

41. Isaacson, *Seed of Sarah*, 117.

42. Isaacson, interview by Eule and Platz.

43. Turgel, interview 39187, segment 127.

44. Weissmann Klein, interview by Ringelheim.

45. Gerda Weissmann to Leo Weissmann, letter, July 2, 1945, in Weissmann Klein and Klein, *The Hours After*, 44.

46. Isaacson, interview by Eule and Platz; also see Isaacson, interview RG-50.227.0006.

47. Isaacman, *Clara's Story*, 74. Also see Anthony, *Compromise of Return*; Auslander, "Coming Home"; Fogg, "Everything Had Ended"; and Krzyzanowski, *Ghost Citizens*.

48. Flory Jagoda, interview by author; Jagoda, interview by Ringelheim.

49. The largest of the anti-Jewish pogroms took place in July 1946 in Kielce, a city in southeastern Poland. Checinski, "The Kielce Pogrom"; Prazmowska, "The Kielce Pogrom 1946"; Tokarska-Bakir, *Pogrom Cries*.

50. Bonder, interview 54741, segment 110; Bonder, interview 40845, segment 161.

51. Herbert Friedman to Charles Rosenbaum, telegram, September 11, 1946, Herbert A. Friedman Papers, MS-763, series A, box 1, folder 4, AJA. On Friedman, see Deblinger, "'In a World Still Trembling.'"

52. Philip S. Bernstein to General McNarney, letter, June 29, 1946, WHB, AA 2, box 20, BHL. Bernstein later served as executive director of CANRA.

53. UNRRA, "General Situation," 6. Also see Königseder, *Flucht nach Berlin*; Königseder and Wetzel, *Lebensmut im Wartesaal*.

54. Judah Nadich, "Report on Conditions of Jews in Berlin," September 16, 1945, JWB, box 22, folder 141. Also see "US Army Aids Refugee Jews in German Zone," *Chicago Tribune*, August 26, 1945, 18; and "Refugees in Berlin," *Berlin Air Line*, December 26, 1945, EJ 5407, IWM.

55. There were forty-five DP camps in the British zone. Bergen-Belsen was the largest, with the greatest number of Jewish DPs. The Hanover Ohestrasse camp was made up mostly of Jewish labor camp survivors. On the Jewish DPs in the British zone, see Lavsky, *New Beginnings*.

56. Pfanzelter, "Between Brenner and Bari," 84; Voigt, *Zuflucht auf Widerruf*, 425.

57. Through much of the spring of 1945, the camps were administered by the UN Relief and Rehabilitation Association (UNRRA), an organization created during the war to repatriate and assist refugees. By the end of the summer, many of their administrations were transferred to other authorities.

58. Pfanzelter, "Between Brenner and Bari," 103.

59. Judith Isaacson, interview by Eule and Platz, 38.

60. Turgel, interview 39187, segment 132.

61. Turgel, "Norman's Chapter."

62. Horvitz, interview by Krulik.

63. Daniel Isaacman to his parents, letter, December 4, 1944, MS-410, box 1, folder 3, AJA; also see Daniel Isaacman to his parents, letter, January 1, 1945, 50/173, box 2, folder 1, UPT.

64. Charlie A. to/from Jack Eisen, letters, February–July 1945, CJCoo1, DA 18, box 23, folder 4, CJA. For privacy purposes, I sometimes use only an initial for the last name.

65. "Was it the pain or the anticipation or both that kept me from clearly recognizing the coming peril?" Kurt wondered. Kurt Klein to Gerda Weissmann Klein, letter, September 15, 1945, in Weissmann Klein and Klein, *The Hours After*, 74–75.

66. Klein, interview by Kuzmack; Klein, interview by Bradley.

67. Klein, interview by Kuzmack.

68. Klein, interview by Kuzmack.

69. Dave B. to Jack Eisen, letter, May 4, 1945, CJCoo1, DA 18, box 23, folder 5, CJA; also see Jack Eisen to Dave B., letter, May 10, 1945, CJCoo1, DA 18, box 23, folder 5, CJA.

70. Bernard B. Cohen to Estelle, letter, April 21, 1945, 0.75, folder 483, item 3540223, YVA.

71. Stone, *The Liberation of the Camps*, 38.

72. Cecil Hornbeck to Hazel Hornbeck, letter, May 6, 1945, O.33, folder 3308, YVA.

73. Akiva Skidell, letter, April 18, 1945, 0.75, folder 139, item 1576, YVA.

74. Unknown author to Faige, letter, May 1945, MS-54, box 3, folder 15, AJA.

75. Harold Saperstein to congregants, letter, December 26, 1944, MS-718, box 8, folder 3, AJA. See Celinscak, *Distance from the Belsen Heap*; Goedde, *GIs and Germans*, 69; Grossmann, *Jews, Germans, and Allies*; and Dash Moore, *GI Jews*. This offered a sharp contrast to UNNRA personnel and to the employees and volunteers of the twenty-three separate voluntary welfare agencies that UNRRA administered, many of whom could not arrive in Europe until late in the summer of 1945. Organizations under UNRRA administration included the Jewish Joint Distribution Committee (JDC), the Hebrew Immigrant Aid Society (HIAS), and the Organization for Rehabilitation through Training (ORT). In late 1945, as

the displaced persons camps received greater autonomy, the voluntary agencies increasingly functioned independently. American Jewish Joint Distribution Committee, "Workbook."

76. Daniel Isaacman to parents, letter, December 4, 1944, MS-410, box 1, folder 3, AJA.

77. Louis Milgrom, June and July 1945 reports, NJWB, box 86, folder 5, AJHS.

78. B. M. Casper to J. H. Hertz, letter, October 18, 1945, Collections of the Office of the Chief Rabbi, ACC 2805/05/01/04, LMA.

79. Herman Dicker, "Recollections of Liberation," *Jewish Chaplain*, November–December 1944, supplement ii–iii. Also see David Max Einhorn to Phil Bernstein, letter, July 13, 1945, NJWB, box 53, folder 5, AJHS; Eugene Lipman to Phil Bernstein, letter, July 1945, NJWB, box 82, folder 3, AJHS.

80. See, e.g., the exchange of letters between Kurt R. Grossman, Committee for Overseas Relief Supplies, and Chaplain Eli Bohnen, WJC, box 65, folder 1, AJA; and American Jewish Joint Distribution Committee, *So They May Live Again*. In fact, Allied Authorities and Jewish communal leaders expressed concern that the chaplains devoted too much time to the DPs and not enough time to the GIs. Leo Jacobs to John Sills, letter, September 3, 1946, I-180, series 6, box 188, folder Austria, AJHS; Aryeh Lev to Mayer Abramowitz, letter, December 24, 1946, NJWB, box 42, folder 7, AJHS; Charlie Appel to Jack Eisen, letter, July 23, 1945, CJC001, DA 18, box 23, folder 4, CJA.

81. Eugene Lipman to Phil Bernstein, letter, July 1945, NJWB, box 82, folder 3, AJHS. Also see Abraham Spiro, report, December 17, 1945, NJWB, box 105, folder 8, AJHS; Abraham Klausner to Sarah Friedman, letter, June 21, 1945, Abraham Klausner Papers, P-879, box 1, folder 1, AJHS; American Jewish Joint Distribution Committee, *So They May Live Again*. On Jewish, Catholic, and Protestant chaplains' reaction to the horrors of war, see Stahl, *Enlisting Faith*, 139–43. Also see Grobman, *Rekindling the Flame*; and Levi, *Breaking New Ground*.

82. Reuben Isaacman to Daniel, letter, January 4, 1945, 50/173, box 2 folder 1, UPT.

83. Abe Bonder to Jack Eisen, letter, October 10, 1945, CJC001, DA 18, box 23, folder 5a, CJA.

84. Kurt Klein to Gerda Weissmann, letter, September 15, 1945, in Weissmann Klein and Klein, *The Hours After*, 75.

85. Daniel Isaacman to parents, letter, April 23, 1945, 50/173, box 2 folder 4, UPT.

86. Daniel Isaacman to parents, letter, April 11, 1945, 50/173, box 2 folder 4, UPT.

87. Dave B. to Eisen, letter, July 30, 1945, CJC001, DA 18, box 23, folder 5, CJA.

88. Roberts shows that while the policy may have formally discouraged fraternization, the practice on the ground was quite different. Roberts, *What Soldiers Do*, 108. Also see Christofferson, *France during World War II*, 181–82.

89. Miri Kugelman, "Report on Countries Other than Germany: Holland," April 5, 1945, JCRA, HA15–2/7, WL.

90. "Directive to the Supreme Commander, Allied Expeditionary Force in Respect of Military Government in Germany for the Pre-surrender Period," May 15, 1944 (London), Department of State, Office of the Historian, https://history.state.gov/historicaldocuments /frus1944v01/d112, accessed October 25, 2017; Jane Levenson, "Report on the Jews in Belgium for the Jewish Committee for Relief Abroad," March 1945, JCRA, HA6A, folder: Jews in Germany, file: Relief Workers Reports, WL.

91. Sydney D. to Jack Eisen, letter, January 18, 1945, CJC001, DA 18, box 23, folder 7, CJA.

92. Bernard Law Montgomery, "Message to 21 Army Group re Non-fraternization," March 1945, NAM 1998–02–30–11, National Army Museum Chelsea, https://collection.nam.ac.uk/detail.php?acc=1998–02–30–11, accessed October 25, 2017; Bernard Law Montgomery, "Letter no. 3 by the Commander in Chief on Non-fraternisation," National Army Museum London, https://collection.nam.ac.uk/detail.php?acc=1996–01–30–2, accessed May 31, 2018.

93. Harold I. Saperstein, letter, April 11, 1945, MS-718, box 8, folder 3, AJA; O'Donnell to Guterbock, letter, May 15, 1945, ADM, file 5370, NAK; "Conclusions of a Meeting of the Cabinet Held at No. 10 Downing St.," July 6, 1945, ADM, file 5370, NAK; "Brief for British Representative on Item 10 of the Agenda: Uniform Regulations on Fraternisation," September 19, 1945, FO 1032, file 1367, NAK; "Memo from the Office of the Chief of Staff, British Zone, to Staff Standard Distribution List," September 24, 1945, FO 1032, file 1367, NAK; "Policy for Non Fraternisation; Draft Issued by the Office of the Allied Secretariat," September 26, 1945, FO 1032, file 1367, NAK; J. Eisen to F. Bassin, letter, September 29, 1945, CJCoo1, DA 18, box 23, file 5b, CJA; Office of the Chief of Staff, British Zone, "Memo from the Office of the Chief of Staff British Zone: Subject Fraternisation," October 1, 1945, FO 1032, file 1367, NAK; "Allow Frauleins in ARC Clubs? Army Is Thinking It Over," *Stars and Stripes*, December 11, 1945, 4; "Red Cross Says No to Frauleins," *Stars and Stripes*, January 24, 1946, 4.

94. B. Bronsohn, letter, November 16, 1945, CJCoo1, DA 18, box 7, folder 7, CJA; "Anti-frat Campaign in Reich Proves a Flop!," *Stars and Stripes*, June 11, 1945, 1; Nadeane Walker, "Meet Some GIs Who Won't Fraternize," *Stars and Stripes*, November 30, 1945, 4; "Frauleins v. WAAF," *Berlin Air Line* 7, December 26, 1945, EJ 5407, IWM. Scholars of fraternization have paid significant attention to these so-called infractions and their meanings in wartime and postwar society. Bauer, "Austria's Prestige"; Bauer, "Frauen, Männer, Beziehungen," 104–7; Biddiscombe, "Dangerous Liaisons"; Esser, "'Language No Obstacle'"; Höhn, *GIs and Fräuleins*; Kleinschmidt, *Do Not Fraternize*; Pfau, *Miss Yourlovin*.

95. H. H. Newman to Commanding General, European Theater of Operations, Confidential Memo, November 25, 1944, RG 498, box 31, folder 291.1, NACP. Also see "Minutes of 2 December 1943," RG 200, folder 618.4, NACP; Jane Levenson, "Report on the Jews in Belgium for the Jewish Committee for Relief Abroad," March 1945, JCRA, HA6A, folder: Jews in Germany, file: Relief Workers Reports, WL; "Office of the Theater Chaplain Information Sheet," January 26, 1945, David M. Eichhorn Papers MS-79, box 12, folder 2, AJA.

96. Vida, *From Doom to Dawn*, 22.

97. Philip Bernstein to Aryeh Lev, letter, July 10, 1945, NJWB, box 76, folder 11, AJHS.

98. Herbert S. Eskin, report, June 1945, NJWB, box 55, folder 15, AJHS. By September, Eskin reported that the policy had been lifted "somewhat." Herbert S. Eskin, report, September 1945, NJWB, box 55, folder 15, AJHS. Also see Bert Steinberg to Herman E. Snyder, letter, May 23, 1945, Herman Eliot Snyder Papers MS-598, box 18, folder 6, AJA; Jack Eisen to F. B., letter, September 29, 1945, CJCoo1 DA 18, box 23, file 5b, CJA.

99. Jewish Hospitality Committee for British and Allied Forces, reports, April and May 1945, CJCoo1, DA 18, box 7, folder 1, CJA; Arieh Tartakower to Luther D. Miller, letter, June 25, 1945, WJC, box 65, folder 1, AJA.

100. Taylor, "'Please Report Only *True* Nationalities,'" 40–41. Interestingly, by 1947, all spheres of influence agreed that the term "German" ought to be defined as "all persons who, during the war, lived in Germany of their own free will." William Haber to Meir Grossman,

letter, June 10, 1948, WHB, AA 2, box 20, BHL; "Inter Service Instruction on Relations with Germans, includes Appendix A," May 22, 1947, FO 1032/1367, NAK; Lestchinsky to Wahraftig, memo, May 9, 1947, WJC, box 64, folder 9, AJA; American Jewish Conference, "The Future of the Legal Position of the Jewish DP's in Germany," WJC, box 16, folder 6, AJA; Louis Levinthal, "Comments on I & E Bulletins," October 31, 1947, WHB, AA 2, box 20, BHL.

101. Dan Stone defines "elderly" survivors as those fifty-five or older. Stone, "'Somehow.'"

102. Bonder, interview 40845, segments 134–49.

CHAPTER TWO

1. Bonder, interview 40845, segments 149–51; Bonder, interview 54741, segments 112–14.

2. Abe Bonder and Jack Eisen, letters, May 10–October 16, 1945, CJC001, DA 18, box 23, folder 5, CJA.

3. Bella Lewkowicz Ostroff and Ray Ostroff, interview by author, March 16, 2009, Philadelphia (hereafter Ostroff and Ostroff, interview by author).

4. Confino, *A World without Jews*.

5. Bernard B. Cohen to his parents, letter, March 31, 1945, O.75, file number 483, item 3540223, YVA; Herman Dicker, "Recollections of Liberation," *Jewish Chaplain*, November–December 1944, supplement ii–iii. Also see David Max Einhorn to Philip Bernstein, letter, July 13, 1945, NJWB, box 53, folder 4, AJHS; Eugene Lipman to Philip Bernstein, letter, July 1945, NJWB, box 82, folder 3, AJHS.

6. Weissmann Klein, interview by Ringelheim.

7. On persistent trauma, see Erikson, *A New Species of Trouble*, 228; Leys, "Image and Trauma"; and Martz, introduction to *Trauma Rehabilitation*, 6–8.

8. Turgel, "Norman's Chapter"; Turgel, *I Light a Candle*, 159.

9. Turgel, *I Light a Candle*, 159; Turgel, interview 39187, segments 160–62.

10. Harry told me he extended the invitation at the suggestion of the British captain with whom he was friendly. Harry Jagoda, interview by author, February 3, 2009, Alexandria, VA.

11. Flory Jagoda, interview by author. Harry Jagoda, interview by author. Kurt Klein and Gerda Weissmann likewise shared a palatable version of their meeting. Klein, interview by Bradley; Weissmann Klein, interview 9725, segments 114–17. Also see Mogan, interview 6666, segments 47–48. Different accounts describe the structure as a factory, shed, and shack.

12. Lala Fishman, interview by author, March 12, 2009, Skokie, IL (hereafter Fishman, interview by author).

13. Judith Summer, interview by author, March 23, 2008, Columbus, OH (hereafter Summer, interview by author); Judith Summer, interview, Columbus Jewish Historical Society, http://columbusjewishhistory.org/oral_histories/judith-summer/, accessed March 26, 2018. When individuals share the same given name, I refer to them by first name and last initial after the first appearance of their full name. So, for example, Judith Summer (née Lederer) becomes simply Judith S. and Judith Magyar Isaacson becomes Judith I.; Sala Bonder (née Solarcz) becomes Sala B. and Sala Kirschner (née Garncarz) becomes Sala K.

14. Flaschka, "Only Pretty Women," 77–78.

15. I did not find examples of refugee soldiers being reunited with loved ones in North Africa.

16. Morris Frank to Florence Frank, letter, January 16, 1945, SC-15430, AJA; Max B. Wall, report, October 1945, NJWB, box 110, folder 26, AJHS; Abraham Spiro, report, December 17, 1945, NJWB, box 105, folder 8, AJHS. There also were cases of reunited partners discovering that the other had remarried. See, e.g., Rose L. Henriques to Rabbi Munk, letter, October 3, 1947, JCRA, HA21–5/23, Miscellaneous: Colonel Solomon's Files, File: Marriages and Deaths, 1946–7, WL.

17. Kohner, Kohner, and Kohner, *Hanna and Walter*, 138–45.

18. Meyer J. Goldman, report, December 1945, NJWB, box 62, folder 6; Pertz (Perry) Milbauer, letter, July 31, 1945, MS-828, box 2, AJA; Ruth Landau, autograph book, 1945, 1849/3, Ruth Kupfer folder, WL; Susan Erlebacher, telephone conversation with author, February 20, 2009.

19. See, e.g., Morris Frank to Florence Frank, letter, May 9, 1945, SC 15430, AJA.

20. Bergman, interview 26752.

21. Jack Eisen to Dave S., July 23, 1945, CJC001, DA 18, box 23, folder 5; Bert A. Klein to Aryeh Lev, letter, October 18, 1946, NJWB, box 71, file Klein, AJHS; Cohen, interview 11.

22. Daniel Isaacman to his parents, letter, April 15, 1945, 50/173, box 2, folder 4, UPT. On his first introducing them, see his letter from April 11, 1945, in the same collection. For other examples, see Horvitz, interview by Krulik; Brenda Karmel to J. Eisen, letter, November 1, 1945, CJC001, DA 18, box 6, file 4, CJA; Sussman, *No Mere Bagatelles*, 93.

23. Garwood, "The Holocaust and the Power of Powerlessness."

24. Ostroff and Ostroff, interview by author.

25. David Miller, report, 1949, JCRA, HA 14–14, Religious Affairs: Chief Rabbis Religious Emergency Council (CRREC), David Miller File, WL; "BAOR," *Menorah*, July 1948, Jewish Memorial Council ACC2999/E4/1–7, LMA; "Confidential Report on the High Holiday Period," October 31, 1951, Central Jewish Fund for World Jewish Relief ACC2793/01/10/07, LMA; Emanuel Schenk, report, May 1945, NJWB, box 97, folder 32, AJHS; Berman, interview.

26. Harold Saperstein, letter, December 26, 1944, MS-718, box 8, folder 3, AJA.

27. He helped organize Rosh Hashanah services with the chief rabbi of Paris and the chief rabbi of France. Aaron Decter, report, October 1944, NJWB, box 52, file 8, AJHS.

28. Jewish Hospitality Committee for British and Allied Forces, report, April 1945, CJC001, DA 18, box 7, file 1, CJA.

29. Central British Fund for World Jewish Relief, Confidential Report on the High Holiday Period, October 31, 1951, Central British Fund for World Jewish Relief, ACC 2793/01/10/07, LMA; Harold Saperstein to congregation, letter, December 26, 1944, MS-718, box 8, folder 3. Also see Meyer J. Goldman, report, February 1945, I-180, series VI, box 188, folder Belgium, AJHS; Meyer J. Goldman, report, May 1945, NJWB, box 62, folder 7, AJHS.

30. Aryeh Lev, journal entry, May 18, 1945, JWB, box 18, folder 106, AJHS. Also see "Yanks Join 400 Jews of Berlin in Rosh Hashana Services," *Chicago Daily Tribune*, September 8, 1945, 2. Lev became the executive director of the National Jewish Welfare Board's Committee on Army and Navy Religious Activities in 1946.

31. Sala Kirschner, interview 33589, segment 39; Kirschner, *Sala's Gift*, 213–16; Ann Kirschner, interview by author, July 10, 2014, New York City (hereafter Kirschner, interview by author).

32. Berman, interview; Bernard Cohen, telephone conversation with author, January 30, 2009; Lydia Servetnick, telephone conversation with author, January 30, 2009; "Oran War

Bride," *Chicago Tribune*, July 26, 1945, 3; "Here and Over There," *Jewish Chaplain*, April–May 1943, 3. Also see "Persian Hospitality," *Jewish Chaplain*, November–December 1944, 7.

33. These also were called "Jewish centers" and "Jewish hospitality clubs."

34. John Sills, "Army and Navy Report for 1945 (JWB)," February 27, 1946, NJWB, box 6, AJHS.

35. "BAOR," *Menorah*, July 1948, Jewish Memorial Council ACC2999/E4/1–7, LMA; S. Brown, "A Chaplain Looks Back on B.A.O.R.," *Jewish Chronicle*, March 10, 1950, HA21–1/14, WL; Herbert Friedman, report, July 1946, MS-763, series A, box 1, file 12, AJA; Joe Friedman to Philip Bernstein, letter, January 13, 1944, JWB, box 17, folder 104, AJHS; Meyer J. Goldman, report, February 1945, I-180, series VI, box 192, folder: overseas Germany 1945, AJHS; Aaron Kahn to Jewish Welfare Board, letter, I-180, series VI, box 188, folder: Austria, AJHS. There was some friction among the leadership. See Joseph Baratz to S. Brodetsky, letter, 1945, Board of Deputies of British Jews ACC3121 E/02/096, LMA.

36. Carl Miller to CANRA, letter, March 5, 1946, NJWB, box 86, folder 8, AJHS; Manuel M. Poliakoff, report, September 1945, NJWB, box 90, folder 4 AJHS; Emanuel George Vida, August–September monthly reports, September 1945, NJWB, box 110, folder 7, AJHS.

37. Jewish Hospitality Committee for British and Allied Forces, report, April 1945; "JWB Synagogue Center Opened," *Center Courier* (Heidelberg, Germany), February 1946, Abraham Klausner Papers P68, File 11, CAHJP; Philip Bernstein, "Executive Directors Report," October 23, 1944, JWB, box 6, folder 12, AJHS; Joseph Shalom Shubow, "Notes Re: Berlin and American-Occupied Germany," June 7, 1946, NJWB, box 101, folder 14, AJHS.

38. Morris Gordon to Frances Gordon, letter, May 1, 1945, P-910, box 1, folder 1, AJHS; Morris Gordon to Frances Gordon, letter, October 24, 1945, P-910, box 1, folder 1, AJHS; Aryeh Lev to Mayer Abramowitz, letter, September 9, 1946, NJWB, box 42, folder 7, AJHS; Carl Miller to CANRA, letter, March 5, 1946, NJWB, box 86, folder 8, AJHS; Aaron Kahn to CANRA, letter, March 1946, I-180, series VI, box 188, folder: Austria, AJHS.

39. Harold Saperstein to Temple Emanuel, letter, September 28, 1944, MS-718, box 8, folder 5, AJA.

40. "JWB Synagogue Center Opened." Also see Carl Miller to CANRA, letter, March 5, 1946, NJWB, box 86, folder 8, AJHS.

41. B. Brohnsohn, letter, November 16, 1945, CJC001, DA 18, box 7 file 7, CJA.

42. "Thoughts of a Jewish Girl in the Center," *Center Courier* (Heidelberg, Germany), February 1946, P68, 11, CAHJP.

43. Their meeting would have been difficult a few months earlier. Then, Shelkan would have been considered an enemy alien under the antifraternization laws, and he and Bertha would have been prohibited from dating.

44. "In Token of Our Appreciation," *Center Courier* (Heidelberg, Germany), February 1946, P68, CAHJP; "Weddings in Heidelberg," *Center Courier*, February 1946, P68, 11, CAHJP. For other examples, see "Wedding Bells in Kassel," JCRA, HA6B, box 3 file 1, WL; Jewish Committee for Relief Abroad to Sam Solomons, letter, March 21, 1949, JCRA, HA2–4/2, JCRA Organisation: Units in Germany, folder: JRU correspondence 1946–9, WL; and David Miller, report, 1949, JCRA, HA 14–14, File: David Miller, WL.

45. Myers Feinstein, *Holocaust Survivors*, esp. 226; Weinberg, "The Reconstruction of the French Jewish Community," 168–86.

46. Kieve (Akiva) Skidell to E., letter, August 20, 1945, 0.75, 139, II, YVA.

47. "Jewish Soldier Weds in Hitler's Room," clipping, October 30, 1945, Jewish Chaplains World War II collection, box 1, folder: clippings, Jewish Military Museum, London; Jewish Committee for Relief Abroad, "Endsleigh Place News," *Volunteers' Newsletter* (London), June–July, JCRA, HA5–6/8, WL; M. R. Villiens to Gollancz, letter, August 25, 1947, JCRA, HA2–4/10, folder: JCRA Organisation: Units in Germany, file: Correspondence with JRU Germany 1945–8, WL.

48. Charlie A. to/from Jack Eisen, letters, July 1945, CJC001, DA 18, box 23, file 4, CJA; Abraham Hyman to Herbert Friedman, letter, January 21, 1948, MS-763, series A, box 1, folder 13, AJA; Mandel Abramowitz, *The Journey*, 100; Horvitz, interview by Krulik; Fishman, interview 2860, segments 90–11.

49. "Holocaust Survivor Talks about Marrying a Soldier (Noga Donat Interview)," *Yad Vashem*, https://www.youtube.com/watch?v=I1oO6fY34zM, accessed 17 February 2023. Also see Rosie Whitehouse, "Italy Seeks to Remember Sheltering Holocaust Survivors—and Aliyah Bet," *Tablet*, May 31, 2018, https://www.tabletmag.com/sections/news/articles/italy-holocaust-survivors-and-aliyah-bet, accessed March 26, 2021. Other members of the surviving remnant were drawn to Zionism as a natural reaction to the Holocaust, and not necessarily from an ideological position or stance. Cohen, "Choosing a Heim"; Ofer, "Past That Does Not Pass"; Patt, *Finding Home*; Weitz, "Jewish Refugees."

50. "Holocaust Survivor Talks about Marrying a Soldier (Noga Donat interview)," *Yad Vashem*, https://www.youtube.com/watch?v=I1oO6fY34zM, accessed February 17, 2023; Marco Cavallarin, "Noga Cohen Donat," *Moked*, February 13, 2017, https://moked.it/blog/2017/02/13/noga-cohen-donat-1922–2017/, accessed March 26, 2021.

51. Daniel Isaacman to his parents, letter, March 26, 1945, 50/173, box 2 folder 3, UPT; Isaacman, interview 24614, segment 149. The first Hachshara meeting he attended in Belgium was in January 1945. Daniel Isaacman to his parents, letter, January 2, 1945, 50/173, box 2, folder 1, UPT. *Hachshara* literally means "preparation" and refers to programs that would train Jews for their immigration to—and lives in—Palestine.

52. Isaacman, interview 24614, segment 149.

53. For Daniel, the term *chaver* referred to a friend within the movement and not simply "a friend." Daniel Isaacman to his parents, letter, March 26, 1945, 50/173, box 2 folder 3, UPT.

54. Meyer Abramowitz to Israel Sol Weisberger, letter, September 9, 1946, NJWB, box 42, folder 7, AJHS; Oscar Lifshutz to Aryeh Lev, letter, June 30, 1947, NJWB, box 81, AJHS; Meyer Abramowitz to/from Aryeh Lev, letters, December 1947, NJWB, box 42, folder 7, AJHS; Bowman, interview by Kent.

55. Most of the inhabitants of the kibbutzim were youths/young adults who had survived the war in Poland or the Soviet Union.

56. Mayer Abramowitz, "A Wedding in Berlin," Jewish Federation of Miami, http://www.ujc.org/page.aspx?id=38547, accessed March 28, 2013; Mandel Abramowitz, *The Journey*, 100; Abraham Hyman to Herbert Friedman, letter, January 21, 1948, MS-763, series A, box 1 folder 13, AJA. Also see Bowman, interview by Kent.

57. See, e.g., Patt, *Finding Home*.

58. Isaacman, interview 24614, segments 147 and 151.

59. Isaacman, interview 24614, segment 156.

60. Daniel Isaacman to his parents, letter, March 26, 1945, 50/173, box 2 folder 3, UPT. Emphasis my own.

61. Isaacman, interview 24614, segment 158. Unlike Daniel, Clara had multiple languages at her disposal: Yiddish, French, Flemish, Rumanian and a smattering of English. See Daniel Isaacman, letter, January 18, 1945, 50/173, box 2 folder 1, UPT.

62. "Holocaust Survivor Talks about Marrying a Soldier (Noga Donat interview)," Yad Vashem, https://www.youtube.com/watch?v=I10O6fY34zM, accessed February 17, 2023; Marco Cavallarin, "Noga Cohen Donat," *Moked*, February 13, 2017, https://moked.it /blog/2017/02/13/noga-cohen-donat-1922–2017/, accessed March 26, 2021.

63. Abraham Klausner to Faigie, letter, May 1945, MS-54, box 3, folder 15, AJA.

64. Abraham Klausner to Faigie, letter, May 1945. Klausner had been born in Tennessee to a Hungarian immigrant father and an Austrian immigrant mother. Growing up in Memphis and then in Denver, he spoke Yiddish at home.

65. Abe Bonder to J. Eisen, letter, October 10, 1945, CJC001, DA 18, box 23, folder 5a, CJA; J. Eisen to Abe Bonder, letter, October 16, 1945, CJC001, DA 18, box 23 folder 5a, CJA.

66. Ostroff and Ostroff, interview by author.

67. Klein, interview by Bradley.

68. Bergman, interview 26752.

69. See Josef Geta, "Refugees in Uniform," *New Statesman*, January 7, 1944, 1158 misc. documents re: aliens in the British Army, WL.

70. Horvitz, interview by Krulik.

71. Certainly, some initial encounters between military personnel and members of the surviving remnant never resulted in further meetings because of the lack of a shared language.

72. Lydia Servetnick, telephone conversation with author, January 30, 2009.

73. Shelkan, interview 15025, segments 19–20.

74. Turgel, interview 39187; Turgel, Holocaust Testimony (HVT-4458); Isaacson, interview 31353, segment 53; Isaacson, interview MOH 027.

CHAPTER THREE

1. Daniel Isaacman to his parents, letter, March 26, 1945, 50/173, box 2, folder 3, UPT. Also see Isaacman, interview 24614, segments 149–50.

2. Daniel Isaacman to his parents, letter, April 3, 1945, 50/173, box 2, folder 4, UPT. Also see Daniel Isaacman to his parents, letter, April 6, 1945, 50/173, box 2, folder 4, UPT. Daniel also wrote to his parents about Clara on April 4 and 5 and earlier during the day on April 6.

3. Daniel Isaacman to his parents, letter, April 21, 1945, 50/173, box 2, folder 4, UPT; Isaacman, interview 24614, segment 158. They married in July. Marriage Certificate, July 30, 1945, A231.544, Archives de l'État, Brussels.

4. Turgel, *I Light a Candle*, 160; Turgel, interview 39187, segments 160–62. Several marriages emerged from the liberation of Belsen, including the marriage of a "male bride" and a British Jewish nurse. M. R. Villiens to Gollancz, letter, August 25, 1947, JCRA, HA2–4/10, folder JCRA Organisation: Units in Germany, File: Correspondence JRU, WL.

5. Daniel Isaacman to his parents, letters, March 26 and 28, 1945, 50/173, box 2, folder 3, UPT.

6. Daniel Isaacman to his parents, letter, April 3, 1945, 50/173, box 2, folder 4, UPT. Similar to Daniel, Morris Fishman grew up in a Brooklyn home where his parents spoke to

one another in Yiddish. He and Lala Weintraub, who had grown up in Poland and was proficient in Polish, German, and Yiddish, communicated in a mix of Yiddish and German. When Morris could not find the appropriate word or phrase in Yiddish, he would rely on his driver to translate into German. Fishman, interview 2860, segments 90–111; Fishman, interview by author.

7. Isaacman, interview 24614, segment 149.

8. Kirschner, interview 33589, segment 164.

9. Kurt Klein to Gerda Weissmann, letter, May 20, 1945, in Weissmann Klein and Klein, *The Hours After*, 36.

10. Bergman, interview 26752. Also see Cohen, interview 11.

11. Bergman, interview 26752.

12. Reims had grown accustomed to devastation. About 85 percent of its buildings, including the Cathédrale Notre-Dame de Reims, had been destroyed during the First World War. While rebuilding efforts had restored the cathedral and several of the city's buildings by 1938, the bombings of the Second World War again destroyed Reims. Overy, *The Bombers and Bombed*, 371–401.

13. Ostroff and Ostroff, interview by author.

14. Daniel Isaacman to his parents, letter, April 9, 1945, 50/173, box 2, folder 4, UPT. On the "malleable medium of food," see Kirschenblatt-Gimblett, "Kitchen Judaism," 77.

15. For another example of home-based courtship activities, see Isaacson, *Seed of Sarah*, 127–31; Isaacson, interview 31353, segment 53.

16. Meyer Abramowitz to Israel Sol Weisberger, letter, NJWB, box 42, folder 7, AJHS; Oscar Lifshutz to Aryeh Lev, letter, June 30, 1947, NJWB, box 81, folder Lifshutz, AJHS; Meyer Abramowitz to/from Aryeh Lev, letters, December 1947, NJWAB, box 42, folder 7, AJHS; Rose, interview 49164, segments 208–15.

17. Bonder, interview 54741, segments 110–20.

18. Both were socialist Zionists, but Clara's Shomrim were known for communing with nature and for their military-like discipline while Daniel's fellow Gordonia enthusiasts called for the redemption of the Jewish people and *Eretz Yisrael* (the land of Israel) through the revival of the Hebrew language and the use of manual labor. See, e.g., Daniel Isaacman to his parents, letter, April 9, 1945, 50/173, box 2, folder 4, UPT.

19. Daniel Isaacman to his parents, letter, May 1, 1945, 50/173, box 2, folder 5, UPT. Also see Daniel Isaacman to his parents, letter, April 19, 1945, 50/173, box 2, folder 4, UPT.

20. Only a few couples studied here discussed patronizing the slowly revitalizing cultural institutions of Europe, visiting art exhibitions, and attending musical performances and the theater. Daniel Isaacman to his parents, vmail, April 15, 1945, 50/173, box 2, folder 4, UPT; Gorewitz, interview 34876, segments 141–57; Isaacman, interview 24614, segments 158–66; Sussman, *No Mere Bagatelles*, 47 and 65–69.

21. Judah Nadich, report, October 1945, NJWB, box 42, folder 5, AJHS; Rose, interview 49164, segment 214. Also see "Weddings in Heidelberg," *Center Courier* (Heidelberg, Germany), March 1946; Benjamin Krasnow, report, September 1946, NJWB, box 73, folder Krasnow, AJHS; "In These Days," *New Jersey Jewish News*, August 28, 1997, https://jhsnj -archives.org/?a=d&d=A19970828-NewJerseyJewishNews-19970828.1.15&s. Also see Mankowitz, *Life between Memory and Hope*, 20; and Zaidman-Dz'ubas, *Be-haftsi'a ha-shaḥar*.

22. A meeting place for Jews who lived outside of the UNRRA-controlled DP camps, the Regensburg center was run by American Jewish chaplain Eugene Lipman. Lipman, interview by Kuzmack.

23. Turgel, *I Light a Candle*, 160; Turgel, interview 39187, segments 160–62.

24. Isaacman, interview 24614, segment 171.

25. Chaplain Herbert Eskin reported that he gave four lectures on sex and morality and had over 600 attendees. Herbert S. Eskin, report, July 10, 1945, NJWB, box 55, folder Eskin, AJHS. Also see Harold Saperstein, report, September 1944, MS-718, box 8, folder 7, AJA.

26. Nathan to Ruth B., letters, May 5 and 22, 1946, B. Family private collection, JPL.

27. Daniel Isaacman to his parents, April 3, 1945, 50/173, box 2, folder 4, UPT.

28. Daniel Isaacman to his parents, vmail, April 16, 1945, 50/173, box 2, folder 4, UPT.

29. Daniel Isaacman to his parents, letter, April 23, 1945, 50/173 box 2, folder 4, UPT.

30. Isaacman, interview 24614, segment 149; Flory Jagoda, interview by author.

31. See, e.g., Bonder, interview 40845, segments 149–51; Bonder, interview 54741, segments 112–14.

32. Grossmann makes clear that such relationships became more visible after 1948, but they still existed before then. Grossmann, *Jews, Germans, and Allies*, 223–30.

33. It was only in 1947 that the Allies could satisfactorily acquire and allocate goods to DPs in Germany. Even then, they were unable to meet the needs of the native German population. See Crago Schneider, "Jewish 'Shtetls' in Postwar Germany," 90. On hunger in postwar Europe, see Burma, *Year Zero*, 53–73; Rothenberger, *Die Hungerjahre*; Stüber, *Der Kampf gegen den Hunger*; and Weinreb, "'For the Hungry Have No Past.'"

34. This was not unique to military-Jewish civilian relationships.

35. When the war ended, between 100,000 and 150,000 Dutch people were suffering from hunger edema. Burma, *Year Zero*, 53–55; Lowe, *Savage Continent*, 43–46; Hitchcock, *The Bitter Road to Freedom*, 119.

36. Rose, *The Tulips Are Red*, 263; Rose, interview 49164, segment 204. They also used them in negotiations with some of the families who had been hiding Jewish children who were now being reclaimed.

37. The canned meat distributed to them barely contained meat; it was composed of nearly 70 percent potatoes. UNRRA, "General Situation," 6. They fared a bit better than German civilians, whose daily rations were quite low. By the end of 1945, the official ration in the US zone of Germany had gone down to 1,550 calories per day, and it fell lower to 1,275 calories by the spring of 1946. In the French zone, the official ration fell below 1,000 calories at the end of 1945 and stayed there for six months. Biddiscombe, "Dangerous Liaisons," 615–16; Lowe, *Savage Continent*, 46; Grossmann, *Jews, Germans, and Allies*, 174–75.

38. Fishman, interview by author; Fishman, interview 2860, segments 90–94. Also see Daniel Isaacman to his parents, letter, April 19, 1945, 50/173, box 2, folder 4, UPT; Kirschner, interview 33589, segment 39; and Sussman, *No Mere Bagatelles*, 48.

39. Mayer Abramowitz, "A Wedding in Berlin," Jewish Federation of Miami, http://www.ujc.org/page.aspx?id=38547, accessed March 28, 2013; Abraham Hyman to Herbert A. Friedman, letter, January 21, 1948, MS-763, series A, box 1, folder 13, AJA.

40. Daniel Isaacman to his parents, letter, May 4, 1945, 50/173, box 2, folder 5, UPT.

41. Flory Jagoda, interview by author. Also see Harry Jagoda, interview by author.

42. Daniel Isaacman to his parents, letter, April 19, 1945, 50/173, box 2, folder 4, UPT, and letter, May 4, 1945, 50/173, box 2, folder 5, UPT; Isaacman, interview 24614, segments 149–51.

43. Daniel Isaacman to his parents, letter, May 13, 1945, 50/173, box 2, folder 5, UPT; Bignon, "Cigarette Money and Black-Market Prices," 7, 9; Geroulanos, "An Army of Shadows"; Klopstock, "Monetary Reform in Western Germany," 278; Roberts, *What Soldiers Do*, 116–25.

44. Summer, interview by author.

45. See, e.g., Bignon, "Cigarette Money and Black-Market Prices"; Pratt, "Medicine and Obedience," 277–78; and Roberts, *What Soldiers Do*, 118–20.

46. After 1946, the occupation authorities prohibited military personnel from converting reichsmarks into pounds or dollars, thus encouraging resourceful military personnel to trade their cigarettes for other goods. Individual cigarettes also could be divided up and made into a larger number of smaller cigarettes.

47. Fishman, interview 2860, segment 99; Fishman, interview by author.

48. Isaacman, interview 24614, segments 165–66. Also see Gerda Weissmann to Kurt Klein, letter, July 20, 1945, in Weissmann Klein and Klein, *The Hours After*, 58.

49. Myers Feinstein, "All under One Roof," 29–48.

50. Isaacson, *Seed of Sarah*, 127; Isaacson, interview 31353, segment 53.

51. Fishman, interview 2860, segments 90–11; Fishman, interview by author; Isaacson, *Seed of Sarah*, 127; Isaacson, interview 31353, segment 53.

52. In December 1945, there were 134 DP camps in the American zone in Germany; by June 1947, there were 416 DP camps. In 1947 there were also 272 camps in the British zone (down from a peak of 443 in December 1946) and 45 in the French Zone; Austria and Italy had a total of 21 and 8 camps, respectively. At its peak in 1947, the Jewish displaced person population reached approximately 250,000. The Soviets did not create DP camps in their zone. Philip S. Bernstein, "Confidential Report on the Situation of Jewish Displaced Persons in US Zones Germany and Austria," WHB, AA 2, box 20, BHL.

53. Submitted in July 1945 by Earl G. Harrison, US representative to the Intergovernmental Committee on Refugees, the Harrison Report was a study concerning the conditions of the DP camps. It criticized the treatment of the Jews in the DP camps and encouraged the Armies of Occupation to consider whether Jews ought to be given their own privileged category.

54. Königseder and Wetzel, *Lebensmut im Wartesaal*, 171; Judah Nadich, "Report on Conditions of Jews in Berlin," September 16, 1945, JWB, box 22, folder 141, AJHS. Two years later, the complaints remained somewhat similar. Benjamin Krasnow, May Report, June 1, 1947, NJWB, box 73, file: Krasnow, AJHS.

55. Herbert Friedman to Charles Rosenbaum, telegram, September 11, 1946, MS-763, series A, box 1, file 4, AJA.

56. Other courtship narratives that emphasized military assistance in claiming new housing can be found in Bergman, interview 26752; Isaacson, *Seed of Sarah*, 127; US Department of Justice, confidential report, May 19, 1947, FBIT.

57. Her landlord would only be allowed to remain in her home as long as Gerda, a survivor, lived there. Gerda Weissmann to Kurt Klein, letter, January 7, 1946, in Weissmann Klein and Klein, *The Hours After*, 191. Allied officials frequently placed former victims in homes belonging to Nazis rather than other Germans as both a form of punishment and

reeducation. As Laura Hilton has established, after the initial housing requisitions of 1945, allied authorities were reluctant to take additional housing from Germans. Hilton, "Who Was Worthy?," 19.

58. For a first description of the room, see Gerda Weissmann to Kurt Klein, letter, September 6, 1945, in Weissmann Klein and Klein, *The Hours After*, 67. On the sense of belonging and unbelonging with DPs, see chap. 4.

59. Abe did not receive permission to marry. Abe Bonder to Jack Eisen, letter, October 10, 1945, CJC001, DA 18, box 23, folder 5a, CJA. Also see Abe Bonder to Jack Eisen, letter, October 16, 1945, CJC001, DA 18, box 23, folder 5a, CJA; Bonder, interview 40845, segments 151–56. Also see Weissmann Klein and Klein, *The Hours After*, 66–74; and Kirschner, interview 33589, segments 39–40.

60. Turgel, interview 39187, segments 160–62; Lydia Servetnick, telephone conversation with author, January 30, 2009.

61. Dave B. to Jack Eisen, letter, February 16, 1945, CJC001, DA 18 box 23, file 5, CJA; Daniel Isaacman to his parents, letter, April 19, 1945, 50/173, box 2, folder 4, UPT; Parfitt family to American Consul (Germany), letter, June 7, 1946, MS-239, box 6, folder 5, AJA; Syd Kirschner to Sala Garnarz, letter, April 23, 1946, Sala Garncarz Kirschner Collection, Dorot Jewish Division, box 1945–1946, NYPL, Abraham Hyman to Friedman, letter, January 21, 1948, MS-763, series A, box 1, folder 13, AJA.

62. Gerda Weissmann to Kurt Klein, letter, October 28, 1945, Weissmann Klein and Klein, *The Hours After*, 117. Also see Rose, interview 49164, segment 212; and Sala Garancz to Kirschner, letter, undated, in Kirschner, *Sala's Gift*, 234–36.

63. R. A. Elliot Jr., directive, August 19, 1944, RG 247, AG 291.1, Marriages Box 198, vol. iv, NACP; Control Commission for Germany British Element to CONFOLK, outgoing restricted message, August 26, 1946, FO 1032/1367, file: Policy for Non Fraternisation, NAK; S. Gershon Levi, certificate, November 3, 1944, CJC001, DA 18, box 6, folder 6, CJA.

64. Committee on the Judiciary House of Representatives Eighty-First Congress, 2nd sess., March 27 and April 3, 1950, Hearings of the Subcommittee no. 1, on H.R. 7614, "A Bill for the Relief of Mrs. Ellen Knauff."

65. See chap. 5.

66. American military commanders, for example, could not approve marriages of "persons of Asiatic or East Indian descent" or permit marriages between individuals of color and white personnel if the latter originated from states that prohibited these marriages. James A. Ulio to Commanding Generals, letter, May 22, 1944, RG 498, AG 291.1, box 31, NACP; also see George R. Merrell to Mark A. Tomas, letter, December 15, 1943, NACP, RG 200, folder 618.4, NACP. Also see the discussion in this book's introduction.

67. All three authorities discussed a wide range of matters concerning marriage, including whether POWs currently interned in their countries could marry local women, if religious ceremonies conducted abroad would be valid in the United States, Canada, or Britain, and whether fiancé(e)s of naturalized or current citizens should be exempted from immigration laws. On POWs, see A. M. Tollefson, memo, August 29, 1944, RG 247, AG 291.1, box 198, vol. 4, NACP; "Wives Will Have to Leave Britain," *Sunday Dispatch*, May 5, 1944, 1158 (Misc. Documents re: Aliens in the British Army), WL. On ceremonies abroad, see Alvie L. McKnight to Haquardo, letter, July 21, 1945, RG 247, AG 291.1, box 198, vol. v, NACP. On

fiancés, see Office of the Deputy Military Governor Control Commission for Germany, memo, February 22, 1946, FO 1052/267, vol. 2, folder: Control Office for Germany and Austria and Foreign Office, file: Administration policy: Displaced Persons: All Nations, NAK.

68. The American military introduced this mandate in June 1942, even though some military commanders had exercised this authority earlier. War Department, Circular 179, June 8, 1942, RG 498, box 52, folder 195, NACP; John CH Lee to LP Collins, letter, August 15, 1942, RG 498, box 53 291.1, NACP; War Department, Circular 307, July 18, 1944, RG 247, AG 291.1, box 198, NACP. Also see Selwyn D. Ruslander, Certificate 120, September 30, 1944, MS-460, series B, box 24, file 3, AJA.

69. Archbishop of Canterbury, letter, May 18, 1943, RG 498, AG 291.1, box 53, folder 228, NACP; Conference of Jewish Chaplains, minutes, January 2–3, 1944, CJC001, DA 18, box 5, folder 18, CJA (hereafter Conference of Jewish Chaplains, minutes); M. B. to I. B. Rose, letter, May 13, 1945, CJC001, DA 18, box 5, folder 10, CJA; Doris Bushnell, letter, June 13, 1944, RG 498, box 200, file 618.31, NACP; Zaltzman to C., letter, September 20, 1944, CJC001, DA 18, box 6, file 6, CJA. Susan Zeiger and Sonya O. Rose tease out the ways American and British officials pushed certain couples together. Zeiger, *Entangling Alliances*; Rose, "Girls and GIs."

70. War Department, Circular no. 307. Susan Zeiger argues that American-British couples had long courtships, even lengthier than the waiting period the United States required. Zeiger, *Entangling Alliances*, 85.

71. Military Government, "Draft of the Military Government—Germany Concerning Marriages with Members of the Allied Expeditionary Forces," December 1944, RG 498, AG 291.1, box 31, folder 27, NACP.

72. Acting Adjutant General to Commanding General, memo (confidential), November 25, 1944, RG 498, AG 291.1, box 31, NACP.

73. "Procedure to Facilitate the Marriage of Certain Persons in Germany by Command of General Eisenhower," October 12, 1945, RG 247, AG 291.1, box 198, vol. 6, NACP. Military personnel stationed in Northwest Europe could marry civilians if the potential spouse was not an enemy alien. Anyone born in Germany or Austria, but now living in Northwest Europe, needed to prove that she or he was "truly" a refugee. "A Directive for the Use of CDN Chaplains Stationed in Northwest Europe," February 21, 1945, CJC001, DA 18, box 5, folder 10, CJA.

74. J. Eisen to Abe Bonder, letter, October 16, 1945. Also see J. Eisen to Charlie A., letter, July 27, 1945, CJC001, DA 18, box 23, folder 4, CJA. The fact that DPs and refugees began imagining that Paris served as a location from which it would be easier to marry and emigrate may have influenced the Canadian chaplain's letter. See chap. 4.

75. B. Rogers to Theater Commander (ETO), letter, May 26, 1944, RG 498, AG 291.1, box 31, folder 121, NACP.

76. J. Eisen to Ralph C., letter, February 16, 1945, CJC001, DA 18, box 23, folder 6a, CJA.

77. R. A. Elliot Jr. to all Commander Officers, Directive, August 19, 1944, AG 291.1, RG 247, box 198, vol. iv, NACP. For an examination of the American chaplaincy's involvement in the private spheres of home and family, see Stahl, *Enlisting Faith*, 106–33.

78. Bertram Klausner, monthly report, June 1945, NJWB, box 71, folder 25, AJHS.

79. Meyer J. Goldman, monthly report, August 1945, NJWB, box 62, folder 7, AJHS; Hirsch Freund, September monthly report, November 1945, NJWB, box 57, folder 42, AJHS;

Hirsch E. L. Freund, July monthly report, November 5, 1945, NJWB, box 57, folder 42, AJHS; Herman Dicker, monthly report, February 1945, NJWB, box 52, folder 29, AJHS. As Ronit Stahl has shown, Christian Science and Church of Latter-Day Saints chaplains in the American military did not possess the right to officiate at weddings between military personnel and civilians. Stahl, *Enlisting Faith*, 124.

80. On postwar Jewish legal debates, see, e.g., Katz, "The Mothers, the Mamzerim, and the Rabbis"; and Zimmels, *The Echo of the Holocaust*.

81. See, e.g., David De Sola Pool, "Jewish Youth Looks at Marriage," JWB, box 23, folder 161, AJHS; B., Marriage Application, October 31, 1945, CJC001, DA 18, box 5, folder 10, CJA; and Ralph H. Blumenthal to Aryeh Lev, letter, March 9, 1949, NJWB, box 47, folder 3, AJHS. A few chaplains, however, allowed for interfaith marriages by removing themselves from the petition process and placing the responsibility for permission in the hands of the commander. See, e.g., Gershon Levi, Review of Marriage Application (AK), February 7, 1944, CJC001, DA 18, box 6, folder 6, CJA.

82. Isaac Rose to David R., letter, July 1, 1945, CJC001, DA 18, box 5, folder 10, CJA. The American reform movement approved of patrilineal descent in 1983 and the UK reform movement in 2015.

83. Oscar M. Lifshutz to Aryeh Lev, letter, March 22, 1946, NJWB, box 81, file Lifshutz, AJHS; also see Herbert Friedman to Abraham Hyman, letter, January 21, 1948, MS-763 series A, box 1, folder 13, AJA.

84. Samuel Cass to Rose, letter, November 7, 1945, CJC001, DA 18, box 6, folder 6, CJA; also see Bertha B. to Robert Marcus, telegram, February 17, 1945, WJC, box 64, folder 3, AJA.

85. "Rabbi Chaplain in Berlin Withholds Sanction of Jewish-German Marriages," *Oregonian*, February 27, 1947, 2.

86. S. Brown, "A Jewish Chaplain in Post War Europe," *Menorah*, January 1951, 16, ACC2999/E4/1–7, LMA.

87. Conference of Jewish Chaplains, minutes.

88. Jack Eisen and B., letters, February 1945, CJC001, DA 18, box 23, file 5b, CJA; Jack Eisen and Max E., letters, April 1945, CJC001, DA 18, box 23, folder 8, CJA. Canadian chaplain Samuel Cass similarly conducted conversions before approving a few marriages between Canadian military personnel and their non-Jewish girlfriends, suggesting that he, too, permitted conversion for marriage's sake. See, e.g., Cass, Marriage Application (S), November 8, 1945, CJC001, DA 18, box 6, file 6, CJA.

89. "Forces Forum: Intermarriage in BAOR," *Menorah*, December 1949, ACC2999 /E4/1–7, LMA; also see Office of the Chief Rabbi, "Confidential Report on the High Holiday Period," October 31, 1951, ACC2793/ 01/10/07, LMA.

90. Joseph Freedman to Philip Bernstein, letter, July 1, 1944, NJWB, box 57, folder 42, AJHS. This is consistent with traditional Jewish law.

91. Division of Religious Activities, *Responsa in War Time*, 22–25; Eugene Lippmann, monthly report, January 1945, NJWB, box 82, folder 3, AJHS; Harold Saperstein to his wife, letter, March 15, 1945, MS-718, box 8, folder 12, AJA; Meyer J. Goldman, monthly report, November 1951, NJWB, box 62, folder 6, AJHS.

92. Philip Pincus, monthly report, November 1949, NJWB, box 89, folder 20, AJHS; Mayer Abramowitz, "Intermarriage in Berlin . . . The Fraulein Kind," Jewish Federation of Miami, http://www.ujc.org/page.aspx?id=38547, accessed March 28, 2013.

93. Joseph Freedman to Philip Bernstein, letter, July 1, 1944, NJWB, box 57, folder 42, AJHS. Also see Gunther Plaut, January chaplains report, February 14, 1946, NJWB, box 89, folder 24, AJHS.

94. For a dated, but useful, comparison of American and Canadian Jewish religious life, see Schoenfeld, "The Jewish Religion in North America."

95. Division of Religious Activities, *Responsa in War Time*, 29–30. If the chaplain himself had objections, he was told to refer the couple to another chaplain or to the commander.

96. Division of Religious Activities, *Responsa in War Time*.

97. Bessner, *Double Threat*, 173.

98. These include the "intermediate days" during the Jewish holidays of Sukkot and Passover, as well as during the three weeks from the seventeenth of Tammuz through Tishah be-Av and the thirty-three-day period from Passover to before Shavuot. While Jewish law forbids weddings between the beginning of the Jewish month of Av until fifteen days later, custom has extended the ban to extend from the seventeenth day of Tammuz until Tishah be-Av. Weddings are legally permissible during the earlier period, but only for urgent reasons. Sephardim prohibit weddings from the second day of Passover through Lag ba-Omer; many Ashkenazim permit weddings until after Rosh Chodesh Iyyar, again on Lag ba-Omer, and beginning with and continuing after Rosh Chodesh Sivan.

99. K., application for marriage, March 5, 1944, CJC001, DA 18, box 6, folder 6, CJA; S. Gershon Levi, review of K.'s application to marry, March 1944, CJC001, DA 18, box 6, folder 6, CJA; A. S., query about marriage authorization, July 1944, ACC 2805/6/6/1/ 42, LMA; I. B. Rose to A. W., letter, July 10, 1945, CJC001, DA 18, box 5, folder 10, CJA; S. Gershon Levi, permission to marry (L.), January 25, 1945, CJC001, DA 18, box 6, folder 6, CJA; Gershon Levi, permission to marry (B. B.), April 13, 1944, CJC001, DA 18, box 6, folder 6, CJA; S. Gershon Levi, permission to marry (G.), March 10, 1944, CJC001, DA 18, box 6, folder 6, CJA.

100. Committee on Army and Navy Religious Activities (CANRA), responsa on marriage ceremony, MSS-675, box 13, file 11, AJA.

101. Katz, "The Mothers, the Mamzerim, and the Rabbis"; Zimmels, *The Echo of the Holocaust*.

102. Munk to Henriques, letter, October 3, 1947, JCRA, HA21–5/23, Miscellaneous: Colonel Solomon's Files, File: Marriages and Deaths, 1946–7, WL; G. Weiss to J. Levine, letter, December 23, 1947, Collection of the Geneva Office, G 45–54 /3 /14 /SM.800, JDCJ; Kantorowsky, *get* and statement, 1947, Pauline Howard Personal Papers 1776, WL.

103. "Weddings in Heidelberg," *Center Courier* (Heidelberg, Germany), March 1946, P68, 11, CAHJP.

104. See, e.g., Manuel M. Poliakoff, monthly report, November 1945, NJWB, box 90, folder 4, AJHS; Weintraub, memo, October 19, 1945, CJC001, DA 18, box 5, folder 10, CJA; and J. Eisen to B. Family, letter, October 16, 1945, CJC001, DA 18, box 23, folder 5b, CJA.

105. Over the course of the summer of 1945, US occupation forces established the category of "assimilees" to designate German-born Jews who could "assimilate" to the status of UN displaced persons. The British, however, were reluctant to offer Jews special consideration because of their Jewishness, as such a move could have been interpreted as envisioning Jews as a nation, which would have significant implications for the British mandate in Palestine. See, e.g., S. Gershon Levi on J. K., statement and letter, November 3, 1944, CJC001, DA 18, box 6, folder 6, CJA.

106. The couple received permission to marry, and Marianne came to Canada in 1946 after her husband's demobilization. Cass to Weintraub, memo, October 19, 1945, CJC001, DA 18, box 5, folder 10, CJA; Weintraub, undated response, CJC001, DA 18, box 5, folder 10, CJA.

107. Reuben Isaacman, "My Daughter," May 9, 1945, 50/173, box 2, folder 8, UPT. For another example, see Parfitt family to American Consul (Germany), letter, June 7, 1946, MS-239, box 6, folder 5, AJA.

108. Kirschner, *Sala's Gift*, 235–36.

109. Horvitz, interview by Krulik. Also see Daniel Isaacman to his parents, letters, April 11 and 18, 1945, 50/173, box 2, folder 4, UPT; Daniel Isaacman to his parents, letters, May 1 and 4, 1945, 50/173, box 2, folder 5, UPT. The support from his father arrived in mid-May. See Daniel Isaacman to his parents, letter, May 12, 1945, 50/173, box 2, folder 5, UPT.

110. For more on the difficulty concerning obtaining residency papers and passing health screenings, see chap. 4.

111. M. Berman to I. B. Rose, letter, May 13, 1945, CJC001, DA 18, box 5, folder 10, CJA.

112. Chaplains also worried that if marriages took place in areas where there was not yet a government recognized by the United States, Britain, or Canada, such as France in the summer of 1944, the weddings would be seen as illegitimate. The AEF determined that if a military chaplain officiated, the weddings would be legitimate. Fred Buttenbaum to Senior Chaplain, letter, August 22, 1944, RG 498, AB 291.1, box 31, NACP.

113. Marriage Certificate of Daniel M. Isaacman and Clara Heller, July 30, 1945, A231.544, Archives de l'État, Brussels.

114. Ostroff and Ostroff, interview by author. Also see Phil C. to Jack Eisen, letter, July 27, 1944, CJC001, DA 18, box 23, folder 6b, CJA.

115. *Canadian Jewish Review*, June 15, 1945, 8.

116. Horvitz, interview by Krulik.

117. On the legal debate, see Katz, "The Mothers, the *Mamzerim*, and the Rabbis."

118. Aryeh Lev to Morris Kertzer, letter, April 18, 1944, MS-709, box 12, file 2, AJA; Committee on Army and Navy Religious Activities, responsa on marriage, MS-675, box 13, folder 11, AJA. While Mort and Helena had a Jewish ceremony when they arrived in the United States, Mort's chaplain could not have foreseen such a development.

119. There also was a concern that she had been previously entered into what was commonly referred to as a "white" or unconsummated marriage (*mariage blanc*).

120. Sydney also faced punishment for leaving without permission. Sydney D. to Jack Eisen, letters, June–December 1945, CJC001, DA 18, box 23, folder 7, CJA.

121. Summer, interview by author.

122. Summer, interview by author.

123. Conference of Jewish Chaplains, minutes.

124. Lydia Servetnick, telephone conversation with author, January 30, 2009.

125. Mayer Abramowitz to Aryeh Lev, letter, December 1947, NJWB, box 42, folder 7, AJHS; Mayer Abramowitz, "A Wedding in Berlin," Jewish Federation of Miami, http://www.ujc.org/page.aspx?id=38547, accessed March 28, 2013.

126. Arthur Brodey, monthly report, November 1945, SC-1390, AJA; Bert A. Klein, monthly report, December 1946, NJWB, box 71, folder Klein, AJHS; Sidney Ballon, monthly reports 1945, NJWB, box 43, folder 24, AJHS; Louis Barish, monthly reports, June 1949–50, NJWB, box 44, folder 8, AJHS.

127. Bert A. Klein to Aryeh Lev, letter, October 18, 1946, NJWB, box 71, folder Klein, AJHS.

128. Ernst Lorge, diary entries, December 7 and October 13, 1945, MS-672, box 1, folder 1, AJA; H. Gevantman, monthly report, October 1945, CJC001, DA 18, box 5, file 18, CJA.

129. Jack Eisen to P. C., letter, July 27, 1944, CJC001, DA 18, box 23, folder 6b, CJA; Meyer J. Goldman, monthly report, February 1945, I-180, series VI, box 188, folder Belgium, AJHS.

130. Division of Religious Activities, *Responsa in War Time*, 26.

131. Canadian chaplaincy conferences never addressed these ceremonies, while the American and British chaplains' meetings did. Jack Eisen to P. Cohen, letter, July 27, 1944, CJC001, DA 18, box 23, folder 6b, CJA.

132. Bert A. Klein to Aryeh Lev, letter, October 18, 1946, NJWB, box 71, AJHS.

133. "Traditional Ceremony Unites PFC, Hungarian," *Wiesbaden (Germany) Post*, May 16, 1947, NJWB, box 52, folder 4, AJHS; Carl Miller to CANRA, letter, March 5, 1946, NJWB, box 86, folder 8, AJHS; "Tryber-Mintz," *Jewish Criterion*, April 13, 1945, 12.

134. Turgel, interview 39187, segments 160–61.

135. Ostroff and Ostroff, interview by author. Also see Fishman and Weingartner, *Lala's Story*, 326.

136. "Jewish Soldier Weds in Hitler's Room," *Jewish Chaplain*, October 30, 1945, Jewish Chaplains World War II, box 1, folder 1 clippings, Jewish Military Museum (London).

137. "Weddings in Heidelberg," *Center Courier* (Heidelberg, Germany), March 1946.

138. Isaacman, interview 24614, segments 166 and 167.

139. Daniel Isaacman to his parents, letter, July 20, 1945, 50/173, box 2, folder 7, UPT.

140. Abraham Klausner officiated at their wedding.

141. Fishman and Weingartner, *Lala's Story*, 323.

142. "Weddings in Heidelberg," *Center Courier* (Heidelberg, Germany), March 1946; Harry Jagoda, interview by author.

143. Fishman, interview by author; also see Fishman and Weingartner, *Lala's Story*, 327.

144. Fishman, interview by author. Lala also emphasized that her wedding dress was a "real" one, given to her by a young German peasant woman from whom they bought produce; it was not a dress handed from DP to DP. Flory Jagoda and Gena Turgel similarly emphasized the uniqueness of their wedding dresses in their interviews.

145. Isaacman, interview 24614, segments 166–68.

146. Kirschner, interview 33589, segments 39–40.

147. Nathan and Edith Litvin Papers, Folder: Correspondence, 1946–1947, 2013.493.1, Litvin 1:7, USHMM; Abe Bonder to Jack Eisen, letter, October 16, 1945, CJC001, DA 18, box 23, file 5a, CJA; Bonder, interview 40845, segments 151–56.

148. Kirschner, interview 33589.

CHAPTER FOUR

1. Sylvia Marsili, memo and letter of instruction, August 24, 1945, MS-410, box 1, folder 7, AJA; Ruby Gorewitz to Daniel Isaacman, letter, September 19, 1945, MS-410, box 1, folder 5, AJA.

2. These countries often relied on the language of "repatriation," even though few of these spouses had ever set foot in any of the countries now claiming them as potential citizens.

3. American Red Cross, "Assistance to War Brides," December 1945, RG 200, 618.4, NACP; H. Dorsey Newson to Thomas Dinsmore, letter, January 14, 1946, RG 200, 618.4, NACP; Dewitt Smith to American Red Cross, letter, April 12, 1946, RG 200, 618.4, NACP.

4. Canada, Debates, House of Commons, October 12, 1945, Canadian Parliamentary Historical Resources, https://parl.canadiana.ca/view/oop.proc_HOC_2001_1/240; Stacey and Wilson, *The Half Million*, 135–41.

5. "Weep No More," *Stars and Stripes Magazine*, June 17, 1945, ii; "US Girls Won't Like You, Wives of GIs Warned," *Chicago Tribune*, January 24, 1946, 9; "Italian Brides' Ship Leads to Protest," *Sunderland (UK) Daily Echo and Shipping Gazette*, March 13, 1946, 1. A more positive assessment can be found in Carl Pierson, "47 Points and a Bride," *Stars and Stripes Magazine*, October 14, 1945, iii.

6. James Forrestal to Basil O'Connor, letter and report, November 15, 1945, RG 200, 618.4, NACP. Also see "Wives Won't Go Next Month," *Stars and Stripes*, November 28, 1945, 1; "Plans to Deploy Brides Remain in Fluid Stage," *Stars and Stripes*, December 29, 1945, 5; Vivien S. Harris to Charlotte Johnson, memo, August 31, 1945, 618.4, 200, NACP. Britain and Canada similarly prioritized bringing veterans home over allowing aliens onto their shores. Sorby, "A Study on Demobilization"; Sparrow, "History of Personnel Demobilization."

7. James Forrestal to Basil O'Connor, letter, November 15, 1945, RG 200, 618.4.

8. "Matrimonial Entanglements of GI's Overseas," *Taunton (UK) Courier and Western Advertiser*, September 8, 1945, 7. In London, it became common for war brides to protest what they envisioned as "delayed" departures. See, e.g., "10,000 British War Brides Will Hire a Hall to Protest Delays in Rejoining Husbands," *New York Times*, October 9, 1945, 15.

9. Few remained in the same location after their wedding or could afford a telephone. Even if they could afford one, many residences lacked the electrical systems that could support its installation. Hadwiger and Cochran, "Rural Telephones in the United States," 222–26; Lauria and Anderson, *Running Wire at the Front Lines*; Ruth B. to Nathan B., letter, May 28, 1946, B. Family Private Collection, JPL.

10. Mail delay was so ubiquitous that complaints about it even appear in US surveillance reports. Surveillance Notes, January 28, 1948, FBIC, vol. 2, 39, NACP.

11. Britain, Canada, and the United States relied on microphotography to handle the massive number of letters. After November 1945, they no longer used the "airgraph" system. Bramley, "Airgraph and Victory Mail Service"; Yell and Fletcher, "Airgraphs and an Airman."

12. Daniel Isaacman to his parents, letter, September 15, 1945, 50/173, box 2, folder 8, UPT; Daniel Isaacman to Ruby Gorewitz, undated letter, MS-410, box 1, folder 5, AJA.

13. The restriction was lifted later in 1945. Kurt Klein to Gerda Weissmann, letter, November 2, 1945, in Weissmann Klein and Klein, *The Hours After*, 123–24.

14. Their reliance on an interlocuter and on a cable format, however, likely prevented the couple from sharing any intimacies. Nathan Litvin to Edith, letter, June 7, 1946, Nathan and Edith Litvin Papers, Folder: Correspondence, 1946–1947, box 1 folder 7, USHMM.

15. Lydia Servetnick, telephone conversation with author, January 30, 2009. Also see Shelkan, interview 15025, segments 23–24.

16. Nathan B. to Ruth, letter, April 9, 1946, B. Family Collection, JPL.

17. Flory Jagoda, interview by author.

18. See, e.g., Marinari, Hsu, and Garcia, *A Nation of Immigrants Reconsidered*; Miles, "Nationality, Citizenship, and Migration"; Steinert and Weber-Newth, "European Immigrants in Britain"; and Yang, *One Mighty and Irresistible Tide*.

19. Each of these countries established immigration policies for spouses and dependents that rested on the military personnel. If the servicemen or veterans were discovered to have been dishonorably discharged, not to be citizens or, in the case of the United States, not race-eligible, then the Europeans or North Africans would be inadmissible. See, e.g., Gardner, *The Qualities of a Citizen*, 226.

20. On where Jewish civilians wished to go, see Cohen, "Choosing a Heim."

21. Schiff, interview by Ringelheim. Also see Judah Nadich, "US Army Report on Conditions of Jews in Berlin," September 15, 1945, P 507, box 3 AJHS; Seibel, interview by Bradley.

22. Gardiner, *"Over Here,"* 140.

23. "History of the Directorate of Repatriation," Directorate of Repatriation, HQ650–124–33, Library Archives Canada. Also see Wolgin and Bloemraad, "'Our Gratitude,'" 53–54. The Canadian support of the transport of wives was something the American Red Cross (ARC) returned to in several of its meetings. Edna Mattox to Charlotte Johnson, committee report, February 12, 1944, RG 200 618.4, NACP.

24. Until 1938, the marriage allowance for soldiers on the Married Quarters Roll of their units varied according to the man's rate of pay and length of service. Brereton, *The British Soldier*, 159.

25. Office of the Deputy Military Governor Control Commission for Germany, "Memo: Marriage in the UK between Alien Women and British Subjects," February 22, 1946, FO 1052/267, Folder: Control Office for Germany and Austria and Foreign Office, Prisoners of War / Displaced Persons Division, File: Administration policy: Displaced Persons: All Nations, NAK. For a period, DPs were not permitted to travel to the United Kingdom to marry British subjects because they lacked passports. Once Britain established passport control offices in the British Zone, such travel was permitted. This was different from the United States and Canada, where the absence of a passport would have been dealt with during the marriage vetting process. Office of the Deputy Military Governor (British Zone), "Memo Concerning Marriage of Foreign Nationals to British Subjects," February 9, 1946, FO 1032/2243, Economic and Industrial Planning Staff and Control Office for Germany and Austria and Successor: Control Commission for Germany (British Element), Military Sections and Headquarters Secretariat: Registered Files (HQ and Other Series), File: Control and Treatment of Displaced Persons, NAK.

26. Charlotte Johnson, minutes, December 17, 1943, RG 200, 618.4, NACP.

27. Charlotte Johnson to Mattox, memo, June 9, 1944, RG 200, 618.31, NACP; Ann S. Petluck, memo, December 27, 1944, RG 248, folder 590, NACP; "GI Brides Who Flock to Paris Give Red Cross a Headache," *Stars and Stripes*, September 30, 1945, 4. During much of the war, there were more applications from the US Army than the Navy. See, e.g., Military Personnel Division Army Services Forces, minutes, December 2, 1943, RG 200, 618.4, NACP.

28. Bell to Shotton, letter, July 29, 1943, RG 200, 618.4, NACP; Attorney General to Commanding Generals Theaters of Operations, letter, May 22, 1944, RG 498, AG 291.1, box 31, NACP.

29. Edith Spray to Emma Jane Whipple, letter, November 3, 1944, RG 200, 618.4, NACP.

30. When the United States, Britain, and Canada permitted military personnel serving in Germany and Austria to marry German civilians, the number of war bride immigration applications from those countries increased considerably as well. McNarney to Commanding General Continental Base Section, letter, December 20, 1946, RG 498, 291.1, box 310, NACP; G. H. Garde, "Memo Subject: Processing German Fiancées under Public Law 471," RG 260, 291.1, box 201, NACP.

31. Department of State, report, December 28, 1945, RG 200, 618.4, NACP.

32. USNA, "Special Information Bulletin," December 5, 1947, WJC, box 3, folder 9, AJA. The policy was extended briefly.

33. Department of State, report, December 28, 1945, RG 200, 618.4, NACP; USNA, "Special Information Bulletin," December 5, 1947, WJC, box 3, folder 9, AJA. For a discussion of the role of race in these policies, see this book's introduction and Wolgin and Bloemraad, "'Our Gratitude,'" 27–60.

34. Charles Strull to Bert Bravman, letter, June 24, 1944, MS-239, box 1, folder 12, AJA; J. Eisen to Ralph C., letter, February 16, 1945, CJC001, DA 18, box 23, folder 6a, CJA; Stephen E. Krasa to AG Travel Branch, cable, March 31, 1947, RG 260, 291.1, box 202, NACP.

35. By November 1945, there were already thirty-two brides clubs in England and Scotland. The bureau was dismantled in 1947, by which time most of the dependents had already reached Canada. Jarratt, *Captured Hearts.*

36. Charlotte Johnson to Home Service Staff, memo, September 13, 1943, RG 200, 618.31, NACP; Robert Bondy to Charles Gamble, letter and policy draft, December 28, 1943, RG 200, 618.31, NACP.

37. Vivien S. Harris to A. E. Clattenburg, letter, September 29, 1945, RG 200, 618.4, NACP.

38. The American Red Cross pushed back at the notion that its workers should be involved in investigating the backgrounds of grooms or brides, suggesting that such an endeavor might jeopardize its capital of "international good will." Robert Bondy to Charles Gamble, letter and policy draft, December 28, 1943, RG 200, 618.31, NACP. Also see American Red Cross, "Assistance to War Brides," RG 200, 618.4, NACP; Vivien Harris to Charlotte Johnson, memo, August 31, 1945, RG 200, 618.4, NACP; Charles Strull to DBG, letter, May 14, 1945, MS-239, box 3, folder 3, AJA.

39. JIAS Montreal Immigrant Case Files, 1922–1951, 10037, 93–22670, Canadian National Archives. Couples also worked with several non-Jewish refugee groups such as the United Service for New Americans and the American Committee for the Protection of the Foreign Born (ACPFB). Bert Bravman to Charles Strull, letter, February 24, 1944, MS-239, box 1, folder 12, AJA; Charles Strull to Bert Bravman, letter, June 24, 1944, MS-239, box 1, folder 12, AJA; Charles Strull to the Commissioner of Immigration and Naturalization (Philadelphia), letter, September 17, 1945, MS-239, box 1, folder 10, AJA; USNA, "Special Information Bulletin," December 5, 1947, WJC, box 3, folder 9, AJA.

40. He could not fly to Munich to marry her because US civilians could not visit Germany. DPs could not exit Germany without permission. Nathan Litvin to Edith, letter, June 7, 1946, Nathan and Edith Litvin Papers, folder: Correspondence, 1946–1947, 1:7, USHMM. Gerda and Kurt similarly had trouble reuniting because the United States had not yet passed the fiancée legislation. Kurt Klein to Gerda Weissmann, letter, November 13, 1945, in Weissmann Klein and Klein, *The Hours After,* 132–33

41. Extant military regulations prohibited his fiancée from traveling to him.

42. Dave B. to J. Eisen, letter, July 31, 1945, CJC001, DA 18, box 23, folder 5; also see Dave B. to J. Eisen, letters, March 12, April 18, April 23, June 12, July 30, and August 20, 1945, CJC001, DA 18, box 23, folder 5; and J. Eisen to Dave B., letters, March 2, April 24, July 31, August 3, and September 21, 1945, CJC001, DA 18, box 23, folder 5. Jeanine finally received her paperwork, traveling to England, then Halifax, and finally to Toronto.

43. Charlotte Johnson, minutes, August 19, 1943, RG 200, 618.4, NACP; Howard Travers to Lewis Barrett, letter, March 1945, RG 200, 618.4, NACP.

44. See, e.g., Morris Aushitz, memo, February 21, 1946, MS-410, box 1, folder 7, AJA; Lala Fishman, identification card, December 18, 1947, Morris and Lala Fishman Papers, series I, box I, folder I, USHMM; Military Government for Germany, temporary travel document 42183, Morris and Lala Fishman Papers, series I, box I, folder I, USHMM; A. Lehmann, certificate of identity, March 28, 1947, private papers of A. Lehmann, collection 9653, 01/3/1, IWM; Pauline Lilly Howard, certificate of identity, Pauline Howard Personal Papers 1776, WL; Rose, *The Tulips Are Red*, 263; Rose, interview 49164, segment 204.

45. Kurt Klein to Gerda Weissmann, letters, November 7 and 22, 1945, in Weissmann Klein and Klein, *The Hours After*, 128–29, 138–40; Gerda Weissmann to Kurt Klein, letter, November 27, 1945, in Weissmann Klein and Klein, *The Hours After*, 141–43. She later lost her papers while trying to go to France illegally. Gerda commented to Kurt about the ubiquity of her situation; most DPs were "unable to get documents from their largely destroyed communities." Gerda Weissmann to Kurt Klein, letter, May 20, 1946, in Weissmann Klein and Klein, *The Hours After*, 258–59.

46. Daniel Isaacman to his parents, letter, May 13, 1945, 50/173, box 2, folder 5, UPT; Gerda Weissmann to Kurt Klein, letter, November 3, 1945, in Weissmann Klein and Klein, *The Hours After*, 124–25; Morris Auschitz, memo, February 21, 1946, MS-410, box 1, folder 7, AJA.

47. Gerda Weissmann to Kurt Klein, letter, October 16, 1945, in Weissmann Klein and Klein, *The Hours After*, 109; Edith Festinger to Nathan Litvin, letters, March 10 and 13, 1946, Nathan and Edith Litvin Papers, Folder: Correspondence, 1946–1947, Litvin 1:7, USHMM.

48. Kirschner, interview by author.

49. Elaine B. to Gershon Levi, letter, February 7, 1945, CJCOO1, DA 18, box 6, file 6, CJA; Daniel Isaacman, "Application for Family Allowances," July 30, 1945, MS-410, box 1, folder 7, Misc., AJA; Gerda Weissmann to Kurt Klein, letter, February 16, 1946, in Weismann Klein and Klein, *The Hours After*, 216; Isaacson, *Seed of Sarah*, 127. Some remained in the residences obtained for them by their military fiancés or spouses.

50. "History of S.A.A.C. Office and Directorate of Repatriation, 1942–1947," n.d., RG24-C-1-a 30-reel C-5220, National Archives Canada, Ottawa; Knowles, *Strangers at Our Gates*, 162; Edna Mattox to Charlotte Johnson, committee report and letter, February 12, 1944, RG 200, 618.4, NACP; Edith Spray to Emma Jane Whipple, letter, November 3, 1944, RG 200, 618.4, NACP. Also see Daniel Isaacman to Clara Isaacman, letter, January 7, 1946, MS-410, box 1, folder 4, AJA.

51. Before the war, commercial forays into transatlantic air service had focused more on the South Atlantic because that region offered aviators shorter distances, better weather conditions, and more intermediate stopping points. In late June 1939, Pan American Airlines began regular transatlantic passenger service between New York and Marseille, and in July it introduced travel between New York and Southampton, England. Bender and Altschul, *The Chosen Instrument*; Reed, "First Transatlantic Commercial Flight."

52. American Export Airlines was the first to offer these flights, but all three companies soon scheduled up to seven flights each week to and from La Guardia and Hurn Airports. Bowen and Rodrigue, "The Rise of Air Transportation"; Courtwright, *Sky as Frontier*, 89–132; Watson, "British Overseas Airways Corporation."

53. There were a few cases when the United States chartered flights to La Guardia, particularly as the deadline for the end of the program approached. Gardiner, *"Over Here,"* 140; Raska, "Movement of War Brides."

54. Ostroff and Ostroff, interview by author. Also see Nathan Litvin to his parents, telegram, August 6, 1946, Nathan and Edith Litvin Papers, Folder Documents Related to European Wedding, 1:8, USHMM; Susan Erlebacher, telephone conversation with the author, February 20, 2009; Burke, interview 9515.

55. "Red Cross Greets Brides of Soldiers," *Gazette* (Cedar Rapids, IA), March 1, 1945, 11; "GI Brides Who Flock to Paris"; "Fail to Reach Decision on War Bride Transportation," *Beatrice (NE) Times*, October 17, 1945, 6; "3000 GI Brides in France May Sail in 2 Months," *Chicago Tribune*, January 2, 1946, 11. Also Emde, interview 9510.

56. Summer, interview by author. Other examples can be found in Bonder, interview 40845, segments 152 and 156–57; Klein, interview 9725, segment 134.

57. "Rescued from US Ship," *Belfast News-Letter*, March 18, 1946. 5; "54 Saved from Ship," *New York Times*, March 18, 1946, 9; "Bryon Darnton."

58. Elisabeth Walton to Mary Rose Ryan, letter, March 1, 1946, RG 200, 618.4, NACP; Don Smith to Wesselius, memo, March 5, 1946, RG 200, 618.4, NACP; William Lee to Don Smith, letter, March 5, 1946, RG 200, 618.4, NACP; "New Army System on Wives' Arrivals," *New York Times*, March 9, 1946, 13; "Cargo Carrying Allowed: North Atlantic Service Liners Get WSA Authorization," *New York Times*, March 31, 1946, 47.

59. Elphick, *Liberty*; Herman, *Freedom's Forge*, 176–91.

60. Nathan B. to Ruth, letter, April 9, 1946, B. Family Collection, JPL. Also see Ruth B. to Nathan, letter, April 27, 1946, B. Family Collection, JPL; "Brides' Ship Gets Repair," *Maple Leaf*, January 4, 1946, 1. Despite Nathan's suggestion that only the liberty ships were at fault, many types of vessels experienced mechanical problems. See, e.g., "Brides Are Held Up," *Maple Leaf*, January 5, 1946, 1; and "Tears, Kisses End GI Brides' Nightmare Trip," *Chicago Tribune*, February 5, 1946, 7.

61. Elisabeth Walton to Mary Rose Ryan, letter, March 1, 1946, RG 200, 618.4, NACP; Don Smith to Wesselius, memo, March 5, 1946, RG 200, 618.4, NACP; William Lee to Don Smith, letter, March 5, 1946, RG 200, 618.4, NACP; "New Army System"; "Cargo Carrying Allowed."

62. Charlotte Johnson to Home Service Staff, letter, June 17, 1944, RG 200, 618.4, NACP; "Canadian War Brides Arriving 'Home,'" *Maple Leaf*, June 19, 1945, 3; "50,000 Wives Want Their Husbands," *Sunday Mirror*, October 7, 1945, 1.

63. "45,000 War Brides in U.S.," *New York Times*, August 8, 1946, 21; "Brides and Kiddies Canada Bound," *Maple Leaf*, February 5, 1946, 1; US Department of Justice, "Immigration and Naturalization Service (U.S. Department of Justice) *Annual Reports* (Fiscal Year Ending June 30, 1947)," Department of Citizenship and Immigration Fonds, RG 26, vol. 143, file 3–40–21, NACP; Knowles, *Strangers at Our Gates*, 162.

64. John Potts, report, January 7, 1946, RG 200, 618.4, NACP; C. J. Kleinegger, "Survey of Bride Staging Facilities," December 20, 1946, RG 498, AG 291.1, box 310, folder 291, NACP. Also see "New Army System."

65. Gorewitz, interview 34876, segments 156–57; Isaacman, interview 24614, segment 183.

66. Canadian Wives Bureau (Civilian Repatriation Section) to Ruth B., letter, July 11, 1946, B. Family Collection, JPL.

67. They had been quickly constructed in 1944 and rebuilt in 1945 to accommodate Occupation troops, returning POWs, and spouses. Kaplan, *The Interpreter*, 142; Guise, "Camp Lucky Strike"; Patriquin, "My Dear Young Lady."

68. Long, interview 9444/2; Harisiades, interview 9446.

69. When, in December 1946, the US military surveyed the facilities in Bremerhaven, for example, they determined that the current facilities, which accommodated 125 infants and 560 adults, needed to be increased by at least 500 beds. C. J. Kleinegger, "Survey of Bride Staging Facilities," December 20, 1946, RG 498, AG 291.1, box 310, file 10, NACP.

70. Flory Jagoda, interview by author.

71. Isaacman, interview 24614, segment 183; Kirschner, interview 33589, segment 41.

72. H. Dorsey Newson to Thomas Dinsmore, letter, January 14, 1946, RG 200, 618.4, NACP; Dewitt Smith, letter, April 12, 1946, RG 200, 618.4, NACP; "GI Brides Start Shipping to US Early in February," *Stars and Stripes*, December 14, 1945, 1; "60,000 GI Brides and Tots Have US Pacing the Floor," *Stars and Stripes*, January 15, 1946, 8; "2 Army Transports Here," *New York Times*, October 18, 1946, 23; Wicks, *Promise You'll Take Care of My Daughter*.

73. "First Shipment of UK Brides Sails January," *Stars and Stripes*, December 31, 1945, 5; "Cargo Carrying Allowed"; Irene Orlaska, interview by author, June 12, 2014, Columbus, OH (hereafter Orlaska, interview by author).

74. A. R. (Avice R.) Wilson, diary entry, July 29, 1946 (9:30 pm), 3403, 86/68/1, IWM.

75. Jagoda, interview by Ringelheim; Flory Jagoda, interview by author.

76. J. Eisen to Irwin Rosen and Herbert Katzki, memo; Nathan B. to Ruth B., letter, February 11, 1946, B. Family Collection, JPL; Kirschner, interview 33589, segment 41; Paroutaud, "Is Your Marriage Really Necessary? (A War Bride's Story)," 1896, 86/5/1, Monterey, CA, December 1, 1984, IWM (hereafter Paroutaud, "Is Your Marriage").

77. Ginnis, interview 9505.

78. Flory Jagoda, interview by author. Also see Harisiades, interview 9446.

79. Undated ship manifesto, undated, CJC001, DA 18, box 7, folder 7, CJA.

80. Paroutaud, "Is Your Marriage." Also see A. R. (Avice R.) Wilson, diary entry, July 27, 1946 (5:30 a.m.), 86/68/1, IWM.

81. Isaacman, interview 24614, segment 183; Jagoda, interview by author; Paroutaud, "Is Your Marriage"; Kirschner, interview by author.

82. Charters, "Just Imagine," 122–23; Flory Jagoda, interview by author; Kirschner, interview 33589, segment 41; A. R. Wilson, diary entry, August 1, 1946, IWM.

83. Arlene Judd, interview by author, January 10, 1989, Yonkers, NY; Ostroff and Ostroff, interview by author.

84. Charters, "Just Imagine," 122–23. Also see Annie C., letter, April 5, 1946, CJC001, DA 18, box 7, file 15, CJA; Auger, "'That's My Story,'" 121.

85. Flory Jagoda, interview by author. Also see A. R. Wilson, diary entry, August 5, 1946, 86/68/1, IWM; Dwyer, interview 9443.

86. Ann Kirschner, interview by author; Isaacman, interview 24614, segment 183.

87. Isaacman, interview 24614, segment 183.

88. J. Eisen to I. Rosen and Herbert Katzki, memo, June 2, 1947, Records of the Stockholm office of the American Jewish Joint Distribution Committee, I 5B/3 43, JDCJ.

89. Hegarty, *Victory Girls*; Littauer, *Sex Anarchy*. Also see Kramm, *Sanitized Sex*.

90. Dwyer, interview 9443; Long, interview 9444/2; Roach Pierson, "*They're Still Women After All*," 189.

91. By 1946, American and Canadian authorities agreed that war brides could not travel beyond their sixth month of pregnancy, nor could infants under the age of three months. Orlaska, interview by author.

92. The first journey witnessed the greatest number of hospitalizations and deaths, with over twenty children hospitalized at Fort Hamilton in Brooklyn immediately upon disembarkation. The second and third *Vance* voyages saw dozens of infants seriously ill upon arrival and two passing away at sea. "Deaths of 3 Babies, Illness of 16 Others Investigated after Bride Ship Arrival," *New York Times*, May 22, 1946, 23; "5 Babies' Deaths on Ship Bring 2 Inquiries: Weinstein Sees No Threat to City Children," *New York Times*, May 23, 1946, 23; "The Bride Ship Tragedy," *Toledo (OH) Blade*, May 25, 1946, 7; "Death of Sixth Baby Spurs Army Inquiry into Cause of Illness on 2 Bride Ships," *New York Times*, May 24, 1946, 38; "4 More Babies Ill aboard a Bride Ship," *New York Times*, May 31, 1946, 25; "Infants Ill on Transport," *New York Times*, August 28, 1946, 16; Lee, *Bittersweet Decision*, 132–33; Bryan Vonstrahl, "Horrors on Board the *Zebulon B. Vance*."

93. "War Bride Baby Toll Now 9 as 2 More Die," *New York Times*, May 27, 1946, 18; "War Bride Travel Slowed by Army," *New York Times*, July 12, 1946, 37; "816 Passengers Are Safe after US Ship Explosion," *Shields Daily News* (Tynemouth, UK), September 7, 1946, 7.

94. "Brides Blamed for Deaths of Babies at Sea," *Tampa Morning Tribune*, June 6, 1946, 15; Orlaska, interview by author.

95. "Army Urges Not to Bring Brides with Infants Less than Year Old," *New York Times*, June 6, 1946, 20.

96. They also complained that the public transport of these women (and men) delayed the demobilization of Allied soldiers, that these women would cause a "spinster crisis" in North America, and that the brides and fiancées of soldiers could be communist spies in disguise. Lila B. to Nathan B., letter, July 8, 1945, B. Family Collection, JPL; "Chaplain Says Experts Fear 75 Pct. of War Marriages Will Fail," *Chicago Tribune*, November 14, 1945, 27; "Wives or GIs?," *Stars and Stripes*, November 28, 1945, 2; "Matrimonial Entanglements of GI's Overseas," *Taunton (UK) Courier, and Western Advertiser*, September 8, 1945, 7.

97. Arlene Judd, interview by author, January 10, 1989, Yonkers, NY; Arlene Judd, interview by author, October 15, 2002, Albany, NY; Flory Jagoda, interview by author.

98. On this, see chap. 6.

99. Lariviere, interview 9529; Harisiades, interview 9446; A. R. (Avice R.) Wilson, diary entries, July and August 1946, 3403, 86/68/1, IWM.

100. Dror and Linn, "The Shame Is Always There"; Ephgrave, "On Women's Bodies," 14. There were not enough male war brides to merit separate processing offices or barracks.

101. Division of Women's Voluntary Services, *Canada Cookbook*; Division of Women's Voluntary Services, *From Dock to Destination*; British Ministry of Information, *Make Do and Mend*; Repatriation Committee, *Information for Wives of Soldiers*; *A War Bride's Guide to the USA*.

102. A. R. (Avice R.) Wilson, diary entry, July 28, 1946, 3403, 86/68/1, IWM. Also see "War Brides Form a Club While Waiting to Go to Canada," *Kent & Sussex (UK) Courier*, January 25, 1946, 3.

103. Harisiades, interview 9446; "Former French Bride Recalls How Red Cross Assisted Her," *Douglas County (CO) News*, March 14, 1957.

104. A. R. Wilson, diary entries, July 29, August 2, August 4, and August 5, 1946, 3403, IWM; Long, interview 9444/2; Kirschner, interview 33489, segment 41.

105. *Brides Asides—Ship Newsletter* (E. B. Alexander) nos. 1–19, 86/5/1, IWM; *Wives Aweigh Newsletter* (*Queen Mary*), February 5, 1946, in Lily Rothman, "See a Newspaper Written for World War II Brides," *Time*, November 11, 2015, https://time.com/4099810/wives-aweigh-veterans-day/; Lariviere, interview 9529; Lily Schacter, interview by author, July 5, 2012, Montreal; Orlaska, interview by author.

106. Elisabeth Walton to Mary Rose Ryan, letter, March 1, 1946, RG 200, 618.4, NACP; Long, interview 9444/2. I have not found any programs that focused on the male war brides.

107. Flory Jagoda, interview by author.

108. Ostroff and Ostroff, interview by author.

109. Schacter, interview by author, July 5, 2012, Montreal; Flory Jagoda, interview by author.

110. Some also discussed their husbands' (and families') failing to "claim" them. See, e.g., Jarratt, *War Brides*, 28; Berthiaume Shukert and Scibetta, *War Brides of World War II*, 75–84; and Winfield and Wilson Hasty, *Sentimental Journey*, 62–84.

111. In her work, Beth Cohen suggests that many DPs had no family to greet them when they disembarked in America. Cohen, *Case Closed*, 19.

112. A few couples traveled together. Lala and Gena, for example, arrived in New York and London with their husbands. For their husbands' families, this was the first moment when they could see the young men after a prolonged absence.

113. Flory Jagoda, interview by author; Harry Jagoda, interview by author.

114. Ostroff and Ostroff, interview by author.

115. "November 1945 List of Passengers, SS *Mingo Seam*," New York, U.S., Arriving Passenger and Crew Lists (including Castle Garden and Ellis Island), 1820–1957 (database), Ancestry.com; Lydia Servetnick, telephone conversation with author, January 30, 2009.

116. Department of National Defense to Jewish Chaplain, Montreal, Military District 4, letter, March 1, 1946, CJCoo1, DA 18, box 7, file 15, CJA.

117. Lydia Servetnick, telephone conversation with author, January 30, 2009.

118. Flory Jagoda, interview by author.

119. Kirschner, interview 33589, segments 40–42.

120. Brander, interview 39.

121. Fishman, interview by author.

122. Ellen had suffered from a miscarriage earlier in the year. Knauff, *The Ellen Knauff Story*, 3–8.

CHAPTER FIVE

1. Archival records include two different dates for Valerie's birth: May 27, 1946, and June 28, 1946. Birth certificate, June 3, 1946, Franciszka Friedel Rosenthal Bilotta T175042, ITS, WL; Certificate, November 24, 1947, Franciszka Friedel Rosenthal, T175042, ITS, WL; Identity

Card, American Joint Distribution Committee Location Service Belsen Camp, March 10, 1948, Francizka Friedel Rosenthal Bilotta T175042, ITS, WL.

2. Bilotta, *Friedel Rosenthal*; FBI, confidential report, May 19, 1947, file no. 100-12931, US Department of Justice, FBIT; Henry Ortner to Boston HIAS, letter, February 5, 1947, I-96, Boston HIAS, box 124, folder 18, AJHSB; War Department, confidential report, February 19, 1948, FBIC, vol. 1, 169, NACP.

3. Edward Soucy to John Stokes, letter, September 14, 1943, FBIC, vol. 1, 8, NACP; Donald B. Woods to Boston FBI, letter, January 3, 1947, FBIC, vol. 1, 48, NACP.

4. Daniel Groden to Helen Alpert, letter, December 8, 1947, I-96, box 124, folder 18, AJHSB. For much of 1946 and 1947, Boston officials insisted that there was nothing untoward about James's service. Donald Woods to Boston FBI, letter, January 3, 1947, FBIC, vol. 1, 48, NACP. To make things more complicated, Friedel needed to be in the United States before mid-March, when her grace period to marry James would expire. FBI, confidential report, May 19, 1947, FBIT.

5. John Edgar Hoover to Jack D. Neal, letter, February 1948, FBIT.

6. That sister had participated in the Kindertransport, the organized effort that began in 1938 to bring refugee children, most of them Jewish, from German-controlled territory to the United Kingdom.

7. James C. Bilotta to Jacob Landau, letter, June 12, 1948, WJC, box 38, folder 23, AJA; FBI, memo, January 20, 1948, FBIT; James A. Brennan, "Report on James Bilotta," June 29, 1949, FBIT.

8. SAC Boston to FBI, letter, March 3, 1949, FBIT; John Edgar Hoover to Jack D. Neal, letter, March 23, 1949, FBIT; James C. Bilotta to ITS (Arolsen), letter, August 7, 1953, 87451001_01, T175042, ITS, WL.

9. See, e.g., "It's Love, Love, Love!," *Sunday Stars and Stripes Magazine*, September 2, 1945, 4; and "British Brides Reunited Here with Husbands," *Hamilton (ON) Spectator*, August 17, 1945, 1.

10. This was especially true among those couples who had received permission to marry but had been unable to do so before demobilization. Phil Rothschild, "It Happened in Paris," *Detroit Jewish Chronicle*, July 26, 1946, 13; "Happily Ever After: European Bride Flies to City from a Bitter Past," *Detroit Free Press*, August 10, 1946, 9; "Love Wins Out," *Pittsburgh Sun-Telegraph*, August 12, 1946, 2; "Jewish GI Finally Wins Bride He Met in Munich in 1945," *National Jewish Post*, August 16, 1946, 18, "Mt. Clemens Vet and Refugee Bride He Flew Back to Europe to Wed," *Jewish News*, August 16, 1946, 8. Scholarly works that complicate these triumphant narratives include Friedman, *Citizenship in Cold War America*, chap. 2; and Zeiger, *Entangling Alliances*.

11. *Shaughnessy v. United States ex rel. Mezei*, 345 U.S. 206 (1953), followed three years later. Ignatz Mezei was married to an American citizen and, in 1948, left his home in Buffalo to visit his mother in Romania. When he returned to the United States, he was detained at Ellis Island. In May 1950, the attorney general ordered him excluded without a hearing. Ignatz filed a series of five habeas corpus petitions, and, eventually, his case made its way to the Supreme Court. Weisselberg, "The Exclusion and Detention of Aliens."

12. *Knauff v. Shaughnessy*, 338 US 537 (1950), https://supreme.justia.com/cases/federal/us/338/537/case.html#T9; Weisselberg, "The Exclusion and Detention of Aliens," 936–54;

Fisher, "To Have and to Hold." While the Supreme Court considered *Knauff*, it denied Judith Coplon's concomitant request that the Justice Department show cause as to why she did not deserve a new trial. A former Justice Department employee, she was found guilty of sharing secret documents with the USSR. Robert K. Walsh, "High Court in Recess after Upholding US in Disputes on Aliens," *Evening Star* (Washington, DC), January 17, 1950, 5.

13. Weisselberg, "The Exclusion and Detention of Aliens."

14. Mary Alice Baldinger to Alan Reitman, letter, February 15, 1950, ACLUP; ACLU to/from Edward Harris, letter, February 1950, ACLUP. Founded in 1920 soon after US attorney general Mitchell Palmer rounded up and deported alleged radicals (the Palmer Raids), the ACLU offered legal assistance to "defend and preserve" individual rights and liberties. The ACLU's response during World War II was mixed; some of its leadership pushed back against the possibility of defending Japanese Americans in court, although its West Coast offices refused to back down.

15. For the ACPFB, the question of the government's ability to deport and exclude was consistent with other causes they embraced. Founded in the 1930s to combat the harassment and persecution of people born outside of the United States and to help those who faced deportation, it now worked to defend foreign-born communists and trade unionists whom the United States sought to deport, and it attempted to "do everything" it could for Friedel. Abner Green to James Bilotta, letter, January 12, 1949, ACFBP.

16. "Late News Bulletin: War Bride Ban Upheld," *Evening Star* (Washington, DC), January 16, 1950, 1; Walsh, "High Court in Recess."

17. Bilotta, *Friedel Rosenthal*; Knauff, *The Ellen Knauff Story*. While Britain and Canada witnessed no case like Ellen Knauff's or Friedel Rosenthal's, their newspapers devoted attention to the stories of military spouses who were temporarily or permanently separated from their loved ones for political reasons and expressed a macabre interest in the spouses who died—or who were accused of crimes—soon after reaching their new homes. See, e.g., "Russia in Chains: The Poignant Story of a Woman Who Escaped to Britain after Compulsory Spy Work for Stalin," *Sheffield (UK) Weekly Telegraph*, July 8, 1950, 11–15; and "Truth about War Brides," *Ottawa Citizen*, December 18, 1946, 28.

18. Manz and Panayi, *Civilian Internment in the British Empire*, 24.

19. Fahrmeir, "Immigration and Immigration Policy in Britain," 50. Also see Bevan, *The Development of British Immigration Law*.

20. Dove, "'A Matter Which Touches the Good Name,'" 12. Also see Steinert and Weber-Newth, "European Immigrants in Britain"; Miles, "Nationality, Citizenship, and Migration"; and Tayler, "Courts and the Executive."

21. They labeled them as Class 2 prisoners of war. Avery, *Reluctant Host*; Brunnhuber, "After the Prison Ships"; Iacovetta and Perin, "Italians and Wartime Internment"; Kordan, *Enemy Aliens*.

22. Krammer, *Undue Process*. After December 1917, J. Edgar Hoover ran the Enemy Alien Registration Section.

23. A hearing was not required. Konvitz, *Civil Rights in Immigration*, 143–45; Jackson Chin, Romero, and Scaperlanda, *Immigration and the Constitution*, 92.

24. "Executive Order 9066," February 19, 1942, File Unit: Executive Orders 9041–9070, January 26, 1942–February 24, 1942, National Archives Catalog, https://catalog.archives .gov/id/5730250; Kashima, *Judgment without Trial*; Tayler, "Courts and the Executive."

25. "Uproar after Procession," *Western Morning News* (West Country, UK), February 20, 1950, 3. Also see Murray, *I Spied for Stalin*; "Russia in Chains."

26. J. Edgar Hoover to Harry Hawkins Vaughan, memo, May 23, 1947, President's Secretary's Files, box 146, FBI Subject File, Truman Library, Harry S. Truman Collection. My appreciation to Christopher Elias for finding and sharing this material with me.

27. "War Bride Free for Yule: Russian Held as Undesirable Makes Bail, Meets Mate," *New York Times*, December 24, 1949, 5; "War Wife Faces Second Christmas under Arrest for a Wrong Answer," *St. Louis Post-Dispatch*, December 22, 1949, 5; "Russian War Bride Freed after 13 Month Detention," *Press and Sun Bulletin* (Binghamton, NY), December 24, 1949, 2; "War Bride Victorious in Fight to be Formally Admitted to US," *St. Louis Post-Dispatch*, August 16, 1950, 3. At around the same time, US immigration officials incarcerated Chinese war bride Leong Bick Ha and her fifteen-year-old son when they arrived from China. After months of internment, the war bride committed suicide, resulting in a widespread protest in San Francisco among Chinese-born women.

28. Herbert Brownwell Jr., "A Report to the Nation on the Fight against Communism," transcript, April 9, 1954, 12, justice.gov, https://www.justice.gov/sites/default/files/ag/legacy/2011/09/12/04-09-1954.pdf. Also see "Mrs. Gebhardt Ordered Deported," *Times Record* (Troy, NY), March 16, 1954, 24; "Mrs. Gebhardt to Be Deported on April 6," *Times Record*, March 25, 1954, 44; "British War Bride to Be Deported," *Yorkshire (UK) Post and Leeds Mercury*, March 17, 1954, 5; "Deported Wife Will Pay Own Fare," *Yorkshire Post*, March 26, 1954, 1; and "Mrs. Mary Esther Gebhardt Detained in USA Pending Deportation," report, 1954, Foreign Office Consular Department, FO 369/5056, NAK.

29. John Edgar Hoover to Jack D. Neal, February 1948, FBIT.

30. Irving, *Citizenship, Alienage, and the Modern Constitutional State*, 124.

31. After he published the October letter, he was terminated from his position in the Signal Corps and forced to return to the United States. FBI, confidential report, May 19, 1947, FBIT.

32. John Edgar Hoover to Jack D. Neal, letter, February 1948, FBIT; James C. Bilotta, letter, June 12, 1948, WJC, box 38, folder 23, AJA.

33. FBI, notes, January 18, 1948, US Department of Justice, FBIC, vol. 2, 40, NACP; FBI Legal Attaché, London, to John Edgar Hoover, memo and letter, July 30, 1958, FBIT.

34. William C. Hacker and Marvin L. Rissinger, "Confidential Memo re Ellen Boxhornova," May 21, 1948, RG 319, box 411, folder 1, NACP; L. R. Forney to FBI (Reynolds), memo, July 15, 1948, RG 319, box 411, folder 2, NACP. According to Ellen Schrecker, INS officials initially made a mistake when detaining Knauff and then spent three years trying to justify their decision. Schrecker, "Immigration and Internal Security," 405. I think it unlikely; Knauff had come to the attention of the FBI as early as 1948.

35. European Command Headquarters, "Internal Route Slip File: D-236869," June 25, 1948, RG 319, box 411, folder 1, NACP.

36. L. R. Forney to Commander in Chief, European Command, "Confidential Memo re Ellen Boxhornova," July 14, 1948, RG 319, box 411, folder 1, NACP.

37. Relator's Exhibit 8, US Court of Appeals for the Second Circuit, *United States of America ex rel. Ellen Knauff vs. W. Frank Watkins*, transcript of record, ACLUP; Gunther Jackson, "1950 Petition to the United District Court Southern District of New York, United States of America ex rel. Ellen Knauff Relator against Philip Forman, as Supervisor of the Ellis Island Detention Station and Edward Shaughnessy, as District Director of the Immigration and

Naturalization Service of the New York District, and against whoever may have the custody of the body of Ellen Knauff," 1950, ACLUP.

38. ACLU, handwritten notes on hearing, undated (1950), ACLUP; ACLU, report on Knauff proceedings, August 14, 1951, ACLUP. Also see Friedman, *Citizenship in Cold War America*, 47–79.

39. Supposedly the two continued to work together even after the security office had been disbanded. Forney to Commander in Chief, European Command, "Confidential Memo re Ellen Boxhornova," July 14, 1948, RG 319, box 411, folder 1, NACP.

40. Bernard A. Tormey to Intelligence Division (Headquarters, European Command), memo, March 14, 1951, RG 319, box 411, folder 2, NACP; ACLU, report on Knauff proceedings, August 14, 1951, ACLUP.

41. See, e.g., "Memo for Record," April 10, 1951, RG 319, box 411, folder 1, NACP.

42. Ellen had met the Bauers when they were detained on Ellis Island; she wrote to them once they settled in Germany. Louis C. Salz, CIC memo, April 19, 1951, RG 319, box 411, folder 1, NACP; Ellen Knauff to Bauers, letter, undated, RG 319, box 411, folder 1, NACP.

43. *US ex rel. Knauff vs. Shaughnessy*; ACLU, handwritten notes on hearing, undated (1950), ACLUP.

44. SAC (Boston) to John Edgar Hoover, memo, September 16, 1948, FBIT. Also see SAC (Boston), notes, January 21, 1948, FBIC, vol. 2, 35, NACP.

45. Friedman, *Citizenship in Cold War America*. Also see "Fraulein Accused of Marital Fraud," *Detroit Free Press*, December 2, 1948, 15; and Doris E. Brown, "Story of Much Married Women Related in Book by Investigator," *New Brunswick (NJ) Sunday Times*, February 26, 1950, 5.

46. They also described those women abandoned by their husbands and a few cases when women murdered their spouses. "Deserted British War Brides in Canada," *Lincolnshire (UK) Echo*, April 11, 1945, 4; "War Brides Returning," *Gloucester (UK) Citizen*, June 29, 1946, 7; "Brides Come Home to Mother," *Dundee (UK) Courier*, July 10, 1946, 3; "Position of Stranded GI Brides," *Coventry (UK) Evening Telegraph*, August 22, 1946, 3; "Self-Defense Trend Seen as Jurors Are Chosen in War Bride's Murder Trial," *Quad City Times* (Davenport, IA), October 22, 1946, 1; "Murder Trial," *Des Moines Register*, July 27, 1947, 4; "War Bride Murder Trial Hears Girl," *Montreal Star*, October 20, 1948, 2; Zeiger, *Entangling Alliances*, 144–46.

47. Howard Erion to INS, letter, January 31, 1946, MS-239, box 2, folder 7, AJA. Also see "Ottawa," *Maple Leaf*, February 20, 1946, 4; "Files in 1947 Suits," *Louisville Courier-Journal*, December 18, 1947, 29; Charles Strull to Messing, letter, August 27, 1947, MS-239, box 5, folder 12, AJA. In 1953, military marriages again came under national scrutiny when the Supreme Court considered *Lutwak et al. v. United States*, a case concerning three military "couples" indicted for marriage fraud and conspiracy. *Lutwak et al. v. United States* (344 U.S. 604), 1953, Cornell Law School, https://www.law.cornell.edu/supremecourt/text/344/604. See Abrams, "Family Reunification and the Security State," 261–65; and Wardle, "Involuntary Imports," 783–87. For an understanding of the contemporary place of *Lutwak*, see Kelly, "Marriage for Sale."

48. Zeiger, *Entangling Alliances*, 158–59.

49. Allied Control Council Law No. 1 nullified all Nazi racial laws, including those that had stripped Jews (and German- or Austrian-born refugees) of their citizenship. The application of the Allied Law was inconsistent at best, with some entities treating German-born

Jews inside and outside of Germany as if their citizenship never had been revoked and others imagining German-born Jews as stateless. See Fraser and Caestecker, "Jews or Germans?"; and Grossmann, *Jews, Germans, and Allies*, chap. 3.

50. Knauff, *The Ellen Knauff Story*, 12. She had lost her German citizenship when she married her first husband, a Czech citizen, and then lost her Czech citizenship after the Nazi seizure of power. The Board of Immigration Appeals refers to her as a native of Germany. See US Department of Justice Board of Immigration Appeals, File A-6947571, 1, NACP.

51. US Congress, Senate, *The Immigration and Naturalization Systems of the United States*, Report of the Committee on the Judiciary, Report no. 1515, 81st Cong., 2nd sess.(Washington, DC: 1950). Also see "Conviction of Bribers Upheld, *Casper (WY) Star-Tribune*, May 2, 1949, 3; "High Court Bars War Bride as Security Risk," *Des Moines Tribune*, January 16, 1950, 4. The FBI sought to demonstrate Kurt's disloyalty to his adopted country, but they were unable to do so. Kurt was naturalized in April 1943. Opinion of Hulbert, D.J., US District Court, Southern District of New York, ACLUP; Knauff, *The Ellen Knauff Story*, 18.

52. John Edgar Hoover to Jack D. Neal, letter, February 1948. Some supporters also emphasized her Germanness. William T. Evjue, "Hello Wisconsin!," *Capital Times* (Madison, WI), July 14, 1948, 1; Abner Green to President Truman, letter, February 8, 1949, ACFBP.

53. Certainly, by the time James had left Germany for the United States, relationships among Allied soldiers and Jewish refugees had worsened. GIs serving in the American zone were not the same soldiers who had liberated the victims of the Nazi camps; they had absorbed antisemitic rhetoric, imagining the Jews as left-leaning, dirty, manipulative, and greedy. William Haber, 1948 Summaries of Conversations (with General Huebner on April 14; with General Clay on April 15; with General Harrold on April 13 and 20; and with Colonel Sage on April 20), WHB, AA 2, box 20, BHL.

54. SAC (Boston) to John Edgar Hoover, memo, September 16, 1948, FBIT. Also see SAC (Boston), notes, January 21, 1948, FBIC, vol. 2, 35, NACP. In his attempts to generate sympathy for Friedel, James omitted the fact that he had been formerly married, that he had two children with his first wife, or that he and Friedel had become pregnant before marriage. Instead, his descriptions of Friedel emphasized her fragile mental state.

55. SAC (Boston), notes, January 21, 1948, FBIC, vol. 2, 35, NACP; US Department of Justice, letter and memo, February 8, 1948, FBIT. Jewish participation on the black/gray market had attracted notice. In 1947 and 1948, the adviser on Jewish affairs in the American zone identified the black market and GI antisemitism as top priorities. I. S. Kenin to Louis E. Levinthal, letter, October 6, 1947, WHB, AA2, box 20, BHL; William Haber to Meir Grossman, letter, February 24, 1948, WHB, AA2, box 20, BHL; Lucius D. Clary to William Haber, letter, March 2, 1948, WHB, AA2, box 20, BHL.

56. James Bilotta, "I Cannot Do Less," *Wisconsin Jewish Chronicle*, December 21, 1945, 14. Here James suggested that Friedel had been married and that her first husband had been murdered. That is not a narrative that gets repeated later (or is upheld by the evidence).

57. Harold Putnam, "Lawrence G.I. Writes *Globe* of Fiancée's Visa Troubles," *Boston Globe*, July 1, 1948, 16.

58. George Marion, "The Cold War on Friedel Rosenthal," *National Guardian*, March 14, 1949, 10. Also see James C. Bilotta to Abner Green, letter, undated (1948), ACFBP; William T. Evjue, "Veteran Pleads Case for Entry of Refugee Fiancée into US," *Gazette and Daily* (York, PA), July 24, 1948, 5.

59. Elizabeth Gurley Flynn, "Life of the Party," *Daily Worker*, February 4, 1949, 10; Putnam, "Lawrence G.I. Writes."

60. James C. Bilotta to Abner Green, letter, undated February 1948, ACFBP.

61. "Vet Will Fly to Girl He Saved at Dachau, Now Near Death," *Boston Globe*, February 25, 1949, 1.

62. Evjue, "Veteran Pleads Case."

63. 1948 Petition for Writ of Certiori, Jacobson, *US ex rel. Ellen Knauff v. Frank Watkins*, Brief in Support of Petition for Writ of Certiorari, ACLUP; "Why?," *Asheville (NC) Citizen-Times*, March 1, 1950, 12; "House Group Won Over by GI Bride," *Hartford (CT) Courant*, April 4, 1950, 2.

64. Knauff Hearing, 338 US 542 (1950), 10.

65. Edward A. Harris, "F.D.R. Jr. Taking Hand to Stay Deportation of Ellen Knauff: Congressman Asking for Delay Until He Can Act on Any Legislation He May Wish to Introduce," *St. Louis Post-Dispatch*, February 8, 1950, 3. Also see Marquis Childs, "Case of the GI Bride: Bar without Hearing," *Washington Post*, February 17, 1950, 22; "Will No One Call a Halt?," *St. Louis Post-Dispatch*, February 26, 1950, 26; and Paul Healy, "House Acts to Block Bride's Deportation," *New York Daily News*, April 4, 1950, 3.

66. "For a Review of the Ellen Knauff Case," *St. Louis Post-Dispatch*, March 23, 1950, 21.

67. Flynn, "Life of the Party."

68. Flynn, "Life of the Party."

69. The act also "mortgaged" the still extant 1924 quotas and allowed up to 50 percent of future quota spaces to be used on behalf of DPs. Neither Friedel nor Ellen would have been impacted by the bill's chronological and geographic restriction. Committee on the Judiciary, "Displaced Persons in Europe," Report of the Committee on the Judiciary pursuant S. Res 137, Report no. 950, 80th Cong., 2nd sess., March 2, 1948 (Washington, DC: 1948); "Displaced Persons," Hearings before the Subcommittee on Amendments to the Displaced Persons Act of Committee on the Judiciary, US Senate, 81st Cong., 1st and 2nd sess., March 25, 1949–March 16, 1950 (Washington, DC: 1950), 1115.

70. Many Americans continued to push back against opening up immigration. See, e.g., Mary Stephanie McDermott, letter to the editor, *St. Louis Post-Dispatch*, May 31, 1950, 24.

71. Abner Green to membership, undated letter (1949?), LC, ACFBP; also see James Bilotta to Jacob Landau, letter, June 12, 1948, ACFBP.

72. Childs, "Case of the GI Bride."

73. James C. Bilotta to Abner Green, January 10, 1949, ACFBP.

74. Evjue, "Veteran Pleads Case." *Boston Globe* reporter Harold Putnam suggested that it was James's anti-German stance that led to Friedel's immigration difficulties in the first place. Putnam, "Lawrence G.I. Writes."

75. Estelle Brand, "Off the Record," *Wisconsin Jewish Chronicle*, January 27, 1950, 6.

76. Gunther Jackson, "Petition to the United District Court Southern District of New York, United States of America ex rel. Ellen Knauff Relator against Philip Forman, as Supervisor of the Ellis Island Detention Station and Edward Shaughnessy, as District Director of the Immigration and Naturalisation Service of the New York District, and against whoever may have the custody of the body of Ellen Knauff," September 28, 1950, ACLUP.

77. "For the Information of Official Washington," *Evening Star* (Washington, DC), March 26, 1950, A21; ACLU, "Press Release," October 2, 1950, ACLUP; "Now for a Showdown," *St. Louis Post-Dispatch*, February 14, 1951, 24; ACLU, notes on Knauff, undated (1951), ACLUP.

78. "Now for a Showdown."

79. Knauff Hearing (338 US 542 (1950)); also see "Legislators Open US Doors to German-Born Wife of GI," *Battle Creek (MI) Enquirer*, April 4, 1950, 1.

80. "Justice Comes Slowly to Mrs. Ellen Knauff," *Salt Lake Tribune*, March 1, 1951, 8. Also see "Will No One Call a Halt?"; and "Happy Ending," *Asheville (NC) Citizen-Times*, November 9, 1951, 20.

81. "What about Ellen Knauff," *Indianapolis Star*, February 8, 1951, 16.

82. Marion, "Cold War on Friedel Rosenthal."

83. Marion, "Cold War on Friedel Rosenthal"; Abner Green to membership, letter, date /month unlisted, ACFBP; James Bilotta to ACPFB, July 30, 1948, ACFBP; James Bilotta to Jacob Landau, letter, June 12, 1948, ACFBP.

84. Abner Green to President Truman, letter, February 8, 1949, ACFBP; James Bilotta to ACPFB, letter, 1948 (date/month unlisted), ACFBP.

85. Evjue, "Veteran Pleads Case."

86. Evjue, "Veteran Pleads Case."

87. James Bilotta to Jacob Landau, letter, August 26, 1948, MS-361, WJC; "Happy Ending."

88. US Immigration and Naturalization Service, *Annual Report*, 34.

89. ACLU, letter to Senators, May 19, 1950, ACLUP; ACLU, "Press Release," October 2, 1950.

90. Kurland, "Robert H. Jackson."

91. Robert H. Jackson, *United States ex rel. Knauff v. Shaughnessy* (1950), Cornell Law School, https://www.law.cornell.edu/supremecourt/text/338/537#writing-type-16 -JACKSONBLACKFRANKFURTER. Also see John C. Granbery to Lyndon Johnson, letter, 1950, ACLUP.

92. Harris, "F.D.R. Jr. Taking Hand."

93. "Will No One Call a Halt?"

94. Patrick Murphy Malin, statement, November 2, 1950, ACLUP. Ellen similarly insisted that the promises of the US Declaration of Independence spoke to all of "the oppressed peoples of the world," particularly those who were "behind the Iron curtain." Knauff, *The Ellen Knauff Story*, 89–90.

95. In her deft study *Citizenship in Cold War America*, Friedman argues that the Knauffs' pleas for public support centered on the assumption that a threat to the integrity of the nuclear family could destabilize the national security state. Friedman, *Citizenship in Cold War America*. Also see Zeigler, *Entangling Alliances*, 159–60.

96. "Abrupt and Brutal," *Washington Post*, January 18, 1950, 12.

97. In Jackson's schema, the US government had presented Kurt with an untenable choice to "abandon his bride to live in his own country or forsake his country to live with his bride." *US ex rel. Knauff v. Shaughnessy*, https://www.law.cornell.edu/supremecourt/text/338/537.

98. Arthur Garfield Hays, introduction to Knauff, *Ellen Knauff Story*, xvi.

99. "Review of the Ellen Knauff Case." In 1951, the attorney general extended another offer to Kurt Knauff: he could live with Ellen at Ellis Island, or she could be released into his custody if she agreed to exclusion. The couple rebuffed both possibilities and, after much back and forth, Attorney General McGrath temporarily released Ellen into Kurt's custody. "Ellen Knauff to Reject US 'Parole' Offer," *St. Louis Post-Dispatch*, January 20, 1951, 1; Friedman, *Citizenship in Cold War America*, 29. See a different perspective in "Vacation or Fight," *Press and Sun Bulletin* (Binghamton, NY), January 19, 1951, 16.

100. Abner Green to President Truman, letter, February 8, 1949, ACFBP. Also see Monica Pearson, " . . . Never Parted Again," *National Guardian*, March 14, 1949, 10.

101. Friedman, *Citizenship in Cold War America*, 67.

102. "Vet Will Fly to Girl." Also see Evjue, "Hello Wisconsin!"

103. Marion, "Cold War on Friedel Rosenthal."

104. SAC Boston to FBI, letter, March 3, 1949, FBIT.

105. Knauff Hearing, 338 US 542 (1950), 14.

106. Knauff, *Ellen Knauff Story*, 175.

107. "Mrs. Knauff Leaves Ellis Island after Winning Fight to Enter US," *New York Times*, November 3, 1951, 1.

108. *US ex rel. Ellen Knauff v. Frank Watkins*, Brief in support of Petition for Writ of Certiorari (1948), ACLUP. Also see "Now for a Showdown"; Gunther Jackson, draft of petition, 1950, ACLUP.

109. *US ex rel. Ellen Knauff v. Frank Watkins*, Brief in support of Petition for Writ of Certiorari, ACLUP.

110. "Now for a Showdown."

111. "Feature Press Service: Weekly Bulletin #1492," June 4, 1951, ACLUP.

112. "Mrs. Knauff Temporarily Paroled," ACLU press release, February 5, 1951, ACLUP. Also see ACLU, "Memo: The Ellen Knauff Case," February 5, 1951, ACLUP.

113. Bilotta, *Friedel Rosenthal*, 6–8; Abner Green to President Truman, letter, February 8, 1949, ACFBP. Also see Abner Green to membership, draft letter, undated (1949?), ACFBP; "Civil Liberties Newsletter," August 5, 1948, ACLUP. James Bilotta to ACPFB, letter, undated (1948), ACFBP.

114. "Vet Will Fly to Girl." When he appealed for her care in 1945, James expressed concern that if he were not to provide her care, she would resort to prostitution "as so many others have." Bilotta, "I Cannot Do Less."

115. Marion, "Cold War on Friedel Rosenthal."

116. Supposedly he wrote five times a week. Evjue, "Veteran Pleads Case"; "Vet Will Fly to Girl"; "Lawrence Vet Flies to London, Ailing Fiancé," *Boston Globe*, February 25, 1949, 6; US Department of Justice, report, January 18, 1948, FBIT; FBI, notes, January 21, 1948, FBIT.

117. March 27 and April 3, 1950, Hearings of the Subcommittee no. 1, Committee on the Judiciary House of Representatives Eighty-First Congress, 2nd sess., on H.R. 7614, "A Bill for the Relief of Mrs. Ellen Knauff," 50, knauffhearinghrg-1950-hjh-0002 from_1_to_19.pdf, 2; Franklin D. Roosevelt, note, 1950, ACLUP; Harris, "F.D.R. Jr. Taking Hand."

118. See, e.g., Cho, "Disappearing Acts"; Marchetti, *Romance and the "Yellow Peril"*; Chung Simpson, "'Out of an Obscure Place'"; and Simpson, "American Orientalisms."

119. Healy, "House Acts"; "Legislators Open US Doors"; "Mrs. Knauff Leaves Ellis Island."

120. "Legislators Open US Doors." Also see "House Unit Approves Ellen Knauff's Entry," *Times-Tribune* (Scranton, PA), April 4, 1950, 26.

121. Putnam, "Lawrence G.I. Writes."

122. "Will No One Call a Halt?"

123. Edward A. Harris, "Ellen Knauff's Chances of Being Admitted to US Appear a Little Bit Brighter," *St. Louis Post-Dispatch*, May 18, 1950, 1.

124. Knauff, *The Ellen Knauff Story*, 233–34.

125. Knauff, *The Ellen Knauff Story*, 89–90.

126. James Bilotta to Abner Green, letter, January 10, 1949, ACFBP.

CHAPTER SIX

1. Lala Fishman, identification and traveling papers, 1945–1948, Morris and Lala Fishman Papers, series 1, file 1, USHMM.

2. Fishman, interview by author.

3. Fishman, interview by author.

4. Turgel, interview 39187, segments 171–72, 177–78; Turgel, interview 16080.

5. Keith, *Politics and the Housing Crisis*, 58. Also see Allport, *Demobbed*, 10; Brushett, "Where Will the People Go"; Klemek, *The Transatlantic Collapse of Urban Renewal*; and McEnaney, "Nightmares on Elm Street."

6. Allport, *Demobbed*, 74.

7. "Housing Dilemma," *Fort-Worth Star-Telegram*, April 8, 1946, 10; "Housing Hubbub," *Huronite and Daily Plainsman* (Huron, SD), December 22, 1947, 4; "Houses before Cinemas!," *Sunday Times* (London), August 26, 1948, 5; Patricia Hornsby-Smith, "What Women Want," *Sunday Times*, December 9, 1948, 4.

8. Works that challenge nostalgic histories of the "greatest generation" include Adams, *The Best War Ever*; Lipsitz, *Rainbow at Midnight*; and Polenberg, "The Good War?"

9. "Canada Not Utopia, Brides Find," *Derby (UK) Daily Telegraph*, November 16, 1945, 5; "Mothers-in-Law Anger GI Brides," *Hull Daily Mail* (East Yorkshire, UK), October 22, 1946, 1; "'Young Mrs. Barrington': Family Play at Hippodrome," *Eastbourne Herald* (Wellington, NZ), February 7, 1948, 4.

10. Millis Duvall, *In-Laws*.

11. Jean Bird cited in Allport, *Demobbed*, 76.

12. Bonder, interview 40845, segment 170.

13. Kirschner, interview 33589, segment 42.

14. Kirschner, interview by author. Also see Kirschner, interview 33589, segments 42–43.

15. Isaacman, interview 24614, segment 170.

16. Fishman, interview by author.

17. Ostroff and Ostroff, interview by author.

18. Turgel, *I Light a Candle*, 176.

19. Kirschner, interview 33589, segments 41–42.

20. Gerda Weissmann Klein, "Coming to Buffalo," in Weissmann Klein, *A Boring Evening at Home*, 9.

21. Ostroff and Ostroff, interview by author.

22. Bonder, interview 40845, segment 170.

23. Kirschner, interview 33589, segments 41–43.

24. Flory Jagoda, interview by author; Harry Jagoda, interview by author; Lydia Servetnick, telephone conversation with author, January 30, 2009.

25. Lydia Servetnick, telephone conversation with author, January 30, 2009.

26. Flory Jagoda, interview by author.

27. Turgel, interview 16080.

28. Kirschner, interview 33589, segments 41–44.

29. Horvitz, interview by Krulik; Horvitz, interview by Zarlin.

30. Naomi Litvin, "Pictures on the Wall (Interviews of Edith and Nathan Litvin)," Nathan and Edith Litvin Papers, box 2, USHMM.

31. On the laws and policies, see chaps. 3 and 4.

32. "Roud-Lipson," *Jewish Criterion*, October 18, 1946, 17; Bob Klein, "Confidentially," *Y.M. & W.H.A. Weekly*, November 1, 1946, 3.

33. Rose, *The Tulips Are Red*, 273; "Former Ottawa Man to Wed Dutch Heroine," *Ottawa Journal*, January 17, 1947, 10; "Canadian Chaplain Takes Overseas Bride," *Ottawa Citizen*, January 24, 1947, 5.

34. Klein, "Confidentially."

35. Kirschner, interview 33589, segment 42.

36. "Roud-Lipson," *Jewish Criterion*, October 18, 1946, 17; Klein, "Confidentially."

37. Langer, *Holocaust Testimonies*.

38. Rose, *The Tulips Are Red*, 273; Rose, interview, RG-50.477.1588.

39. Turgel, *I Light a Candle*, 136.

40. This was akin to child survivors who became parents after the war. Clifford, *Survivors*, 190–91.

41. Fishman and Weingartner, *Lala's Story*, 337.

42. Ostroff and Ostroff, interview by author.

43. Turgel, *I Light a Candle*, 175.

44. Turgel, *I Light a Candle*, 175. Lala, who had gone to Boston for a weekend to see her husband, expressed surprise that she had become pregnant during that visit. Fishman, interview by author. Also see Jean Komaiko, "A War Bride Looks at America: Polish Born Wife of Ex-GI Sees Nothing But the Good in Her Adopted Country," *Chicago Tribune*, June 5, 1955, 35.

45. Turgel, *I Light a Candle*, 175.

46. Summer, interview by author.

47. Ostroff and Ostroff, interview by author. Also see Brander, interview 39.

48. The couple eventually adopted a son. Isaacman, interview 24614, segment 172.

49. Kleinplatz and Weindling, "Women's Experiences of Infertility after the Holocaust," 211–17. Also see Pasternak and Brooks, "The Long-Term Effects of the Holocaust."

50. Turgel, *I Light a Candle*, 179; Turgel, interview 39187, segments 178–80.

51. Fishman and Weingartner, *Lala's Story*, 338.

52. Scientists have found that four to five years is the most common lag time for tuberculosis to bloom or for there to be a relapse of the disease if not fully treated.

53. Summer, interview by author.

54. Turgel, interview 39187, segment 179.

55. Summer, interview by author; Turgel, interview 39187, segment 179.

56. Kirschner, interview 33589, segment 44. Also Kirschner, interview by author.

57. Turgel, *I Light a Candle*, 175.

58. Cohen, *Case Closed*, 133. Also see Clifford, *Survivors*, 158; and Goldberg, *Holocaust Survivors in Canada*, 70–71.

59. "Hysterical D.P. Girl on Forty Foot Perch Rescued by Firemen," *Toronto Star*, May 2, 1949, 1; "Pole Sitter Mental Case," *Windsor (ON) Star*, May 3, 1949, 28; "Pole Sitting Girl

Rescued from Perch by Firemen," *StarPhoenix* (Saskatoon, SK), May 3, 1949, 10; "Girl on Forty Foot Perch Rescued by Firemen," *Times Colonist* (Victoria, BC), May 4, 1949, 2. Also see Cohen, *Case Closed*, 115–54; and Salamon, "Denial and Acceptance."

60. Abraham Klausner to Faige, letter, May 1945, MS-54, box 3, folder 15, AJA.

61. Paul Friedman, "The Road Back for the DPs," cited in Cohen, *Case Closed*, 137.

62. Clifford, *Survivors*, 410.

63. Schneer, "Is Seeing Believing?"; Schröder, "From Illustrations to Sources."

64. Komaiko, "War Bride Looks at America."

65. Komaiko, "War Bride Looks at America."

66. "Rabbi Rose Will Wed Heroic Dutch Girl," *Ottawa Journal*, January 16, 1947, 11.

67. "Holland Heroine Will Wed Here," *Ottawa Citizen*, January 17, 1947, 5; Murray Goldblatt, "Shepherds People from 12th to 20th Century," *Ottawa Citizen*, July 25, 1951, 17.

68. See, e.g., "Former Ottawa Man to Wed"; and "Canadian Chaplain Takes."

69. I have not discovered a Canadian or British radio or television show that featured a Jewish war bride who was a survivor; this is consistent with scholarship concerning television and radio coverage of the Holocaust. See Jordan, "And the Trouble Is Where to Begin."

70. "I'm an American Day" had its roots in a 1939 Wisconsin program. In 1940, Congress passed a resolution declaring the third Sunday in May "I Am an American Day." The INS produced the earliest war time broadcasts, while Voice of America produced later productions. Jenkins, "I'm an American."

71. Friede's first appearance coincided with the show's honoring Eleanor Roosevelt. Gorewitz, interview 34876.

72. Shelkan, interview 15025.

73. Bonder, interview 40845, segment 175.

74. Bergman, interview 26752.

75. Kirschner, interview 33589, segments 43–44.

76. See, e.g., Dashorst et al., "Intergenerational Consequences of the Holocaust."

77. On postwar trauma and posttraumatic stress disorder among war veterans, see Allport, *Demobbed*, 191.

78. Ostroff and Ostroff, interview by author; Flory Jagoda, interview by author; Harry Jagoda, interview by author.

79. Bonder, interview 40845, segment 149.

80. Kirschner, interview by author. Sala's own language can be seen in Sala Garancz to Kirschner, letter, undated, in Kirschner, *Sala's Gift*, 234–36.

81. Kirschner, interview 33589, segment 43.

82. Kirschner, interview 33589, segment 43. Also see Gerda Weissmann Klein, "Coming to Buffalo," in Weissmann Klein, *A Boring Evening at Home*, 9.

83. Bergman, interview 26752.

84. Fishman and Weingartner, *Lala's Story*, 338; Ostroff and Ostroff, interview by author.

85. On the GI Bill, see Larsen et al., "War and Marriage." On the Veteran's Rehabilitation Act, see Lemieux and Card, "Education, Earnings and the 'Canadian G.I. Bill.'"

86. Turgel, *I Light a Candle*, 140.

87. Kirschner, interview by author.

88. Ostroff and Ostroff, interview by author.

89. These clubs focused on female war brides. I found no evidence of male war bride participation.

90. Isby, interview 9516.

91. Fishman, interview by author.

92. Ostroff and Ostroff, interview by author.

93. "Home Chats and News," *North Hudson (NY) Post*, March 1, 1944, 5; "Under the Harvest Moon," *New York Daily News*, August 23, 1945, 11.

94. L. A. Weintraub to S. Werkzie, letter, January 25, 1946, CJC001, DA 18, box 7, folder 7, CJA; Lily Schachter, interview by author, July 5, 2012, Montreal; Charlotte K., interview by author, July 8, 2012, Montreal. The majority of Jews in Montreal were English speakers, and Jewish war brides became part of the city's English-speaking Jewish community.

95. Some Jewish women's organizations insisted on their status as the rightful wives of available or returning American and Canadian servicemen. National Federation of Temple Sisterhoods, Transcript of Conference, February 26, 1945, WRJ, box 21, folder 2, AJA; Lichtenstein, letter, undated 1947, I 7A/1 8, JDCJ.

96. Survivors in the United States and Canada also attended English and citizenship classes through public libraries, school boards, YMHAs, and YMCAs. These programs did not cater specifically to survivors but rather served new Americans and Canadians of all religions and ethnicities.

97. Some instructors supplemented the already-provided course materials with their own supplemental materials. Adara Goldberg asserts that the JIAS classes "tried to transform the survivors into Canadians first, Jews second." Goldberg, *Holocaust Survivors in Canada*, 63. Also see Abramson and Lynch, *The Montreal Shtetl*, 174; Rogow and Bronk, *Gone to Another Meeting*, 173–78; and Switzer, "*Faith and Humanity*," 111–16.

98. "Field Advisor of Girl Scouts to Visit City," *Herald Statesman* (Yonkers, NY), September 26, 1945, 10; "NCJW Speaks for International Control of Energy," *Herald Statesman*, November 28, 1945, 11; "Mrs. Hanau Is Chairman," *Herald Statesman*, December 21, 1945, 17; "NCJW Group Learns about Religious Work," *Herald Statesman*, March 11, 1948, 23.

99. "Adult Students Entertain for Student Canteen," *Herald Statesman* (Yonkers, NY), December 22, 1949, 17; "Adult Students Elect Officers," *Herald Statesman*, June 10, 1950, 7; "Adult Students Club Returns Officers for Another Term," *Herald Statesman*, May 22, 1951, 11; "NCJW Hears Cookery Expert on Jewish Food," *Herald Statesman*, March 12, 1953, 11; Arlene Judd, interview by author, December 23, 1989, Albany, NY.

100. Bonder, interview 40845, segments 169–71; Arlene Judd, "Questionnaire," March 1989, author's personal collection; Arlene Judd, interview by author, December 23, 1989, Albany, NY; Arlene Judd, interview by author, October 15, 2002, Albany, NY.

101. Ostroff and Ostroff, interview by author.

102. Kirschner, interview 33589, segments 43–44.

103. Kirschner, interview by author.

104. Turgel, interview 39187, segments 177–78.

105. I have found no examples of war brides participating in resettlement programs run by the United Service for New Americans (USNA).

106. Many agencies made similar assumptions about single female survivors or those married to male survivors.

107. Turgel, interview 39187, segments 171–78; Turgel, *I Light a Candle*, 178.

108. Gorewitz, interview 34876, segment 168. Also see Isaacman, interview 24614, segment 193.

109. Kushner, "Holocaust Survivors in Britain."

110. Turgel, interview 39187, segments 171–72. Also see Brander, interview 39; and Bergman, interview 26752.

111. Abella and Troper, *None Is Too Many*.

112. Ruth B. to Nathan B., letter, March 16, 1946, B. Family Collection, JPL.

113. Its obstructive nature persisted after the passage of the Displaced Persons Act in 1948.

114. Auerbach, *The Admission and Resettlement of Displaced Persons*, 14–18.

115. Travel Report no. 225159 (1948), Archives de l'État File, no. 1541040, Algemeen Rijksarchief / Archives générales du Royaume, Brussels; Isaacson, interview RG-50.227.0006; Isaacson, interview MOH 027; Summer, interview by author.

116. Summer, interview by author.

117. Ostroff and Ostroff, interview by author.

118. Anne F. to Charles Strull, letter, August 11, 1949, MS-239, box 5, folder 12, AJA. Also see Charles Strull to Ann S. Petluck, letter, July 26, 1949, MS-239, box 5, folder 12, AJA.

119. Girard, "If Two Ride a Horse," 35.

120. An exception, however, might be if they married enemy aliens.

121. The Cable Act of 1922 may have "restored" the citizenship of American-born white women, but it denationalized Chinese American women. See Lewis Bredbenner, *A Nationality of Her Own*, 80–110; Cott, "Marriage and Women's Citizenship"; Motomura, *Americans in Waiting*, 5; and Volpp, "Divesting Citizenship." Also see Cho, *Uncoupling American Empire*, 1–2; and DiStasi, "Derived Aliens."

122. Komaiko, "War Bride Looks at America."

123. British Nationality and Status of Aliens Act (1914), The National Archives, https://www.legislation.gov.uk/ukpga/Geo5/4–5/17/enacted. To be British was to owe allegiance to the monarch. A 1918 amendment allowed a British-born wife of an enemy alien to become naturalized as a British subject after she underwent the naturalization process. After the passage of the 1935 Irish Nationality and Citizenship Law, which stipulated that marriage did not result in an Irish woman's loss of Irish citizenship, British women who were married to aliens could have different statuses. Baldwin, "Subject to Empire," 552.

124. Among other things, the Act reinstated a woman's right to retain her British nationality. Baldwin, "Subject to Empire"; Gibney, "'A Very Transcendental Power'"; Hansen, "The Politics of Citizenship"; Tabili, "Outsiders in the Land of Their Birth."

125. Bergman, interview 26752. The shift in British law was due, in part, to the Canadian Citizenship Act, which defined Canadian citizenship and only secondarily provided that Canadian citizens would be British subjects. Hansen, "The Politics of Citizenship," 69.

126. Girard, "If Two Ride a Horse," 52.

127. Canadian war brides received mixed messages concerning how one would become a citizen, which caused its own difficulties. Matrix, "Mediated Citizenship," esp. 73. This issue became publicly known during the early 2000s.

128. Komaiko, "War Bride Looks at America"; Bergman, interview 26752.

129. Summer, interview by author.

130. Fishman, interview by author.

131. Fishman, interview by author; Kirschner, interview 33589, segment 42; Rose, interview 49164, segment 212.

132. Leesha, for example, spoke with newspaper reporters when first coming to Canada, but by the early 1950s she had ceased speaking about her experiences in the resistance. "Holland Heroine Will Wed Here," *Ottawa Citizen*, January 17, 1947, 5; G. Murray Goldblatt, "Shepherds People from 12th to 20th Century," *Ottawa Citizen*, July 25, 1951, 17. For an interesting comparison of Leesha's memoir and interview, see Linden, "In the Name of the House of Orange"; and Linden, "Reflections on 'In the Name of the House of Orange.'"

133. See, e.g., Jagoda, *The Flory Jagoda Songbook*; and Weissmann Klein, *The Promise of a New Spring*.

134. Rose, interview RG-50.477.1588.

135. Schwartzman, "Sutured Identities."

136. Allport, *Demobbed*, 191.

CONCLUSION

1. Weissmann Klein, *All but My Life*; Isaacson, *Seed of Sarah*; Levi, *Survival in Auschwitz*; Rose, *The Tulips Are Red*; Turgel, *I Light a Candle*; Wiesel, *Night*.

2. As I discuss in the introduction, this reluctance was common.

3. It was likely that he, my grandmother, and my father had been moving toward Košice, the region where my paternal great-grandmother and many of my aunts, uncles, and cousins had been living at the beginning of the Hungarian occupation.

4. Anna's son Gershon did not want to immigrate to the United States and instead went to Palestine. Ron, *My Little Blue Tattoo*; Ron, interview by Zarlin.

5. Mishnah Torah, Laws of Yibbum and Halizah 6:4; Maimonides, Mishneh Torah, 2:1.

6. Arlene Judd, interview by author, January 10, 1989, Yonkers, NY; Arlene Judd, "Questionnaire," March 1989, author's personal collection; Arlene Judd, interview by author, December 23, 1989, Albany, NY; Arlene Judd, interview by author, October 15, 2002, Albany, NY.

7. My deep appreciation to Gershon Ron for sharing his stories and enthusiasms over the years and to Christine Schmidt for helping me to navigate the ITS records of Arlene and Gary Judd.

8. Tara M. Zrinski, "The Hidden Children, 70 Years after the Holocaust," *Elucidator* 47 (Winter 2015–16), http://www.elucidator.net/feature/the-hidden-children/.

9. After my grandmother moved out of her apartment, we discovered a group of letters that had been in Joe's possession, charting his and Harry's attempts to bring his family to the United States.

10. For much of my youth and young adulthood, my grandmother insisted that she spoke no German, an assertion she only recanted when I was a graduate student. Arlene Judd, interview by author, October 15, 2002, Albany, NY.

11. Arlene Judd, "Questionnaire," March 1989, author's personal collection; Arlene Judd, interview by author, December 23, 1989, Albany, NY.

12. I found one couple that divorced in the late 1940s or early 1950s.

BIBLIOGRAPHY

PRIMARY SOURCES

Archives and Libraries

Alex Dworkin Canadian Jewish Archives, Montreal
    Canadian Jewish Congress Organizational Records, CJC001
    Jewish Community Council of Montreal, I00033
    Montreal B'nai Brith Women, I0046
American Jewish Archives, Cincinnati, Ohio
    David M. Eichhorn Papers, MS-79
    Herbert A. Friedman Collection, MS-763
    Daniel M. Isaacman Papers, MS-410
    Harry Kaplan Papers, MS-54
    Eugene J. Lipman Collection, SC-7280
    Peretz Milbauer Correspondence, MS-828
    Selwyn D. Ruslander Papers, MS-460
    Harold I. Saperstein Papers, MS-718
    Herman Eliot Snyder Papers, MS-598
    Charles Strull Papers, MS-239
    Women of Reform Judaism, MS-73
    World Jewish Congress Records, MS-361
American Jewish Historical Archives, New York City
    Isadore Breslau Papers, P-507
    Morris Gordon Papers, P-910
    Abraham Klausner Papers, P-879
    National Jewish Welfare Board, I-337
    National Jewish Welfare Board, Army-Navy Division Records, I-180
    National Refugee Service, RG-248
    Records of the Jewish Welfare Board Chaplaincy, I-249

American Jewish Historical Society, Boston
  Hebrew Immigrant Aid Society Collection, I-96
Bentley Historical Library, Ann Arbor, Michigan
  William Haber Collection, 85198
Central Archives for the History of the Jewish People, Jerusalem
  Abraham Klausner Papers, P-68
Harry S. Truman Presidential Library and Museum, Independence, Missouri
  Harry S. Truman Collection
Imperial War Museum, London
  Berlin Air Line, EJ 5407
  Private Papers of A. Lehmann, 9653
  Private Papers of V. A. Long, 9742
  Private Papers of M. D. Paroutaud, 1896
  Private Papers of M. A. Turnbull, 2422
  Private Papers of A. R. Wilson, 3403
Jewish Military Museum, London (now housed at the Jewish Museum)
  Jewish Chaplains World War II Collection
Jewish Public Library, Montreal
  B* Family Collection
Joint Distribution Committee Archives, Jerusalem
  Geneva Office, Chaplains, 1947–1948, G 45–54/3/14/SM.800
  Geneva Office, Misc. Inquiries, G 45–54/3/6/SM.914
  Records of the Stockholm Office of the AJJDC
Leo Baeck Institute, New York City
  Judith Fraenkel-Bravman Collection, PID 1655161
  Hugo Stransky Collection, AR 7039
Library and Archives of Canada, Ottawa
  Directorate of Repatriation, RG24-C-1-a
London Metropolitan Archive, City of London
  Board of Deputies of British Jews, ACC 3121
  Central British Fund for World Jewish Relief, ACC 2793
  Jewish Memorial Council, ACC 2999
  Office of the Chief Rabbi, ACC 2805
McGill University, Montreal
  Living Testimonies Project
Mudd Library, Princeton University, Princeton, New Jersey
  ACLU Papers 1912–1990, MS Years of Expansion, online at Gale
    Primary Sources at https://www.gale.com/primary-sources
National Archives, Kew, Richmond, United Kingdom
  Admiralty Record Cases ADM 116
  Control Office for Germany and Austria and Foreign Office: Control
    Commission for Germany, Political Division, Records, FO 1049
  Control Office for Germany and Austria and Foreign Office: Control
    Commission for Germany (British Element), Prisoners of War
    / Displaced Persons Division: Registered Files, FO 1052

Economic and Industrial Planning Staff and Control Office for Germany and
 Austria and Successor: Control Commission for Germany, FO 1032
Foreign Office Consular Department, General Correspondence from 1906, FO 369
National Archives College Park, College Park, Maryland
 Chief of Chaplains, RG 247
 Abraham G. Duker / Irving Dwork Papers, RG 200
 Federal Bureau of Investigation, James C. Bilotta, 100-BS 12931
 Federal Bureau of Investigation, Transfer Call 421, 100-HQ 328147
 General Records of the United States Government, RG 11
 Knauff, Ellen, RG 319
 Records of Headquarters, European Theater of Operations,
  US Army (World War II), RG 498
 Records of the Immigration and Naturalization Service, RG 85
 Records of the National American Red Cross, NAID 783
 Records of the US Coast Guard, RG 26
 Records of US Occupation Headquarters, RG 260
 Records of the War Shipping Administration, RG 248
National Archives of Belgium, Brussels
 Heller, Clara, A231.544
 Ramet, Felicia, A2.060.639
 Wagman, Sylvia, A2.198.001
National Museum of American Jewish Military History, Washington, DC
 Morton Horvitz Collection
New York Public Library, New York City
 Fight for Racial Justice and the Civil Rights Congress
 Sala Garncarz Kirschner Collection, Dorot Jewish Division
United States Holocaust Memorial and Museum, Washington, DC
 Brian Coleman Collection, 2009.46
 Morris and Lala Fishman Papers, 1999.51
 Jeff and Toby Herr Oral History Archive
 Nathan and Edith Litvin Papers, Folder: Correspondence, 1946–1947, 2013.493.1
University of Michigan, Labadie Collection, Ann Arbor, Michigan
 Papers of the American Committee for the Foreign Born
University of Pennsylvania Archives and Records Center, Philadelphia
 Daniel Isaacman Collection, 50/173
University of Pittsburgh Archives Center, Pittsburgh
 American Left Ephemera Collection, 1894–2008, AIS.2007.11
USC Shoah Foundation Institute, Los Angeles
 Visual History Archive
Wiener Library, London
 Pauline Howard Personal Papers, 1776
 International Tracing Service Collection
 Jewish Committee for Relief Abroad, Papers, WL 1232
 Ruth Landau Collection, 1849/3
 Refugee Voices Collection

William Breman Jewish Heritage Museum, Atlanta
  Cuba Family Archives
Yad Vashem Archives, Jerusalem
  American Civil Liberties Union Papers, 1912–1990, Years of Expansion
  Gale Primary Sources, online
  Letters and Postcards Collection, 0.75
  Righteous among the Nations Database, online at https://righteous.yadvashem.org
  Testimonies, Diaries, and Memoirs Collection, 0.33

Interviews

Bergman, Anna. Interview 26752. Interview by Lyn Smith. February 5, 2004. Imperial War Museum, London.

Berman, Annette. Interview. Undated. RG-50.157.0002. Jeff and Toby Herr Oral History Archive. United States Holocaust Memorial and Museum, Washington, DC.

Bloch, Gottfried. Interview 107. Interview by Dana Schwartz. September 23, 1994. Visual History Archive, USC Shoah Foundation, Los Angeles. https://vha.usc.edu.

Bonder, Sala. Interview 54741. October 20, 1993. Living Testimonies Project, McGill University, and Visual History Archive, USC Shoah Foundation, Los Angeles. https://vha.usc.edu/partners/mcgill.

Bonder, Sala. Interview 40845. Interview by Rachel Alkallay. April 22, 1998. Visual History Archive, USC Shoah Foundation, Los Angeles. https://vha.usc.edu.

Bowman, Penina. Interview by John Kent. July 31, 2000. Esther and Herbert Taylor Oral History Collection. William Breman Jewish Heritage Museum, Atlanta.

Brander, Dorothea. Interview 39. Interview by Rosalyn Livshin. November 16, 2003. AJR Refugee Voices. Wiener Library, London.

Cohen, Hannelore. Interview 11. Interview by Rosalyn Livshin. March 23, 2003. AJR Refugee Voices. Weiner Library, London.

Dwyer, Mary Joyce. Interview 9443. June 9, 1986. Imperial War Museum, London.

Emde, Cicely Francesca. Interview 9510. Interview by Jan R. Stovold. September 26, 1986. Imperial War Museum, London.

Fishman, Lala. Interview 2860. Interview by Margaret Littman. May 25, 1995. Visual History Archive, USC Shoah Foundation, Los Angeles. https://vha.usc.edu.

Ginnis, Muriel. Interview 9505. September 27, 1986. Imperial War Museum, London.

Gorewitz, Freide. Interview 34876. Interview by Ed Lessing. November 2, 1997. Visual History Archive, USC Shoah Foundation, Los Angeles. https://vha.usc.edu.

Harisiades, Coline. Interview 9446. Interview by Jan R Stovold. September 27, 1986. Imperial War Museum, London.

Horvitz, Halina. Interview by Brad Zarlin. June 4, 2009. RG-90.063.0661. United States Holocaust Memorial Museum Collection, Washington, DC.

Horvitz, Morton. Interview by Jeff Krulik (Discovery Channel). Morton Horvitz file. National Museum of American Jewish History, Washington, DC.

Isaacman, Clara. Interview 24614. Interview by Irene Dansky. January 10, 1997. Visual History Archive. USC Shoah Foundation, Los Angeles. https://vha.usc.edu.

Isaacson, Irving. Interview MOH 027. Interview by Don Nicoll, Rob Chavira, and Stuart O'Brien. June 24, 1988. Bates College, Lewiston, ME.

Isaacson, Judith Magyar. Interview by Norma Eule and Paula Marcus Platz. March 24, 1988. Holocaust Human Rights Center. https://bates-archives.libraryhost.com/repositories/2/archival_objects/33699.

Isaacson, Judith Magyar. August 26, 1993. RG-50.227.0006. Jeff and Toby Herr Oral History Archive. United States Holocaust Memorial Museum Collection, Washington, DC.

Isaacson, Judith Magyar. Interview 31353. Interview by Rosalie Franks. July 23, 1997. Visual History Archive, USC Shoah Foundation, Los Angeles. https://vha.usc.edu.

Isby, Peggy Ada. Interview 9516. Interview by Jan Stovold. September 27, 1986. Imperial War Museum, London.

Jagoda, Flory. Interview by Joan Ringelheim. August 10, 1995. RG-50.030*0342. United States Holocaust Memorial Museum Collection, Washington, DC.

Jagoda, Flory. Interview by Howard Bass. May 7, 2014. Library of Congress (website). https://www.loc.gov/item/webcast-6271/.

Kirschner, Sala. Interview 33589. Interview by Susie Grama. September 18, 1997. Visual History Archive, USC Shoah Foundation, Los Angeles. https://vha.usc.edu.

Klein, Kurt. Interview by Linda Kuzmack. October 11, 1990. RG-50.030.0106. United States Holocaust Memorial Museum Collection, Washington, DC.

Klein, Kurt. Interview by Sandra Bradley. March 13, 1992. RG-50.042.0015. United States Holocaust Memorial Museum Collection, Washington, DC.

Lariviere, Violet Joyce. Interview 9529. Interview by Jan Stovold. October 20, 1986. Imperial War Museum, London.

Lipman, Eugene. Interview by Linda G. Kuzmack. February 8, 1990. RG-50.030*0135. United States Holocaust Memorial Museum Collection, Washington, DC.

Long, Vera. Interview 9444/2. Interview by Jan R. Stovold, September 27, 1986. Imperial War Museum, London.

Mogan, Harry. Interview 6666. Interview by Tanya Sherman. September 12, 1995. Visual History Archive, USC Shoah Foundation, Los Angeles. https://vha.usc.edu.

Ron, Gershon. Interview by Brad Zarlin. Undated. RG-90.063.1252. Gift of Brad Zarlin, United States Holocaust Memorial Museum Collection, Washington, DC.

Rose, Leesha. Interview. June 15, 1981. RG-50.477.1588. United States Holocaust Memorial Museum Collection, Gift of Jewish Family and Children's Services of San Francisco, the Peninsula, Marin and Sonoma Counties.

Rose, Leesha-Chava. Interview 49164. Interview by Naaman Belkind. January 31, 1999. Visual History Archive, USC Foundation, Los Angeles. https://vha.usc.edu.

Schiff, Charlene. Interview by Joan Ringelheim. March 23, 1993. RG 50.030.0203. United States Holocaust Memorial Museum Collection, Washington, DC.

Seibel, Richard. Interview by Sandra Bradley. RG-50.035.02.0006. February 23, 1995. United States Holocaust Memorial Museum Collection, Washington, DC.

Shelkan, Gregor. Interview 15025. Interview by Jill Greenberg. June 11, 1996. Visual History Archive, USC Shoah Foundation, Los Angeles. https://vha.usc.edu.

Turgel, Gena. Holocaust Testimony (HVT-4458). Fortunoff Video Archive for Holocaust Testimonies, Yale University Library, New Haven, CT.

Turgel, Gena. Interview 16080. Interview by Lyn E. Smith. August 30, 1995. Reel 3. Imperial War Museum, London.

Turgel, Gena. Interview 39187. Interview by Carol Hurst. March 17, 1998. Visual History Archive, USC Shoah Foundation, Los Angeles. https://vha.usc.edu.

Weissmann Klein, Gerda. Interview by Joan Ringelheim. March 13, 1992. RG 50.042*01. United States Holocaust Memorial Museum Collection, Washington, DC.

Weissmann Klein, Gerda. Interview 9725. Interview by Louise Bobrow. December 7, 1995. Visual History Archive, USC Shoah Foundation, Los Angeles. https://vha .usc.edu.

Periodicals

ACLU Newsletter

Asheville (NC) Citizen-Times

Battle Creek (MI) Enquirer

Beatrice Times

Belfast News-Letter

Berlin Air Line

Boston Globe

Brisbane Telegraph

Canadian Jewish Review

Capital Times (Madison, WI)

Casper (WY) Star-Tribune

Center Courier (Heidelberg, Germany)

Chicago Tribune

Courier-Journal (Louisville, KY)

Courier News (Somerville, NJ)

Coventry Evening Telegraph

Daily Worker (New York)

Derby Daily Telegraph

Des Moines (IA) Tribune

Detroit Free Press

Detroit Jewish Chronicle

Douglas County News (Denver, CO)

Dundee Courier

Eastbourne Herald

Evening News (Sault Sainte Marie, MI)

Evening Star (Washington, DC)

Expositor (Brantford, ON)

Forbes

Fort-Worth Star-Telegram

Gazette (Montreal)

Gazette and Daily (York, PA)

Gloucester Citizen

Hamilton Spectator

Hartford (CT) Courant

Herald Statesman (New York)

Hull Daily Mail (Hull, ON)

Huronite and Daily Plainsman
   (Huron, SD)

Indianapolis Star

Jewish Chaplain (New York)

Jewish Criterion (Pittsburgh)

Jewish News (Detroit)

Kent & Sussex Courier

Lincolnshire Echo

Menorah: A Magazine for Jewish
   Members of H.M. Forces (London)

Montreal Star

Nanaimo Daily News

National Guardian (New York)

National Jewish Post (Indianapolis)

New Jersey Jewish News

New Statesman (London)

New York Daily News

New York Times

North Hudson Post

Oregonian (Portland)

Ottawa Citizen

Ottawa Journal

Pittsburgh Sun-Telegraph

Press and Sun Bulletin (New York)

Salt Lake Tribune

Sheffield Weekly Telegraph

Shields Daily News
   (Tynemouth, Northumberland, UK)

St. Louis Post-Dispatch

StarPhoenix (Saskatoon, SK)

Stars and Stripes Magazine
   (Altdorf, Germany)

Stars and Stripes Newspaper
   (Altdorf, Germany)

Sunday Mirror (London)
Sunday Times (London)
Sunday Times (New Brunswick)
Sunderland Daily Echo and
   Shipping Gazette
Sun Sentinel (Deerfield Beach, FL)
Tampa Morning Tribune
Taunton (UK) Courier and
   Western Advertiser
Times Colonist (Victoria, BC)
Times Record (Brunswick, ME)
Times Sunday Supplement (New York)

Times-Tribune (Scranton, PA)
Toledo (OH) Blade
Toronto Star
Valley Morning Star (Harlingen, TX)
Washington Post
Western Morning News
   (West Country, UK)
Wiesbaden Post (Germany)
Windsor (ON) Star
Wisconsin Jewish Chronicle
Y.M. & W.H.A. Weekly (Pittsburgh)
Yorkshire Post and Leeds Mercury (UK)

Printed Materials

American Jewish Joint Distribution Committee. *So They May Live Again: 1945 Annual Report of the American Joint Distribution Committee.* New York: AJDC, 1946.

———. "Workbook: Table of Contents, Thirty-First Annual Meeting Joint Distribution Committee, December 8 and 9th 1945." New York: AJDC, 1946.

Bilotta, James C. *Friedel Rosenthal: US Hostage in Germany.* With Accompanying Letter from the Author. American Left Ephemera Collection, 1894–2008. AIS.2007.11, box 2, folder 127, Archives Service Center, University of Pittsburgh.

British Ministry of Information. *Make Do and Mend.* London: Ministry of Information, 1943.

Division of Religious Activities, National Jewish Welfare Board. *Responsa in War Time.* New York: National Jewish Welfare Board, 1947.

Division of Women's Voluntary Services. *Canada Cookbook for British Brides.* Ottawa: Department of National War Services, 1945.

———. *From Dock to Destination.* Ottawa: Department of National War Services, n.d.

Parliamentary Debates. 4th series. *Second Session of the 28 Parliament.* Vol. 170. London: Wyman and Sons, 1907.

Raney, E. F. *Marriage and Divorce Laws of Canada.* Toronto: Social Service Council of Canada, 1914.

Repatriation Committee. *Information for Wives of Soldiers.* Canada: 1919, rpt. 1945.

Roosevelt, Franklin D. "Executive Order 9066, Authorizing the Secretary of War to Prescribe Military Areas." Washington, DC: 1942.

Sorby, Alice. *A Study on Demobilization and Rehabilitation of the Canadian Armed Forces in the Second World War, 1939–1945.* Army Headquarters Report No. 97. May 31, 1960.

UNRRA (UN Relief and Rehabilitation Administration). "General Situation of D.P. US and Military and German Authorities." In *DPs, Germany, 6.* New York: United Nations, 1946.

US Immigration and Naturalization Service. *Annual Report of the Immigration and Naturalization Service for the Fiscal Year Ended June 30, 1953.* Washington, DC: US Government Printing Office, 1953.

A War Bride's Guide to the USA. Good Housekeeping, 1945.

Books and Dissertations

Abella, Irving, and Harold Troper. *None Is Too Many: Canada and the Jews of Europe, 1933–1948*. Toronto: Lester, 1983.

Abramson, Zelda, and John Lynch. *The Montreal Shtetl: Making Home after the Holocaust*. Toronto: Between the Lines, 2019.

Adams, Michael C. C. *The Best War Ever: America and World War II*. Baltimore: Johns Hopkins, 1994.

Adler, K. H. *Jews and Gender in Liberation France*. Cambridge: Cambridge University Press, 2003.

Allport, Allan. *Demobbed: Coming Home after the Second World War*. New Haven, CT: Yale University Press, 2009.

Anthony, Elizabeth. *The Compromise of Return: Viennese Jews after the Holocaust*. Detroit: Wayne State University Press, 2021.

Arendt, Hannah. *Eichmann in Jerusalem: A Report on the Banality of Evil*. New York: Penguin, 1963.

Armstrong-Reid, Susan, and David Murray. *Armies of Peace: Canada and the UNRRA Years*. Toronto: University of Toronto Press, 2008.

Auerbach, Frank. *The Admission and Resettlement of Displaced Persons in the United States*. New York: Common Council for American Unity, 1950.

Auger, Lauren Beth. "'That's My Story': Unpacking Canadian War Bride Veterans' Life Histories." PhD diss., University of Brighton, 2017.

Avery, Donald. *Reluctant Host: Canada's Response to Immigrant Workers, 1896–1994*. Toronto: McLelland and Stewart, 1995.

Bardgett, Suzanne, and David Cesarani, eds. *Belsen 1945: New Historical Perspectives*. London: Vallentine Mitchell, 2006.

Bender, Marilyn, and Selig Altschul. *The Chosen Instrument: Pan Am, Julian Trippe. The Rise and Fall of an American Entrepreneur*. New York: Simon and Schuster, 1982.

Berkowitz, Michael. *The Crime of My Very Existence: Nazism and the Myth of Jewish Criminality*. Berkeley: University of California Press, 2007.

Berthiaume Shukert, Elfrieda, and Barbara Smith Scibetta. *War Brides of World War II*. Novato, CA: Presidio, 1988.

Bessner, Ellin. *Double Threat: Canadian Jews, the Military, and World War II*. Toronto: New Jewish Press, 2018.

Bevan, Vaughan. *The Development of British Immigration Law*. London: Routledge, Kegan & Paul, 1986.

Blank, Ralf. *Bitter Ends: Die letzten Monate des Zweiten Weltkriegs im Ruhrgebiet, 1944/45*. Essen, Germany: Klartext, 2015.

Brereton, J. M. *The British Soldier: A Social History from 1661 to the Present Day*. London: Bodley Head, 1986.

Browning, Christopher R. *Collected Memories: Holocaust History and Postwar Testimonies*. Madison: University of Wisconsin Press, 2003.

Burma, Ian. *Year Zero: A History of 1945.* New York: Penguin, 2013.

Celinscak, Mark. *Distance from the Belsen Heap: Allied Forces and the Liberation of a Nazi Concentration Camp.* Toronto: University of Toronto Press, 2015.

Cho, Yu-Fang. *Uncoupling American Empire: Cultural Politics of Deviance and Unequal Difference, 1890–1910.* New York: SUNY Press, 2014.

Christofferson, Thomas. *France during World War II: From Defeat to Liberation.* New York: Fordham University Press, 2006.

Clifford, Rebecca. *Survivors: Children's Lives after the Holocaust.* New Haven, CT: Yale University Press, 2020.

Cohen, Beth B. *Case Closed: Holocaust Survivors in Postwar America.* New Brunswick, NJ: Rutgers University Press, 2007.

Cohen, Shaye D. *The Beginnings of Jewishness: Boundaries, Varieties, Uncertainties.* Los Angeles: University of California Press, 2001.

Confino, Alon. *A World without Jews: The Nazi Imagination from Persecution to Genocide.* New Haven, CT: Yale University Press, 2015.

Cooperman, Jessica. *Making Judaism Safe for America: World War I and the Origins of Religious Pluralism.* New York: New York University Press, 2018.

Courtwright, David. *Sky as Frontier.* College Station: Texas A&M University Press, 2004.

Crago Schneider, Kierra. "Jewish 'Shtetls' in Postwar Germany: An Analysis of Interactions among Jewish Displaced Persons, Germans, and Americans between 1945 and 1957 in Bavaria." PhD diss., University of California, Los Angeles, 2013.

Dash Moore, Deborah. *GI Jews: How World War II Changed a Generation.* Cambridge, MA: Harvard University Press, 2004.

Dean, Carolyn J. *The Moral Witness: Trials and Testimony after Gender.* Ithaca, NY: Cornell University Press, 2019.

Deblinger, Rachel Beth. "'In a World Still Trembling': American Jewish Philanthropy and the Shaping of Holocaust Survivor Narratives in Postwar America (1945–1953)." PhD diss., University of California, Los Angeles, 2014.

Elphick, Peter. *Liberty: The Ships That Won the War.* Annapolis, MD: Naval Institute Press, 2006.

Engelking, Barbara, and Jack Leociak. *The Warsaw Ghetto: A Guide to a Perished City,* translated by Emma Harris. New Haven, CT: Yale University Press, 2009.

Erikson, Kai T. *A New Species of Trouble: The Human Experience of Modern Disasters.* New York: Norton, 1994.

Fishman, Lala, and Steven Weingartner. *Lala's Story: A Memoir of the Holocaust.* Evanston, IL: Northwestern University Press, 1998.

Fox, Anne L. *My Heart in a Suitcase.* London: Vallentine Mitchell, 1996.

Friedman, Andrea. *Citizenship in Cold War America: The National Security State and the Possibilities of Dissent.* Amherst: University of Massachusetts Press, 2014.

Friedman, Barbara G. *From the Battlefront to the Bridal Suite: Media Coverage of British War Brides, 1942–1946.* Columbia: University of Missouri Press, 2007.

Gardiner, Juliet. *"Over Here": The GIs in Wartime Britain.* London: Collins & Brown, 1992.

Gardner, Martha Mabie. *The Qualities of a Citizen: Women, Immigration, and Citizenship: 1870–1965.* Princeton, NJ: Princeton University Press, 2005.

Goedde, Petra. *GIs and Germans: Culture, Gender, and Foreign Relations, 1945–1949.* New Haven, CT: Yale University Press, 2003.

Goldberg, Adara. *Holocaust Survivors in Canada: Exclusion, Inclusion, Transformation, 1947–1955.* Winnipeg: University of Manitoba Press, 2015.

Goldstein, Ivo, and Slavko Goldstein. *The Holocaust in Croatia.* Pittsburgh: University of Pittsburgh Press, 2016.

Grobman, Alex. *Rekindling the Flame: American Jewish Chaplains and the Survivors of European Jewry, 1944–1948.* Detroit: Wayne State University Press, 1993.

Grossmann, Atina. *Jews, Germans, and Allies: Close Encounters in Occupied Germany.* Princeton, NJ: Princeton University Press, 2007.

Grube, Frank, and Gerhard Richter. *Die Schwarzmarktzeit: Deutschland zwischen 1945 and 1948.* Hamburg: Hoffmann und Campe, 1979.

Halpern, Sara. "Saving the Unwanted: Australia, the United States, and Shanghai's Jewish Refugee Problem, 1943–1951." PhD diss., Ohio State University, 2020.

Hartman, Geoffrey, ed. *Holocaust Remembrance: The Shapes of Memory.* Oxford, UK: Blackwell, 1995.

Hegarty, Marilyn E. *Victory Girls, Khaki-Wackies, and Patriotutes: The Regulation of Female Sexuality during World War II.* New York: New York University, 2007.

Hennessy, John, Jr. *The Bride and the Beetle.* Pittsburgh: Dorrance, 2010.

Herman, Arthur. *Freedom's Forge: How American Business Produced Victory in World War II.* New York: Random House, 2012.

Hitchcock, William. *The Bitter Road to Freedom: The Human Cost of Allied Victory in World War II Europe.* New York: Free Press, 2008.

Höhn, Maria. *GIs and Fräuleins: The German-American Encounter in 1950s West Germany.* Chapel Hill: University of North Carolina Press, 2002.

Hurl-Eamon, Jennine. *Marriage and the British Army in the Long Eighteenth Century: The Girl I Left behind Me.* Oxford: Oxford University Press, 2014.

Irving, Helen. *Citizenship, Alienage, and the Modern Constitutional State: A Gendered History.* Cambridge: Cambridge University Press, 2016.

Isaacman, Clara. *Clara's Story.* New York: Jewish Publication Society, 1994.

Isaacson, Judith. *Seed of Sarah: Memoirs of a Survivor.* Urbana: University of Illinois Press, 1991.

Jackson, Paul. *One of the Boys: Homosexuality in the Military.* 2nd ed. Montreal: McGill-Queen's University Press, 2010.

Jackson Chin, Gabriel, Victor C. Romero, and Michael A. Scaperlanda. *Immigration and the Constitution: Shark Infested Waters: Procedural Due Process in Constitutional Immigration Law.* New York: Taylor & Francis, 2001.

Jagoda, Flory. *The Flory Jagoda Songbook: Memories of Sarajevo.* New York: Tara, 1993.

Jarratt, Melynda. *Captured Hearts: New Brunswick's War Brides.* Fredericton, NB: Goose Lane, 2008.

———. *War Brides: The Stories of the Women Who Left Everything behind to Follow the Men They Loved.* Stroud, UK: Tempus, 2007.

Kaiser, Hilary. *French War Brides in America: An Oral History.* Westport, CT: Praeger, 2008.

Kaplan, Alice. *The Interpreter.* Chicago: University of Chicago Press, 2005.

Kashima, Tetsuden. *Judgment without Trial: Japanese American Imprisonment during World War II.* Seattle: University of Washington Press, 2003.

Keith, Nathaniel S. *Politics and the Housing Crisis since 1930.* New York: Universe, 1973.

Kirschner, Ann. *Sala's Gift: My Mother's Holocaust Story.* New York: Free Press, 2006.

Kleinschmidt, Johannes. *Do Not Fraternize: Die schwierigen Anfänge deutsch-amerikanischer Freundschaft, 1944–1949.* Trier, Germany: WVT Wissenschaftler, 1997.

Klemek, Christopher. *The Transatlantic Collapse of Urban Renewal: Postwar Urbanism from New York to Berlin.* Chicago: University of Chicago Press, 2012.

Knauff, Ellen Raphael. *The Ellen Knauff Story.* New York: W. W. Norton, 1952.

Kneeland, Paulette S. *Paulette: The Story of a War Bride.* London: Athena, 2010.

Knowles, Christopher. *Winning the Peace: The British in Occupied Germany, 1945–1948.* London: Bloomsbury Academic, 2018.

Knowles, Valerie. *Strangers at Our Gates: Canadian Immigration and Immigration Policy, 1540–2015.* 4th ed. Toronto: Dundurn, 2016.

Kohner, Hanna, Walter Kohner, and Julie Kohner. *Hanna and Walter: A Love Story.* New York: iUniverse, 2008.

Kohs, Samuel C. *Jews in the United States Armed Forces, 1945.* Yiddish Scientific Institute. New York: YIVO, 1945.

Königseder, Angelika. *Flucht nach Berlin: Jüdische Displaced Persons, 1945–1948.* Berlin: Metropol, 1998.

Königseder, Angelika, and Juliane Wetzel. *Lebensmut im Wartesaal: Die jüdischen DPs im Nachkriegsdeutschland.* Frankfurt am Main: Fischer, 1995.

Konvitz, Milton R. *Civil Rights in Immigration.* Ithaca, NY: Cornell University Press, 1953.

Kordan, Bohdan. *Enemy Aliens, Prisoners of War: Internment in Canada during the Great War.* Montreal: McGill-Queen's University Press, 2003.

Kramm, Robert. *Sanitized Sex: Regulating Prostitution, Venereal Disease, and Intimacy in Occupied Japan, 1945–1952.* Oakland: University of California Press, 2017.

Krammer, Arnold. *Undue Process: The Untold Story of America's German Alien Internees.* Lanham, MD: Rowman & Littlefield, 1997.

Krzyzanowski, Lukasz. *Ghost Citizens: Jewish Return to a Postwar City,* translated by Madeline G. Levine. Cambridge: Harvard University Press, 2020.

Langer, Lawrence L. *Holocaust Testimonies: The Ruins of Memory.* New Haven, CT: Yale University Press, 1991.

Lauria, Louis J., and Amanda Page Anderson. *Running Wire at the Front Lines: Memoir of a Radio and Telephone Man in World War II.* Jefferson, NC: McFarland, 2010.

Lavsky, Hagit. *New Beginnings: Holocaust Survivors in Bergen-Belsen and the British Zone in Germany, 1945–1950.* Detroit: Wayne State University Press, 2002.

Lee, Erika. *At America's Gates: Chinese Immigration during the Exclusion Era, 1882–1943.* Chapel Hill: University of North Carolina Press, 2003.

Lee, Helene R. *Bittersweet Decision: The War Brides—40 Years Later.* Lockport, NY: Roselee, 1985.

Levi, Gershon. *Breaking New Ground: The Struggle for a Canadian Jewish Chaplaincy.* Montreal: National Archives, Canadian Jewish Congress, 1994.

Levi, Primo. *Survival in Auschwitz.* Phoenix: Orion, 1959.

Lewis Bredbenner, Candice. *A Nationality of Her Own: Women, Marriage, and the Law of Citizenship*. Berkeley: University of California Press, 1998.

Lilly, J. Robert. *Taken by Force: Rape and American GIs in Europe during World War II*. New York: Palgrave Macmillan, 2007.

Lipsitz, George. *Rainbow at Midnight: Labor and Culture in the 1940s*. Urbana: University of Illinois Press, 1994.

Littauer, Amanda H. *Sex Anarchy: Women, Girls, and American Sexual Culture in the Mid-Twentieth Century*. Chapel Hill: University of North Carolina Press, 2015.

London, Louise. *Whitehall and the Jews, 1933–1948: British Immigration Policy, Jewish Refugees and the Holocaust*. Cambridge: Cambridge University Press, 2001.

Lowe, Keith. *Savage Continent: Europe in the Aftermath of World War II*. New York: St. Martin's, 2012.

Mandel Abramowitz, Mona. *The Journey of Rabbi and Rachel Abramowitz*. Bloomington, IN: Authorhouse, 2012.

Mankowitz, Zeev W. *Life between Memory and Hope: The Survivors of the Holocaust in Occupied Germany*. New York: Cambridge University Press, 2002.

Manz, Stefan, and Panikos Panayi. *Civilian Internment in the British Empire during the First World War*. Oxford: Oxford University Press, 2020.

Marchetti, Gina. *Romance and the "Yellow Peril": Race, Sex, and Discursive Strategies in Hollywood Fiction*. Los Angeles: University of California Press, 1994.

Marinari, Maddalena, Madeline Y. Hsu, and Maria Cristina Garcia. *A Nation of Immigrants Reconsidered: US Society in an Age of Restriction, 1924–1965*. Urbana: University of Illinois Press, 2019.

McManus, John C. *Hell before Their Very Eyes: American Soldiers Liberate Concentration Camps in Germany, April 1945*. Baltimore: Johns Hopkins University Press, 2015.

Michman, Dan. *Holocaust Historiography: A Jewish Perspective: Conceptualizations, Terminology, Approaches and Fundamental Issues*. London: Vallentine Mitchell, 2003.

Millis Duvall, Evelyn. *In-Laws, Pro and Con: An Original Study of Interpersonal Relations*. New York: Associated Press, 1954.

Motomura, Hiroshi. *Americans in Waiting: The Lost Story of Immigration and Citizenship in the United States*. Oxford: Oxford University Press, 2006.

Murray, Nora Korzhenko. *I Spied for Stalin*. London: Odhams, 1950.

Myers Feinstein, Margarete. *Holocaust Survivors in Postwar Germany, 1945–1957*. Cambridge: Cambridge University Press, 2010.

Naimark, Norman. *The Russians in Germany: The History of the Soviet Zone of Occupation*. Cambridge, MA: Harvard University Press, 1995.

Nakano Glenn, Evelyn. *Issei, Nisei, War Bride: Three Generations of Japanese American Women in Domestic Service*. Philadelphia: Temple University Press, 1986.

Overy, Richard. *The Bombers and Bombed: Allied Air War over Europe, 1940–1945*. New York: Penguin, 2013.

Patt, Avinoam. *Finding Home and Homeland: Jewish Youth and Zionism in the Aftermath of the Holocaust*. Detroit: Wayne State University Press, 2009.

Pfau, Ann Elizabeth. *Miss Yourlovin: GIs, Gender, and Domesticity during World War II*. New York: Columbia University Press, 2008.

Prais, Lea. *Displaced Persons at Home: Refugees in the Fabric of Jewish Life in Warsaw, September 1939–July 1942*. Jerusalem: Yad Vashem, 2015.

Pratt, William John. "Medicine and Obedience: Canadian Army Morale, Discipline, and Surveillance in the Second World War, 1939–1945." PhD diss., University of Calgary, 2015.

Reinisch, Jessica. *The Perils of Peace: The Public Health Crisis in Occupied Germany*. Oxford: Oxford University Press, 2013.

Roach Pierson, Ruth. *"They're Still Women After All": The Second World War and Canadian Womanhood*. Toronto: McClelland and Stewart, 1986.

Roberts, Mary Louise. *What Soldiers Do: Sex and the American GI in World War II France*. Chicago: University of Chicago Press, 2013.

Rogow, Faith, and Joan Bronk. *Gone to Another Meeting: The National Council of Jewish Women, 1893–1993*. Birmingham: University of Alabama Press, 2005.

Ron, Gershon G. *My Little Blue Tattoo*. Plymouth, MA: AFDP Publishing, 2006.

Rose, Leesha. *The Tulips Are Red*. South Brunswick, NJ: Barnes, 1978.

Rose, Sonya O. *Which People's War? National Identity and Citizenship in Britain, 1939–1945*. Oxford: Oxford University Press, 2003.

Rothenberger, Karl-Heinz. *Die Hungerjahre nach dem Zweiten Weltkrieg: Ernähhrungs- und Landwirtschaft in Rheinland-Pfalz, 1945–1950*. Boppart am Rhein, Germany: Boldt, 1980.

Sander, Helke, and Barbara Johr. *Befreier und Befreite: Krieg, Vergewaltigung, Kinder*. Frankfurt am Main: Fischer, 2005.

Schrijvers, Peter. *Liberators: The Allies and Belgian Society, 1944–1945*. Cambridge: Cambridge University Press, 2009.

Shandler, Jeffrey. *While America Watches: Televising the Holocaust*. New York: Oxford University Press, 1999.

Shepard, Ben. *The Long Road Home: The Aftermath of the Second World War*. London: Bodley Head, 2010.

Simpson, Caroline Sue. "American Orientalisms: The Gender and Cultural Politics of America's Postwar Relationship with Japan." PhD diss., University of Texas at Austin, 1994.

Slomovitz, Albert. *The Fighting Rabbis: Jewish Military Chaplains and American History*. New York: New York University, 1998.

Stacey, C. P., and Barbara M. Wilson. *The Half Million: The Canadians in Britain, 1939–1946*. Toronto: University of Toronto Press, 1987.

Stahl, Ronit Y. *Enlisting Faith: How the Military Chaplaincy Shaped Religion and State in Modern America*. Cambridge, MA: Harvard University Press, 2017.

Stone, Dan. *The Liberation of the Camps: The End of the Holocaust and Its Aftermath*. New Haven, CT: Yale University Press, 2015.

Stüber, Gabriele. *Der Kampf gegen den Hunger, 1945–1950: Die Ernährungslage in der britischen Zone Deutschlands, insbesondere in Schleswig-Holstein und Hamburg*. Neumünster, Germany: K. Wachholtz, 1984.

Sussman, Jeffrey. *No Mere Bagatelles: Telling the Story of Handbag Genius Judith Lieber and Modernist Artist Gerson Lieber*. New York: Judith Lieber, 2009.

Thibault, Andréanne, et al. *Spouse and Partner Immigration to Canada: History and Current Issues in Canadian Immigration Policy*. Montreal: Centre de Recherche en Immigration, Ethnicité et Citoyenneté, 2017.

Tokarska-Bakir, Joanna. *Pogrom Cries: Essays on Polish-Jewish History, 1939–1946.* Berlin: Peter Lang, 2019.

Tomasevich, Jozo. *War and Revolution in Yugoslavia, 1941–1945, Occupation and Collaboration.* Palo Alto, CA: Stanford University Press, 2001.

Turgel, Gena. *I Light a Candle: The Inspiring True Story of "The Bride of Belsen."* London: Grafton, 1987.

Veranneman de Watervliet, Jean-Michel. *Belgium in the Second World War.* Barnsley, UK: Pen & Sword Military, 2017.

Vida, George. *From Doom to Dawn: A Jewish Chaplain's Story of Displaced Persons.* New York: Jonathan David, 1967.

Virden, Jenel. *Good-bye Piccadilly: British War Brides in America.* Urbana: University of Illinois Press, 1996.

Voigt, Klauf. *Zuflucht auf Widerruf: Exil in Italien, 1933–1945.* Vol 2. Stuttgart, Germany: Klett-Cotta, 1993.

Ward Crawford, Miki, Katie Kaori Hayashi, and Shizuko Suenaga. *Japanese War Brides in America: An Oral History.* Santa Barbara, CA: Praeger, 2010.

Webster, Wendy. *Imagining Home: Gender, "Race," and National Identity, 1945–1964.* London: University College London Press, 1998.

Weindling, Paul. *Epidemics and Genocide in Eastern Europe.* Oxford: Oxford University Press, 2000.

Weissmann Klein, Gerda. *All but My Life: A Memoir.* Expanded ed. New York: Hill and Wang, 1995.

———. *A Boring Evening at Home.* Washington, DC: Leading Authorities, 2004.

———. *The Promise of a New Spring: The Holocaust and Renewal.* Dallas: Rossel, 1982.

Weissmann Klein, Gerda, and Kurt Klein, eds. *The Hours After.* New York: St. Martin's, 2000.

Wicks, Ben. *Promise You'll Take Care of My Daughter: The Remarkable War Brides of World War II.* Toronto: Stoddart, 1992.

Wiesel, Elie. *Night.* New York: Hill and Wang, 1960.

Winfield, Pamela, and Brenda Wilson Hasty. *Sentimental Journey: The Story of the GI Brides.* London: Constable, 1984.

Yang, Jia Lynn. *One Mighty and Irresistible Tide: The Epic Struggle over American Immigration, 1924–1965.* New York: W. W. Norton, 2020.

Zaidman-Dz'ubas, Rut. *Be-haftsiʻa ha-shaḥar: Ha-ḥazarah la-ḥayim ve-sipurim ʻal yeladim be-ʻidan ḥurban Yahadut Eropah.* Jerusalem: Minhat Yisrael, 1998.

Zakić, Mirna. *Ethnic Germans and National Socialism in Yugoslavia in World War II.* Cambridge: Cambridge University Press, 2017.

Zeiger, Susan. *Entangling Alliances: Foreign War Brides and American Soldiers in the Twentieth Century.* New York: New York University Press, 2010.

Zimmels, H. J. *The Echo of the Holocaust in Rabbinic Literature.* New York: Ktav, 1977.

Articles and Chapters

Abrams, Kerry. "Family Reunification and the Security State." *Constitutional Commentary,* 2017, 261–65.

Auslander, Leora. "Coming Home: Jews in Postwar France." *Journal of Contemporary History* 40, no. 2 (2005): 237–59.

Baldwin, Annabelle. "Sexual Violence and the Holocaust: Reflections on Memory and Witness Testimony." *Holocaust Studies* 16, no. 3 (2010): 112–34.

Baldwin, M. Page. "Subject to Empire: Married Women and the British Nationality and Status of Aliens Act." *Journal of British Studies* 40, no. 4 (October 2001): 522–56.

Bauer, Ingrid. "Austria's Prestige Dragged into the Dirt? The GI Brides and Postwar Austrian Society (1945–1955)." In *Women in Austria*, edited by Günter Bischof, Anton Pelinka, and Erika Thurner, 41–55. New Brunswick, NJ: Transaction, 1998.

———. "Frauen, Männer, Beziehungen: Sozialgeschichte der Geschlechterverhältnisse, in der Zweiten Republik." In *1945–1955: Entwicklungslinien der Zweiten Republik*, edited by Johann Burger and Elisabeth Morawek, 104–7. Vienna: Springer, 1995.

Biddiscombe, Perry. "Dangerous Liaisons: The Anti-fraternization Movement in the US Occupation Zones of Germany and Austria, 1945–1948." *Journal of Social History* 34, no. 3 (2001): 611–47.

Bignon, Vincent. "Cigarette Money and Black-Market Prices during the 1948 German Miracle." In *EconomiX*, 2009, 1–37.

Bothe, Alina, and Markus Nesselrodt. "Survivor: Towards a Conceptual History." *Leo Baeck Institute Year Book* 61 (2016): 57–82.

Bowen, John, and Jean-Paul Rodrigue. "The Rise of Air Transportation." In *The Geography of Transport Systems*, 5th ed., edited by Jean-Paul Rodrigue, 181–95. New York: Routledge, 2020.

Bramley, Elisabeth. "Airgraph and Victory Mail Service during World War II, 1939–1945." Museums Victoria Collections, https://collections.museumsvictoria.com.au/articles/16591. Accessed February 14, 2023.

Branstetter, Ross W. "Family Law: Military Constraints upon Marriages of Service Members Overseas, or, If the Army Had Wanted You to Have a Wife . . ." *Military Law Review* 102, no. 5 (1983): 5–22.

Brunnhuber, Nicole M. T. "After the Prison Ships: Internment Narratives in Canada." In *"Totally Un-English?" Britain's Internment of "Enemy Aliens" in Two World Wars*, edited by Richard Dove, 165–78. Amsterdam: Rodopi, 2005.

Brushett, Kevin. "Where Will the People Go: Toronto's Emergency Housing Program and the Limits of Canadian Social Housing Policy, 1944–1957." *Journal of Urban History* 33, no. 3 (March 2007): 375–99.

Bryan Vonstrahl, Joyce. "Horrors on Board the *Zebulon B. Vance*." US Warbrides, http://www.oocities.org/us_warbrides/WW2warbrides/vance.html. Accessed July 18, 2018.

"Bryon Darnton: Boiler Reef, Sanda Island, Firth of Clyde." Canmore: National Record of the Historic Environment, Historic Environment Scotland. https://canmore.org.uk/site/114911/bryon-darnton-boiler-reef-sanda-island-firth-of-clyde. Accessed May 2, 2017.

Charters, Joan. "Just Imagine if You Had Stayed in England." In *Blackouts to Bright Lights: Canadian War Bride Stories*, edited by Barbara Ladouceur and Phyllis Spence, 122–23. Vancouver: Ronsdale, 1995.

Checinski, Michael. "The Kielce Pogrom: Some Unanswered Questions." *Soviet Jewish Affairs* 5 (1975): 57–72.

Cho, Grace M. "Disappearing Acts: An Immigrant History." *Cultural Studies* 18, no. 5 (2018): 307–13.

Chung Simpson, Caroline. "'Out of an Obscure Place': Japanese War Brides and Cultural Pluralism in the 1950s." *Differences: A Journal of Feminist Cultural Studies* 10, no. 3 (1998): 47–81.

Cohen, Sharon Kangisser. "Choosing a Heim: Survivors of the Holocaust and Post-war Immigration." *European Judaism: A Journal for the New Europe* 46, no. 2 (Autumn 2013): 32–54.

Cott, Nancy. "Marriage and Women's Citizenship in the United States, 1830–1934." *American Historical Review* 103, no. 5 (1998): 1440–74.

Cunningham-Sabot, Emmanuèle, and Sylvie Fol. "Shrinking Cities in France and Great Britain: A Silent Process?" In *The Future of Shrinking Cities: Problems, Patterns and Strategies of Urban Transformation in a Global Context*, edited by Karina Pallagst, 17–27. Berkeley, CA: Institute of Urban and Regional Development, 2009.

Dashorst, Patricia, et al. "Intergenerational Consequences of the Holocaust on Offspring Mental Health: A Systematic Review of Associated Factors and Mechanisms." *European Journal of Psychotraumatology* 10, no. 1 (August 30, 2019). doi:10.1080/20008198.2019.16 54065.

Dinnerstein, Leonard. "The US Army and the Jews: Policies toward the Displaced Persons after World War II." In *America, American Jews, and the Holocaust*, edited by Jeffrey S. Gurock, 7:427–40. New York: Routledge, 1998.

DiStasi, Lawrence. "Derived Aliens: Derivative Citizenship and Italian-American Women during World War II." *Italian Americana* 29, no. 1 (2011): 23–33.

Dove, Richard. "'A Matter Which Touches the Good Name of This Country.'" In *"Totally Un-English"? Britain's Internment of "Enemy Aliens" in Two World Wars*, edited by Richard Dove, 11–15. Amsterdam: Rodopi, 2005.

Dror, Esther, and Ruth Linn. "The Shame Is Always There." In *Sexual Violence against Jewish Women during the Holocaust*, edited by Sonja M. Hedgepeth and Rochelle G. Saidell, 275–92. Waltham, MA: Brandeis University Press, 2010.

Ephgrave, Nicole. "On Women's Bodies: Experiences of Dehumanization during the Holocaust." *Journal of Women's History* 28, no. 2 (2016): 14.

Esser, Raingard. "'Language No Obstacle': War Brides in the German Press, 1945–49." *Women's History Review* 12, no. 4 (December 2003): 577–603.

Fahrmeir, Andreas. "Immigration and Immigration Policy in Britain from the Nineteenth to the Twentieth Centuries." In *European Immigrants in Britain, 1933–1950*, edited by Johannes-Dieter Steinert and Inge Weber-Newth, 50. Munich: DeGruyter, 2003.

Fisher, Louis. "To Have and to Hold." *Legal Times* 32, no. 11 (March 16, 2009), 38–39.

Flaschka, Monika J. "'Only Pretty Women Were Raped:' The Effect of Sexual Violence on Gender Identities in Concentration Camps." In *Sexual Violence against Jewish Women*, edited by Sonja M. Hedgepeth and Rochelle G. Saidell, 77–93. Waltham, MA: Brandeis University Press, 2010.

Fogg, Shannon L. "'Everything Had Ended and Everything Was Beginning Again': The Public Politics of Rebuilding Private Homes in Postwar France." *Holocaust and Genocide Studies* 28, no. 2 (Fall 2014): 277–307.

Fraser, David, and Frank Caestecker. "Jews or Germans? Nationality Legislation and the Restoration of Liberal Democracy in Western Europe after the Holocaust." *Law and History Review* 31, no. 2 (May 2013): 391–422.

Garwood, Alfred. "The Holocaust and the Power of Powerlessness: Survivor Guilt an Unhealed Wound." *British Journal of Psychotherapy* 13, no. 2 (1996): 223–58.

Geroulanos, Stefanos. "An Army of Shadows: Black Markets, Adaptation, and Social Transparency in Postwar France." *Journal of Modern History* 88, no. 1 (2016): 60–98.

Gibney, Matthew J. "'A Very Transcendental Power': Denaturalisation and the Liberalisation of Citizenship in the United Kingdom." *Political Studies* 61 (2012): 637–55.

Girard, Philip. "'If Two Ride a Horse, One Must Ride in Front': Married Women's Nationality and the Law in Canada, 1880–1950." *Canadian Historical Review* 94, no. 1 (March 2013): 28–54.

Goodman, Giora. "'Only the Best British Brides': Regulating the Relationship between US Servicemen and British Women in the Early Cold War." *Contemporary European History* 17, no. 4 (2008): 483–503.

Greenspan, Henry. "The Awakening of Memory: Survivor Testimony in the First Years after the Holocaust and Today." USHMM occasional paper, May 17, 2000. https://collections .ushmm.org/search/catalog/bib49303.

Grossmann, Atina. "A Question of Silence: The Rape of German Women by Occupation Soldiers." *October* 72 (Spring 1995): 43–63.

———. "Trauma, Memory, and Motherhood: Germans and Jewish Displaced Persons in Post-Nazi Germany." In *Life after Death: Approaches to a Cultural and Social History of Europe during the 1940s and 1950s*, edited by R. B. a. D. Schumann, 93–128. Washington, DC: German Historical Institute and Cambridge University Press, 2003.

Guise, Kim. "Camp Lucky Strike: RAMP Camp No. 1." National World War II Museum, June 26, 2020. https://www.nationalww2museum.org/war/articles/camp-lucky-strike.

Hadwiger, Don F., and Clay Cochran. "Rural Telephones in the United States." *Agricultural History* 58, no. 3 (July 1984): 222–26.

Hansen, Randall. "The Politics of Citizenship in 1940s Britain: The British Nationality Act." *Twentieth Century British History* 10, no. 1 (1999): 67–95.

Herzog, Dagmar. "European Sexualities in the Age of Total War." In *The Oxford Handbook of European History, 1914–1945*, edited by Nicholas Doumanis, 407–22. Oxford: Oxford University Press, 2016. https://academic.oup.com/edited-volume/28001 /chapter/211759080.

Heynen, Hilde. "Belgium and the Netherlands: Two Different Ways of Coping with the Housing Crisis, 1945–70." *Home Cultures* 7, no. 2 (2010): 159–77.

Hilton, Laura J. "Who Was Worthy? How Empathy Drove Policy Decisions about the Uprooted in Occupied Germany, 1945–1948." *Holocaust and Genocide Studies* 32, no. 1 (Spring 2018): 8–28.

Holian, Anna. "The Ambivalent Exception: American Occupation Policy in Postwar Germany and the Formation of Jewish Refugee Spaces." *Journal of Refugee Studies* 25 (2012): 452–73.

Hoppe, Jens. "Curzola Island." In *The United States Holocaust Memorial Museum Encyclopedia of Camps and Ghettos, 1933–1945*, vol. 3, edited by Geoffrey P. Megargee and Joseph R. White, translated by Fred Flatow. Bloomington: Indiana University Press, 2018.

Iacovetta, Franca, and Roberto Perin. "Italians and Wartime Internment: Comparative Perspectives on Public Policy, Historical Memory, and Daily Life." In *Enemies Within: Italian and Other Internees in Canada and Abroad*, edited by Franca Iacovetta, Roberto Perin, and Angelo Principe, 3–21. Toronto: University of Toronto Press, 2000.

Jeges, Edit. "Gendering the Cultural Memory of the Holocaust: A Comparative Analysis of a Memoir and a Video Testimony by Olga Lengyel." In *Women and the Holocaust: New Perspectives and Challenges*, edited by Andrea Peto, Louise Hecht, and Karolina Krasuska, 233–53. Budapest: Central European University Press, 2015.

Jenkins, Amanda. "'I'm an American': From Radio Program to Citizenship Day." *Now See Hear!* (blog), National Audio-Visual Conservation Center, November 5, 2018. https://blogs.loc.gov/now-see-hear/2018/11/im-an-american/.

Jordan, James. "'And the Trouble Is Where to Begin to Spring Surprises on You. Perhaps a Place You Might *Least* Like to Remember': *This Is Your Life* and the BBC's Images of the Holocaust in the Twenty Years before *Holocaust*." In *Britain and the Holocaust: Remembering and Representing War and Genocide*, edited by Caroline Sharples and Olaf Jensen, 90–114. London: Palgrave MacMillan, 2013.

Katz, Ethan B. "The Mothers, the Mamzerim, and the Rabbis: A Post-Holocaust Halakhic Debate as Legal and Historical Source." In *When Jews Argue: Between the University and the Beit Midrash*, edited by Ethan B. Katz, Elisha Ancselovits, and Sergey Dolgopolski. London: Routledge, forthcoming.

Kelly, Linda. "Marriage for Sale: The Mail Order Bride Industry and the Changing Value of Marriage." *Journal of Gender, Race, and Justice* 5, no. 1 (2001): 175–96.

Kirschenblatt-Gimblett, Barbara. "Kitchen Judaism." In *Getting Comfortable in New York: The American Jewish Home, 1880–1950*, edited by Jenna Weissman Joselit and Susan L. Braunstein, 77–105. New York: Jewish Museum, 1990.

Kleinplatz, P. J., and P. Weindling. "Women's Experiences of Infertility after the Holocaust." *Social Science & Medicine* 309 (2022). OhioLINK Electronic Journal Center. doi:10.1016/J.SOCSCIMED.2022.115250.

Klopstock, Fred H. "Monetary Reform in Western Germany." *Journal of Political Economy* 57, no. 4 (1949): 277–92.

Kollander, Patricia. "Reflections on the Experience of German Émigré Soldiers in the US Army during World War II." *Yearbook of German-American Studies* (41): 103–16.

Kurland, Philip B. "Robert H. Jackson." In *The Justices of the United States Supreme Court*, edited by Leon Friedman and Fred L. Israel, 1283–311. New York: Chelsea House Publishers, 1997.

Kushner, Tony. "Holocaust Survivors in Britain: An Overview and Research Agenda." *Journal of Holocaust Education* 4, no. 2 (1995): 147–66.

Larsen, Matthew F., et al. "War and Marriage Assortative Mating and the World War II GI Bill." *Demography* 52 (2015): 1431–61.

Lemieux, Thomas, and David Card. "Education, Earnings and the 'Canadian G.I. Bill.'" *Canadian Journal of Economics* 34, no. 2 (May 2001): 313–44.

Levenkron, Nomi. "'Death and the Maidens': Prostitution, Rape, and 'Sexual Slavery' during World War II." In *Sexual Violence against Jewish Women during the Holocaust*, edited by Sonja M. Hedgepeth and Rochelle G. Saidell, 13–28. Waltham, MA: Brandeis University Press, 2010.

Leys, Ruth. "Image and Trauma." *Science in Context* 19, no.1 (2006): 137–49.

Linden, Ruth. "In the Name of the House of Orange: A Life History of Leesha Rose during the Holocaust." In *Making Stories, Making Selves: Feminist Reflections on the Holocaust*, 113–35. Columbus: Ohio State University Press, 1993.

————. "Reflections on 'In the Name of the House of Orange.'" In *Making Stories, Making Selves: Feminist Reflections on the Holocaust*, 136–46. Columbus: Ohio State University Press, 1993.

Lomas, Janis. "'Delicate Duties': Issues of Class and Respectability in Government Policy towards the Wives and Widows of British Soldiers in the Era of the Great War." *Women's History Review* 9, no. 1 (2000): 123–47.

Martz, Erin. Introduction to *Trauma Rehabilitation after War and Conflict: Community and Individual Perspectives*, 6–8. New York: Springer: 2010.

Matrix, Sidney Eve. "Mediated Citizenship and Contested Belongings: Canadian War Brides and the Fictions of Naturalization." *TOPIA: Canadian Journal of Cultural Studies* 17 (April 2007): 67–86.

Matthäus, Jürgen. "Displacing Memory: The Transformations of an Early Interview." In *Approaching an Auschwitz Survivor: Holocaust Testimony and Its Transformations*, edited by Jürgen Matthäus, 49–72. Oxford: Oxford University Press, 2009.

McEnaney, Laura. "Nightmares on Elm Street: Demobilizing in Chicago, 1945–1953." *Journal of American History* 92, no. 4 (March 2006): 1265–91.

Miles, Robert. "Nationality, Citizenship, and Migration to Britain, 1945–1951." *Journal of Law and Society* 16, no. 4 (Winter 1989): 426–42.

Myers Feinstein, Margarete. "All Under One Roof: Persecutees, DPs, Expellees, and the Housing Shortage in Occupied Germany." *Holocaust and Genocide Studies* 32, no. 1 (Spring 2018): 29–48.

Nasiali, Minayo. "Citizens, Squatters, and Asocials: The Right to Housing and the Politics of Difference in Post-Liberation France." *American Historical Review* 119, no. 2 (April 2014): 434–59.

Ofer, Dalia. "The Past That Does Not Pass: Israelis and Holocaust Memory." *Israel Studies* 14, no. 1 (2009): 1–35.

Orgad, Shani. "The Survivor in Contemporary Culture and Public Discourse: A Genealogy." *Communications Review* 12 (2009): 132–61.

Papamichos Chronakis, Paris. "'We Lived as Greeks and We Died as Greeks': Thessalonican Jews in Auschwitz and the Meaning of Nationhood." In *The Holocaust in Greece*, edited by Giorgos Antoniou and A. Dirk Moses, 157–80. Cambridge: Cambridge University Press, 2018.

Pasternak, Alfred, and P. G. Brooks. "The Long-Term Effects of the Holocaust on the Reproductive Function of Female Survivors." *Journal of Minimally Invasive Gynecology* 14, no. 2 (March 2007): 211–17.

Patriquin, Betty. "My Dear Young Lady, Do You Know What You're Doing." In *Blackouts to Bright Lights: Canadian War Bride Stories*, edited by Barbara Ladouceuer and Phyllis Spence, 2–10. Vancouver: Ronsdale, 1995.

Pfanzelter, Eva. "Between Brenner and Bari: Jewish Refugees in Italy 1945 to 1948." *Journal of Israeli History* 19, no. 3 (1998): 83–104.

Polenberg, Richard. "The Good War? A Reappraisal of How World War II Affected American Society." *Virginia Magazine of History and Geography* 100 (July 1992): 295–322.

Popkin, Jeremy D. "From Displaced Persons to 'Secular Saints': Holocaust Survivors, Jewish Identity, and Gender in the Writing of Zelda Popkin." *Studies in American Jewish Literature* 37, no. 1 (2018): 1–20.

Prazmowska, A. "The Kielce Pogrom 1946 and the Emergence of Communist Power in Poland." *Cold War History* 2 (2002): 101–24.

Raska, Jan. "Movement of War Brides and Their Children through Pier 21." Canadian Museum of Immigration at Pier 21, June 22, 2022. https://pier21.ca/research/immigration-history/movement-war-brides-and-children-pier-21.

Reed, Ted. "First Transatlantic Commercial Flight Landed 75 Years Ago Sunday." *Forbes*, August 10, 2013.

Reinisch, Jessica. "Internationalism in Relief: The Birth (and Death) of UNRRA." *Past and Present* supplement 6 (2011): 258–89.

Rose, Sonya O. "Girls and GIs: Race, Sex, and Diplomacy in Second World War Britain." *International History Review* 19, no. 1 (1997): 146–60.

Sabloff, Paula L.W. "How Pre-modern State Rulers Used Marriage to Reduce the Risk of Losing at War: A Comparison of Eight States." *Journal of Archaeological Method and Theory* 25, no. 2 (June 2018): 426–52.

Salamon, Michael J. "Denial and Acceptance: Coping and Defense Mechanisms." In *Holocaust Survivors' Mental Health*, edited by T. L. Brink, 17–26. New York: Haworth Press, 1994.

Salvatici, Silvia. "'Help the People to Help Themselves': UNRRA Relief Workers and European Displaced Persons." *Journal of Refugee Studies* 25 (2012): 452–73.

Schneer, David. "Is Seeing Believing? Photographs, Eyewitness Testimony, and Evidence of the Holocaust." *East European Jewish Affairs* 45, no. 1 (2015): 65–78.

Schoenfeld, Stuart. "The Jewish Religion in North America: Canadian and American Comparisons." *Canadian Journal of Sociology* 3, no. 2 (Spring 1978): 209–31.

Schrecker, Ellen. "Immigration and Internal Security: Political Deportations during the McCarthy Era." *Science and Society* 60, no. 4 (Winter 1996/1997): 393–426.

Schröder, Stefan. "From Illustrations to Sources: A Survey of Photographs of and about Displaced Persons." In *Survivors of Nazi Persecution in Europe after the Second World War*, edited by David Cesarani, 54–67. London: Vallentine Mitchell, 2010.

Schwartzman, Roy. "Sutured Identities in Jewish Holocaust Survivor Testimonies." *Journal of Social Issues* 71, no. 2 (2015): 279–93.

Shandler, Jeffrey. "This Is Your Life: Holocaust Stories." In *This Is Your Life: Preserving Holocaust Survivor Testimonies on Early Television*. https://www.cinema.ucla.edu/sites/default/files/TIYLv8.pdf. Accessed August 25, 2016.

Shepard, Ben. "'Becoming Planning Minded': The Theory and Practice of Relief, 1940–1945." *Journal of Contemporary History* 43, no. 3 (July 2008): 405–19.

———. "The Medical Relief Effort at Belsen." In *Belsen 1945: New Historical Perspectives*, edited by Suzanne Bardgett and David Cesarani, 31–50. London: Vallentine Mitchell, 2006.

Sparrow, John C. "History of Personnel Demobilization in the United States Army." Department of the Army, June 1951.

Steinert, Johannes Dieter, and Inge Weber-Newth. "European Immigrants in Britain, 1933–1950." In *European Immigrants in Britain, 1933–1950*, edited by Johannes-Dieter Steinert and Inge Weber-Newth, 7–16. Munich: K. G. Saur, 2003.

Stone, Dan. "'Somehow the Pathetic, Dumb Suffering of These Elderly People Moves Me More Than Anything': Caring for Elderly Holocaust Survivors in the Immediate Postwar Years." *Holocaust and Genocide Studies* 32, no. 3 (Winter 2018): 384–403.

Switzer, Jack. "*Faith and Humanity*: Calgary's National Council of Jewish Women." *Western States Jewish History* 42, no. 4 (2010): 111–16.

Tabili, Laura. "Outsiders in the Land of Their Birth: Exogamy, Citizenship, and Identity in War and Peace." *Journal of British Studies* 44 (October 2005): 796–815.

Tayler, Amanda L. "Courts and the Executive in Wartime: A Comparative Study of the American and British Approaches to the Internment of Citizens during World War II and Their Lessons for Today." *California Law Review* (2019): 789–866.

Taylor, Lynne. "'Please Report Only *True* Nationalities': The Classification of Displaced Persons in Post–Second World War Germany and Its Implications." In *Survivors of Nazi Persecution*, edited by David Cesarani, Suzanne Bardgett, Jessica Reinisch, and Johannes-Dieter Steinert, 35–53. Edgeware, UK: Vallentine Mitchell, 2010.

Turgel, Norman. "Norman's Chapter." In *I Light a Candle*, by Gena Turgel, 106–21. London: Grafton, 1987.

Volpp, Leti. "Divesting Citizenship: On Asian American History and the Loss of Citizenship through Marriage." *UCLA Law Review* 53, no. 2 (2005): 403-83.

Wardle, Lynn D. "Involuntary Imports: Williams, Lutwak, the Defense of Marriage Act, Federalism, and 'Thick' and 'Thin' Conceptions of Marriage." *Fordham Law Review* (2012): 783–87.

Watson, Dacre. "British Overseas Airways Corporation, 1940–1950, and Its Legacy." *Journal of Aeronautical History* 3 (2013): 136–61.

Weinberg, David. "The Reconstruction of the French Jewish Community after World War II." In *She'erit Hapletah, 1944–1948: Rehabilitation and Political Struggle*, edited by Yisrael Gutman and Avital Saf, 168–86. Jerusalem: Yad Vashem, 1990.

Weindling, Paul. "'Belsenitis': Liberating Belsen, Its Hospitals, UNRRA, and Selection for Re-emigration, 1945–1948." *Science in Context* 19, no. 3 (2006): 401–18.

Weinreb, Alice. "'For the Hungry Have No Past, Nor Do They Have a Political Party': Debates over German Hunger after World War II." *Central European History* 45 (2012): 50–78.

Weisselberg, Charles D. "The Exclusion and Detention of Aliens: Lessons from the Lives of Ellen Knauff and Ignatz Mezei." *University of Pennsylvania Law Review* 143, no. 4 (April 1995): 933–1034.

Weitz, Yechiam. "Jewish Refugees and Zionist Policy during the Holocaust." *Middle Eastern Studies* 30, no. 2 (April 1994): 351–68.

Wolgin, Philip, and Irene Bloemraad. "'Our Gratitude to Our Soldiers': Military Spouses, Family Re-unification, and Postwar Immigration Reform." *Journal of Interdisciplinary History* 41, no. 1 (Summer 2010): 27–60.

Yell, Susan, and Meredith Fletcher. "Airgraphs and an Airman: The Role of Airgraphs in World War II Family Correspondence." *History Australia* 8, no. 3 (January 2011): 117–38.

Films

Chubbock, Lyndon, dir. *The War Bride*. DB Entertainment, 2001.

Fissel, Curt, and Ellen Friedlan, dirs. *Flory's Flame*. Voices and Visions Productions, 2014.

Hawks, Howard, dir. *I Was a Male War Bride*. Twentieth Century Fox, 1949.

"This Is Your Life, Hanna Kohner." May 27, 1953. https://www.youtube.com /watch?v=R4ckFEnn5Bo.

INDEX

Page numbers in italics refer to illustrations.

Bernstein, Philip, 26–27, 35

Bilotta, James, 105–8, 111–23. *See also* Rosenthal, Friedel

Bonder, Abraham "Abe," 31–32, 37–38, 49, 52, 59, 64–67, 81, 86, 93, 128, 138. *See also* Bonder, Sala Solarcz

Bonder, Sala Solarcz, 137, 138; courtship narrative, 37–38, 52, 65; and immigration, 72, 81, 93; and language, 129–30; liberation of, 17–18, 23, 26, 35–36; marriage of, 65, 66–67, 81, 86; participation in war bride clubs, 141; postwar life of, 128; wartime experiences of, 16–17; and Zionism, 59. *See also* Bonder, Abraham "Abe"

Brander, Dorothea, 103

British Control Commissions, 27

British Nationality and Status of Aliens Act, 108–9, 146

British West Indies, 87

Brownwell, Herbert, Jr., 110

Buchenwald, 136

Canada: and acculturation, 8, 113, 123, 139–43; and the Cold War, 108; housing, 127–28; immigration/naturalization laws, 3, 52, 65–67, 83–89, 108–10, 113, 144–46; Jewish soldiers from, 29–33, 47; marriage regulation, 4–7, 37, 42–43, 73, 81; military personnel from, 3, 46, 149; transport to, 12

Canadian Expeditionary Force (Canada Corps), 4

Canadian Royal Air Force, 28–29, 33–34, 49, 68, 94, 103

Canadian War Brides Bureau Repatriation Section, 86

Canadian Wives Bureau, 88–89, 98, 101

cantors, 47, 75

Casper, B. M., 31

Cass, Samuel, 68

Chanukah, 47

chaplains, Jewish: and aid for survivors, 31, 34–35, 135; concern about sexual assault, 24; encouragement of civilian-soldier mixing, 46–47, 60; enforcement of immigration regulations, 67, 81, 89–90, 113; and Jewish recovery, 8, 31–33, 43–46; performance of marriages, 12, 73–77; support of war bride clubs, 140–41; vetting of marriages, 67–72

Charles A., 28, 49

Charlotte R., 140

children: and acculturation, 140–43; and immigration, 3, 6, 84–88, 94–100, 102, 144, 152, 154; and language, 52–53; and legitimacy, 131; and nonfraternization rules, 33–34; orphaned, 49; and parents' Holocaust trauma, 137, 148; and Zionism, 49–51. *See also* parenting; pregnancy

China, 6, 110

cigarette camps, 95, 98, 153

cigarettes, 61–63, 81, 95, 98, 152–53

Clark, Tom, 112

Clay, Lucius, 47

clubs: and courtship, 60; for military personnel, 7, 46; Red Cross, 33–34; for war brides, 88, 92, 139–42, 147, 156; and weddings, 77

Cohen, Eugenia, 49–51

Cold War, 9, 65, 108, 110, 113, 118, 123

Committee on Army and Navy Religious Activities (CANRA), 45, 69–71

communism, 26, 66, 106, 108–13, 118–19, 123; anticommunism, 110

Communist Party: in Czechoslovakia, 112; in Germany, 106; in the United States, 111–12

concentration camps. *See* Auschwitz; Bergen-Belsen; Dachau; Holocaust; liberation

courtship: activities, 58–61; and communication, 57–58; and food, 61–63; path to marriage, 55–57; and privacy, 148, 150, 152; in Rosenthal narrative, 119–20; and sex, 60–61; and synagogue rebuilding, 46; and Zionism, 59

Croatia, 16, 26

Czechoslovakia, 20, 25, 42, 74, 111–12, 115, 151–55; Czech (language), 52, 58, 98, 141

Dachau, 30, 105, 121
Dave B., 89
death march, 18, 21, 25, 28, 41, 71, 105
Decter, Aaron, 45
demobilization, 59, 64, 67, 81, 83–86, 89–90, 93, 126, 131, 154–55
deportation, 2, 9, 17, 29, 32, 43, 49, 87, 107–12, 118–122
disability, 99
disease: among Holocaust survivors, 17, 22–25, 29, 31, 38–39, 62, 133–36, 147; and migration, 22–23, 99–101, 154–56; venereal, 99
displaced persons (DP), 7–10, 35; and chaplains, 31; and community, 95–97, 147; and food, 61–64; illness among, 22, 99–100; and immigration, 86, 89–91, 95–99, 115–16, 144, 154; and marriage, 71, 75, 79; and mental health, 135; movement restrictions for, 21, 35; and national security, 113; and sexual assault, 24, 61; and war brides, 148; and Zionism, 59
DP camps, 8, 77; Allied, 21–27; Harrison Report, 63–64; and housing, 63–64, 71, 138; Jewish personnel in, 33, 125; as Jewish spaces, 33, 37, 40, 46–54, 60
divorce, 69–70, 106, 112–13, 120, 157
Donath, Reuven, 49

Edwards, Ralph, 1
Egypt, 19, 87, 131
Eichmann, Adolf, 10
Eisen, Jack, 68
Eisenhower, Dwight D., 64, 136
Ellis Island, 102, 107, 112–13, 116, 120, 154
engagement, 11, 38, 56–57, 72, 81, 90, 105, 114, 128, 131
England. See United Kingdom
English among nonnative speakers: communication at home, 85, 103, 126–29; communication with military

personnel, 40; and migration, 97–98, 101; and postwar life, 126–29, 139–43, 154–55; at weddings, 75
Europe: Eastern, 21, 51–52, 63; Jews from, 3, 8, 27–35, 69, 77, 99, 135, 144; Western, 21, 62, 147

fascism, 120, 123; antifascism, 111
FBI, 106, 110–14, 118, 120
Fishman, Bessie and Albert, 125–26
Fishman, Lala Weintraub, 91, 134, 147–49; appearance, 40; courtship of, 62–63; immigration of, 49, 152; relationship with in-laws, 103, 125–29; pregnancy, 132, 140; wedding of, 77–81. See also Fishman, Morris
Fishman, Morris, 40, 49, 62–63, 77, 79–81, 79, 126–27, 152
Flynn, Gurley, 114–15
food: and acculturation, 129–30, 133, 157; and courtship, 55–65, 114; on holidays, 46; and liberation, 22–28, 31, 35, 43, 68; and sexual barter, 24, 61; and survival, 16–17; at weddings, 77–81; on war bride ships, 97–98, 101–2. See also malnutrition
France, 19, 88–89, 92–93, 132, 145, 153; chaplains in, 67; French (language), 52–53, 97–98, 103, 140–41, 154; and immigration, 88–89, 92–93, 97, 132, 145; and liberation, 33, 38–39; marriage laws in, 73; military personnel in, 28, 65, 153; underground markets in, 62
Frances C., 141
Freidl (Elfriede) H., 34, 74
Friedman, Henry M., 100
Friedman, Herbert, 26

Gardner, Valentina, 110
Gebhart, Joe, 110
Gebhart, Mary Esther, 110
gender, 8, 45, 47, 65, 119
Germany: Americans in, 29, 39; Communist Party in, 111–12; emigration from, 86, 89, 93, 125–28;

International Relief Organization, 9

Isaacman, Clara Heller, 24, 72, 133, 143; courtship of, 43, 55–63; and immigration, 83–85, 94–95, 98; and liberation, 19–21, 25; relationship with in-laws, 72, 128; wedding of, 73, 77; and Zionism, 33, 49–51. *See also* Isaacman, Daniel

Isaacman, Daniel: in courtship, 43, 55–63; and migration, 83, 85; parents of, 28, 31, 72, 128, 133; wedding of, 73, 77, 81; as Zionist, 24, 13–33, 49–51. *See also* Isaacman, Clara Heller

Isaacman, Reuben, 72, 128

Isaacson, Irving "Ike," 54

Isaacson, Judith Magyar, 24–25, 54, 63, 144

Israel. *See* Palestine; Zionism

Italy: immigration to, 86–88, 95–98, 103; Italian (language), 49, 51; Jewish refugees in, 3, 26–27, 33, 49, 116; and liberation, 19–21; synagogues in, 45–46; in World War II, 9–10, 16, 151–52

Jackson, Robert H., 118–21

Jagoda, Harry (Herschel), 33, 40, 62, 64, 75–76, 85, 102–3, 151–55

Japan, 109–10

Jeanine F., 89

Jewish culture, 3, 7–8, 29, 33, 38, 44, 46, 49–51, 56–58, 64, 75, 90, 113, 126, 129–30, 153, 157; and ideas of Jewish beauty and bodies, 7–8, 38–40, 60, 133. *See also* chaplains, Jewish; Judaism

Jewish Committee for Relief Abroad (JCRA), 89

Jewish Hospitality Committee for British and Allied Forces, 35

Jewish Joint Distribution Committee (JDC), 49, 89–90, 98, 153

Jewish languages, 3, 7–8, 38, 44, 51–54, 64, 129, 134, 147, 153, 157

Jewish Public Library (Montreal), 141

Jewish Telegraph Agency (JTA), 107

Judaism, 11, 47, 68–69, 150, 153; court (*bet din*), 69; Orthodox, 70, 75, 130, 132, 141, 155; Reform, 70, 75; religious affiliation, 7, 11, 70, 75, 157

Judd, Arlene Zipser (Aurelia), 98, 141, 149–57, 156

Judd, Joe, 141, 149–57, 156

Judd, Sophie, 154–56

Judkowicz, Ignatz, 149–52, 157

Kabilio, Flory, 41; courtship of, 40–41, 62, 64; immigration of, 85, 95–98, 102–3; and liberation, 15–20, 24; wedding of, 75, 76. *See also* Jagoda, Harry

Kabilio, Michael, 15–16, 26

Kabilio, Rosa Altarac, 15–16, 26, 55–56, 143

Kerson, Bertha, 47, 53

Kessler, Harold, 48

kibbutzim, 50

kin-conflict, 128

Kirschner, Sala Garncarz, 45–47, 58, 103, 128–34, 137–38, 142, 144

Kirschner, Sidney, 45–46, 58, 72, 81, 128–31, 138, 142

Klausner, Abraham, 52, 135

Klausner, Bert, 67

Klein, Gerda Weissmann: courtship of, 64–65; immigration of, 85, 90, 93, and language, 52, 54, 58, 129; and liberation, 25, 29, 32

Klein, Kurt: and acculturation, 129; and courtship, 54, 64–65; and immigration, 85, 90, 93; and language, 52, 58; and liberation, 29–32

Knauff, Ellen: beauty of, 121; and exclusion narratives, 103–4, 107–11; national security concerns about, 111–14, 121–23; and victimhood narratives, 114–21

Knauff, Kurt, 104, 107–8, 111–12, 116–21

Kohner, Hanna Bloch, 1–5, 42, 137

Kohner, Walter, 2–5, 42–43

Kosowski, Rachel, 49, 62, 75. *See also* Abramowitz, Mayer

Kugelman, Miri, 33

landsmanschaftn, 142, 147, 152

language: and acculturation, 129, 134, 139–41, 147; barriers between partners, 58; and courtship, 56–59, 64; and family, 129–30, 153, 155, 157; and immigration, 85, 95–98, 102; and Jewishness, 3, 7–8; and liberation, 31, 38, 43–44, 51–54; secular, 52; shared, 7, 51–58, 64, 126, 129, 153; and Zionism, 51

Lanzmann, Claude, 10

Lev, Aryeh, 45

Lewkowicz, Bella: acculturation of, 129, 141–45; home life of, 129; immigration of, 92, 101–2; and language, 52, 139; and loss, 38–39; marriage, 73, 77; memoir, 149; pregnancy, 132; and ritual objects, 44–45. *See also* Ostroff, Raymond "Ray"

liberation, 7–8, 13; difficulties associated with, 3, 18–29; immigration after, 35–36; and medical care, 114; meeting of partners during, 56, 58, 97, 119, 121; military personnel experiences, 29–33, 138; and nonfraternization policies, 33–35; photography, 136; and rebuilding, 39, 42, 45–46, 50; and sexual violence, 23–25; survivors' ambivalence toward, 16, 27; and survivors' silence, 149, 151

Liesl, 25

Lifshutz, Oscar, 67

Litvin, Edith Festinger, 81, 85, 89–90, 93. *See also* Litvin, Nathan

Litvin, Nathan, 81, 85, 89–90, 93, 131

loneliness, 17, 25, 126, 129, 134, 139

Lorge, Ernst Mordechai, 75

malnutrition, 22–23, 38, 62, 133

Maple Leaf Association, 139–40, 147

Marcus, Robert, 24

Marianne K., 71

Marion, George, 114, 117

marriage: calendars, 70–73; celebrations or receptions, 77, 81, 130–31; ceremonies, 57, 65–67, 70, 73–81, 130–31; civil, 71–77, 81, 130–31, 138; endogamy, 67; hasty, 8, 106; Jewish marriage laws, 69–71, 93, 150; Kiddushin, 75; Levirate, 150; of noncombatants, 3–5, 11, 21, 28, 33–34, 46; officiants, 73, 75, 77; permission to marry, 4, 6, 11–12, 65–68, 73–74, 81, 145, 153; proposals, 3, 42, 64–65, 150; regulations of soldier marriages, 4–7, 57, 66–69, 73–74; right to marry and victimhood, 71–72; secular, 73–74, 130–31; solemnizing of, 72, 83, 92, 153; wedding vows, 57, 72–74, 77, 83, 92, 130, 153. *See also* interfaith marriage; weddings

Mauthausen, 2

memory, 12, 156–57

Messing, Joseph, 113

Meyer, "Chesty" L., 131–32

Milgrom, Louis, 31

military-civilian relationships, 43, 54, 60, 65, 73, 75

military personnel: defined, 10–11; Jewish, 11, 27–34, 45–48, 53–54, 67–70, 110, 138–39

Nadich, Judah, 64

Nathan, Anna, 43, 52–53, 58, 137–38, 146, 150–56

Nathan B., 144, 146

National Council of Jewish Women (NCJW), 141, 155

National Jewish Welfare Board (NJWB), 24, 45–46

national security: 33, 86, 95, 109–14, 117–18

Nazis: anti-Jewish laws, 2, 15–17; atrocities, 2, 29, 42–44, 108, 136; collaborators, 10, 18, 38, 44–45, 69, 151; destruction of synagogues, 45–46; as epitome of evil, 108; extermination aims of, 17, 32, 40, 46, 114–15; Kristallnacht, 42; perpetrators, 18, 34, 40, 71; in World War II, 15–21. *See also* Holocaust; liberation

Neiderland, William Guglielmo, 10

Netherlands, 2, 10, 19, 45–47, 48, 60, 62, 73, 88, 97–98

housing, 127–28; immigration to, 2–8, 12, 21, 27, 81, 83–89, 92–96, 99–104, 150–57; and marriage, 4, 130–31; and medicine, 134; war bride clubs, 139–45; war bride term, 11

United States government: Air Force, 10, 31; Bill of Rights, 115; Civil Censorship Division, 111–12; Department of Justice, 109–10, 115, 117–21; Department of Labor, 118; Holocaust Memorial Museum, 10; Navy, 84, 97; Office of Immigration and Naturalization Services, 87, 110, 112, 118; Office of War Services, 88; Senate, 89; State Department, 106, 111, 117; Supreme Court, 9, 107–8, 118: War Department, 84, 111. *See also* US Army; US House of Representatives

UN Relief and Rehabilitation Administration (UNRRA), 21, 27, 48, 77, 79

US Army, 3, 10, 25–26, 33, 42, 45–46, 49, 85, 97, 99, 105–6; Army Intelligence, 117; Counter Intelligence Corps (CIC), 111

US House of Representatives, 89; House Judiciary Committee, 115, 117, 121

Va'ad Lemaan Hachayal (Association for the Well-Being of Soldiers), 46

Veteran's Rehabilitation Act, 138;

Victory in Europe (VE) Day, 19–20, 49, 62

Walter, Francis E., 117, 121

war bride: defined, 9–11; legislation, 86–87; media portrayal of, 136–39

War Brides Act (US), 92–93, 121, 153

war fiancée, defined, 11

War Measures Act, 109

weddings: civil, 74, 77, 81, 130–31; civilian-military, 73, 75, 81, 138; events, 75–81; food at, 79–81; Ketubah, 75; officiants, 73, 75, 77. *See also* marriage

whiteness, 1, 6–7, 17, 61, 101, 110, 139–40

widowhood, 69, 86, 150

Wilson, Woodrow, 109

World War I, 4–5, 108–9, 113, 139

worship, 35, 45–48, 60, 75, 95

xenophobia, 26, 68, 100, 110

Yiddish, 9, 29, 38, 44, 51–58; and acculturation, 142; and communication, 85, 98, 102–3; and courtship, 38, 44, 51–58; and in-laws, 102–3, 126, 129–30; and naming survivorship, 9

Yom Kippur, 47, 54, 70

Yugoslavia, 10, 15–16

Zionism: *chalutzim*, 77; and courtship, 49–51, 55–56, 59–60; Gordonia, 24, 51, 59–60; *hachshara*, 55; Hashomer Hatzair, 50; identity, 24; key Zionist terms, 51; and liberation, 33–35; meetings, 37, 44, 48; and rebuilding, 32; *shaliach*, 24; Shromrim/Ha-Shomer, 59; unifying cause, 50–51; youth activities, 7, 31; at weddings, 77. *See also* Abramowitz, Mayer; Isaacman, Clara Heller; Isaacman, Daniel; Palestine